PLAY FOR ALL ™

Guidelines

Planning, Design and Management
of Outdoor Play Settings
for All Children

Play For All Guidelines

Planning, Design and Management
of Outdoor Play Settings for All Children

PLAY FOR ALL GUIDELINES

Planning, Design and Management of
Outdoor Play Settings for All Children

Workbook Edited by:
Robin C. Moore
Susan M. Goltsman
Daniel S. Iacofano

With contributions by:
Jay Beckwith
Lynda Schneekloth

Illustrations:
Yoshiharu Asanoumi

Project Director:
Susan Goltsman

Copyright ©1987, MIG Communications
1824-A Fourth Street, Berkeley, CA 94710, USA, (415) 845–7549

Library of Congress Catalog Card Number: 87–73243
Main Entry Under Title:

Play For All Guidelines: Planning, Design and Management of
Outdoor Play Settings for All Children

1. Play and Playgrounds 2. Environmental Design 3. Child Development
I. Moore, Robin C. II. Goltsman, Susan M. III. Iacofano, Daniel S.

ISBN 0–944661–00–9
Version 2.0

Composed in Palatino ten on thirteen, on an IBM-PC using MultiMate wordprocessor
and Ventura Publisher page composition.

ABOUT THE EDITORS

The editors are partners in the planning and design firm of Moore Iacofano Goltsman, with many years experience in the field of children's environments. Together they founded PLAE, Inc. (Play and Learning in Adaptable Environments) in Berkeley, California, in 1980, through which projects related to children, environment and integration of children with disabilities continue to be sponsored—including Play For All.

Robin Moore holds degrees in Architecture (London University) and City Planning (MIT). His research and development work with children's play environments began in Boston with the Lenox–Camden Experiment in Playground Design (1966); this was followed by his major work, the Environmental Yard (1971–81), in Berkeley, California. In 1984, it was recognized by the National Endowment for the Arts as a Exemplary Design Research Project. Robin is the author of *Childhood's Domain: Play and Place in Child Development* (Croom Helm, London, 1986) and co-author of *Another Way of Learning: Child Devleopment in Natural Settings* (Sierra Club Books, 1988). He is also Associate Professor of Landscape Architecture, North Carolina State University, Raleigh; Vice President and Publications Editor of the International Association for the Child's Right to Play and former chair of the Environmental Design Research Association.

Susan Goltsman, ASLA, holds degrees in Landscape Architecture (North Carolina State University), Environmental Psychology (University of Surrey, U.K.) and Environmental Design (Parsons School of Design, New York City). Susan is Director of PLAE, Inc. For the past fifteen years, she has been creating programs and environments that promote the development of children. She has been recognized by the National Endowment for the Arts and the American Planning Association for her work with children and youth, and received the 1986 California Park and Recreation Merit Award for PLAE's contribution to the field of recreation therapy. Susan teaches at Stanford University in the Program on Urban Studies. She serves on the California Council of Landscape Architects and is a member of the board of the Northern California Chapter of ASLA.

Daniel Iacofano, PhD, AICP, holds degrees in Environmental Planning (University of California, Berkeley), Environmental Psychology (University of Surrey, U.K.) and Urban Planning (University of Cincinnati). Daniel is a Visiting Lecturer at Stanford University and the University of California at Davis. For more than twelve years, Dr. Iacofano has applied his planning and design background to projects in transportation planning, community design, organizational planning and development, strategic planning and public involvement program design. He has consulted and lectured throughout the United States and Europe, and has pioneered many innovative techniques for community participation and inter-agency collaboration. He has been recognized for his work in planning and public information by the American Planning Association. He serves as co-editor of the Citizen Participation and Voluntary Action Abstracts, and Boardmember and newsletter editor of the American Planning Association, Northern California Section.

Jay Beckwith has been creating children's play equipment and environments since 1965. His designs have been manufactured by companies such as BigToys, Iron Mountain Forge and Mexico Forge and distributed in the United States, Canada and Australia. Jay's play sculptures were presented in a month long, one-man show at the DeYoung Museum of San Francisco in 1974. He has published many books and articles on creative play environments and playground safety. He has developed the Playground Risk Management Program, which has been adopted by Burger King Corporation and many recreation departments.

Lynda Schneekloth holds degrees in Landscape Architecture, Child Development and English (University of Wisconsin). She is an Associate Professor of Architecture in the School of Architecture and Environmental Design at the State University of New York at Buffalo. Lynda has conducted pioneering research in design for children with visual impairments and is a principal in the Caucus Partnership, a consulting firm specializing in environmental and organizational change.

CONTENTS

ACKNOWLEDGMENTS

The publication of the *Play For All Guidelines* represents the cumulative result of the efforts of many. First, the U.S. National Endowment for the Arts and the San Francisco Foundation, who were crucial in getting Play For All off the ground.

Second, the members of the Play for All Task Force who were instrumental in mapping the scope of the program and setting the direction. The members were: **Jay Beckwith,** Playground Designer; **Kim Blakley,** Associate Director of Play Environments Research at the Graduate School of the City University of New York; **Phyllis Cangemi,** Director, Whole Access; **Susan Goltsman,** ASLA, Director, PLAE, Inc.; **Roger Hart,** Ph.D., Director of the Center for Human Environments; **Daniel Iacofano, Ph.D.,** AICP, Partner in the planning and design firm of Moore Iacofano Goltsman; **Richard Klink,** ASLA, landscape architect with the Los Angeles Department of Parks and Recreation; **Sally Mc Intyre,** RTR, recreation therapist, PLAE, Inc; **Clare Cooper Marcus,** Professor in the Departments of Architecture and Landscape Architecture at the University of California – Berkeley; **Robin Moore,** Vice President of the International Association for the Child's Right to Play (IPA); **Elaine Ostroff,** Director of the Adaptive Environments Center in Boston, Massachusetts; **Barry Ryan,** Compliance Division, Office of the California State Architect; **Lynda Schneekloth,** Associate Professor in the Department of Architecture at the State University of New York at Buffalo; **Kevin Stoops,** Associate Park Planner for Seattle's Department of Parks and Recreation; and **Fred Etzel,** AICP, of Henn, Etzel & Mellon, Attorneys at Law, serving as counsel to the PLAY FOR ALL Conference and PLAE, Inc.

Third, the working group facilitators, recorders and participants who conducted the review of the draft (version 1.0) of the guidelines at the Stanford Conference, held in September, 1986: **Susan Goltsman,** ASLA, Project Coordinator; **Daniel Iacofano,** AICP, Process Manager; **Robin Moore,** Director of Research; **Sally McIntyre,** RTR, Administrator; **Yoshiharu Asanoumi,** Design Research; and **Kerri Glover,** Clerical; **Carolyn Francis,** Recorder; **Mark Francis,** ASLA, Facilitator; **Joe Frost,** Ph.D., Facilitator; **Sharyl Green,** Facilitator; **Louis Hexter,** Recorder; **Clare Cooper Marcus,** Facilitator; **Jim Oswald,** Recorder; **Mary Jo Porter,** Recorder; **Lynda Schneekloth,** Facilitator; and **Leland Shaw,** Facilitator.

The following people have participated in the development and review of the guidelines:

Suzanne Alexandra	Andrea Angelo	Karen Bagelatos
Jeanette Anders	Yoshiharu Asanoumi	James Barnard
Don Anderson	Jerry Bagelatos	Jay Beckwith

Joan Bergy
John Blackburn
Kim Blakely
Rae Blasquez
Judy Boshoven
Daniel Brenman
Larry Bruya, PhD
Shirley Bulpe, EdD
Karen Bult
John Busch
Don Cadman
Phyllis Cangemi
Rodney V. Castro
Ed Chandler
Rod Corbett
F. Clayton Dade
Charles O. Davis
Harry Dean, Jr.
Edith Dowley
J. Frederick Druck
Felix Drury
Stan Edmister
Jim D. Edwards
Sandra Edwards
Fred Etzel
Morgan Jasper
Susan Ferreyra
Carolyn Francis
Mark Francis
Joe Frost, PhD
Dick Gannon
Marilyn Golden
Selwyn Goldstein
Seymour M. Gold, PhD
Gabriel Goulart
Sharyl Green
Patricia Hadley

Goran Hag
Gary Harrison
Roger Hart, PhD
Horst Henke
Peter Heseltine
Chris Heusser
Louis Hexter
Paul Hogan
John Holborn
Eileen Hooker
Jeff Johnson
Susan Jurgenson
Susan Kaplan
Jennifer King
Steve King
Richard N. Klink
Walter Kocian
Gary Koenig
Susan Landry
Elaine Day LaTourelle
A. Ann Lovell
Deborah Learner
Louis Leff
Mary Lincoln
Denise J. Lynch
Rob Lynch
Dennis Maloney
Clare Cooper Marcus
Lauren Martelli
Kim McAdams
Sally McIntyre
Bill Michaelis, PhD
Robert Morrissey
Ann A. Nathan
Lindsay Nee
James E. Niskanen

Helge B. Olsen
Elaine Ostroff
Jim Oswald
Marlyn Perritt
Ewing Philbin
Dr. William Robert Pitt
Alice Poggi
Mary Jo Porter
Sally Reese
Christine Russell
William Russo
Greg Sagen
Jill Sager
Barbara Sampson, PhD
Lynda Schneekloth
Leland Shaw
Dannette Shoemaker
Amita Sinha
Fran Smith
Laurene Smith, PhD
Troy Squires
Sharon Stine
Kevin B. Stoops
Theodora Briggs Sweeney
Donna Thompson, PhD
Louis Torelli
Tod. W. Turriff
Michael J. Waite
Curt Wear
Cathy Weissberg
Rosemary Wills
Winifred Yen Wood
Marshal R. Wortham, PhD
Sue Wortham, PhD
Connie Zimmerman
Nicholas J. Zirpolo, PhD

Fourth, the almost 200 organizations and institutions (Appendix B) involved in Play For All who continue to lend support to the program in many ways.

Fifth, the following manufacturers of play equipment and surfacing who provided financial as well as informational support: Iron Mountain Forge; Big Toys; Children's Playgrounds, Inc.; Landscape Structures, Wooden Environments, HAGS Play (Sweden); Airspace USA; Kompan; Log Rhythms; Playscapes; Tiger Hug Toys; Reese Industries and Cam-Turf.

From the supporting cast of hundreds, special contributions by a number of individuals to the guidebook must be recognized: Peter Heseltine for his careful review of the manuscript with respect to European experience and literature; Lynda Schneekloth for generously allowing us to adapt sections of her unpublished manuscript, *Play Environments for Disabled Children*; Jay Beckwith for his draft of Chapter 9 and the many other ideas he contributed during the development of the text; and James Tuomey and James Donovan for their thoughtful critique from the manufacturing perspective and Phyllis Cangemi from the access perspective.

Thank you to Cheryl Barton, President, American Society of Landscape Architects, Charles Davis, President, California Parks and Recreation Society, and Barbara Sampson, EdD, Executive Director, The American Alliance for Health, Physical Education, Recreation and Dance, for their time and support in promoting the work of PLAY FOR ALL.

Last but not least, a special garland of recognition goes to the staff at PLAE, Inc.: Yoshiharu Asanoumi, Ann Cuthbertson, Louis Hexter, Keri Glover, Erika Jenssen, Sally McIntyre, Jim Oswald, Dave Driskell and Lowell Kline for his organizational, computer and desktop publishing skills. Without their tireless shouldering of responsibility none of this would have been possible.

PREFACE

A quality children's play environment is more than a piece of play equipment set neatly into a circle of sand in a park, schoolyard or residential development.

Play is the child's way of learning. It is an intricate, intimate process which helps children develop and become socialized. Play is learning in its most experiential sense, but it is only as rich as the supporting social and physical environment. The *Play for All Guidelines* focus attention on the physical environment, where choice and diversity are the keys to success. A good play and learning environment must be designed as a range of settings carefully layered on the landscape. The design of a good play environment requires an interdisciplinary understanding of human development, and how it can respond to the capabilities of both natural and manufactured settings.

The *Play For All Guidelines* are a tool to help professional designers, park and recreation managers and community groups make informed decisions about the planning, design and on-going management of children's play environments.

The *Guidelines* are based on six principal assumptions:

a. Play is a process by which children learn. Good quality play opportunities have a significant impact on child development.

b. The type, quality and diversity of children's physical settings (play value) directly affect the type, quality and diversity of children's play.

c. The type, quality and diversity of the social setting (play leadership and programming) directly affects play value. Play leadership (or animation, as it is sometimes called), refers to the critical role of trained staff, or play leaders, engaging children in creative interaction with each other and their surroundings.

d. Children with physical, mental, emotional and social disabilities have an equal right to play opportunities.

e. Integration of disabled and able-bodied children is based on the concept of accessibility which relates to both the physical and social environment (e.g., the attitudes and awareness of staff towards children with disabilities will greatly affect the rate and depth of integration).

f. The quality of settings and their play value are severely threatened by liability costs and the threat of suit. Risk management strategies and management policies should be developed to protect the quality and value of children's settings.

Addressing the Safety and Liability Crisis

Today, safety, security and liability have become major factors in determining the quality of children's outdoor play environments and play programs. While the safety and security of our children, whether in supervised or unsupervised play environments, justifiably deserves careful attention, the goals of safety and security must be balanced with the goal of providing stimulating and challenging environments for children's play and development. The concept of a healthy, safe environment need not be at odds with child development objectives.

Without taking risks, children cannot learn to their full potential. Settings must challenge them to take risks without being hazardous.

The difference between "hazard" and "challenge" must be understood when creating play settings. Children will use equipment and parts of the environment in all possible ways, regardless of design intentions. Since the idea of play is to explore and maximize the potential of any play setting, children will test its use to the limits of their abilities.

Such testing should present a challenge. It teaches children new skills. Children will run up slides, jump out of swings and climb trees. Well-designed play settings reflect an understanding of children's behavior and provide for risk taking without introducing hazards or unforeseen consequences.

The Purpose of Play For All

Play For All is a national program to develop design guidelines and criteria for children's play environments. The program has an added focus on the needs of children with disabilities, and their integration into the community of all children.

The guidelines are concerned primarily with public play environments. Other sectors of play environment development (day care and child development centers, community-built settings, etc.), while recognized as important, have not been explicitly addressed. The editors encourage those working in these sectors to use these guidelines as a springboard.

In January 1986, PLAE, Inc., with support from NEA, convened a national task force of child development specialists, designers and representatives of the disability field, which met in Berkeley, California. They proposed a National Working Conference which was held at Stanford University, California, in the fall of that same year. The main task of the conference was to review and critique a draft version of these guidelines, prepared by PLAE, Inc., based on an outline developed by the task force.

This extensively revised version of the *Play For All Guidelines* is based on the results of the conference review and additional reviews by experts in the field.

Play For All is funded by the National Endowment for the Arts, the San Francisco Foundation, play equipment manufacturers and other sources. The effort has been endorsed by nearly 200 organizations and universities.

Play For All is now developing a long-term publications program of *Design Bulletins* to provide more technical detail on priority design issues. *Play For All News,* the program newsletter, is published four times a year with up-to-date news of developments in the field (a subscription blank is in the back of the book).

In preparing the *Play For All Guidelines*, the editors have drawn heavily on a number of research publications and other guideline documents (published and unpublished) as referenced in the text. Permission to extract from these documents is gratefully acknowledged. A major source of information, from which the concept play settings was derived, was the ten-year archive of research material (1971–80) from the Environmental Yard, Berkeley, California. Several chapters of this book are based on an earlier manuscript prepared by Robin Moore. A further invaluable source has been the archives of PLAE, Inc., from 1981–87, documenting the operation of a summer play program based at a number of park sites in the City of Berkeley, California.

As much as possible, these guidelines are based on empirical research findings and post-construction evaluations of children's settings. In other cases where empirical research is weak or nonexistent, the guidelines are supported by arguments that stem from child development theories, especially those which emphasize the child's interaction with physical settings (Björklid, 1986).

In cases where PFA experts could not reach agreement on any aspect of a guideline, it has been omitted from the text and earmarked for further discussion. Issues requiring further research are noted in the text.

It is the goal of Play For All to continue updating its information base, both in the form of *Design Bulletins* and in revised editions of the *Guidelines.* To achieve success in this venture, it is essential that close contact be maintained with practitioners in the field: designers, specifiers, park and recreation directors, play equipment manufacturers, disability specialists, school site administrators and parents. Please do not hesitate to write or call PFA at the address and number listed on the inside front cover.

Berkeley, California
December 1987

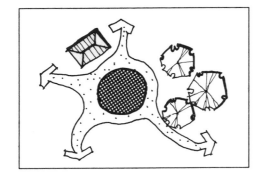

PART A :

Site Planning and Design

I. CHILD DEVELOPMENT OBJECTIVES

A well-designed, well-managed play environment should provide children with the following developmental opportunities (adapted from Schneekloth, 1985; Frost & Klein, 1983):

a. **Opportunities for motor skill development.** Large and fine muscle development, eye-hand-foot coordination, and balancing and locomotion skills must be supported. A range of opportunities to practice and test limits of abilities is required.

Regardless of the abilities of the children playing, they should have opportunities to practice and extend whatever skills they have. There should always be something further to reach. When children accomplish one skill, they can test themselves in new ways.

b. **Opportunities for decision making.** Any environment in which children live should allow them to make decisions about their own activities (Moore, in press). For this to happen:

1) The child must be in control of some or all of the environment.

2) The experiences provided by the environment must not be "dead-ends." They must have decision points that allow the child options for continuing a current activity, terminating it, or initiating a new one.

3) Decision points must be appropriate to different age and skill levels and present a sufficient range of choices so that forced repetition is avoided.

c. **Opportunities for learning.** Properties and relationships among physical objects, space and self can be demonstrated in play settings. With appropriate supervision, children will solve problems, actively manipulate the environment, transform it, dismantle it, and re-create it in order to learn about the nature of the world.

Children need opportunities to change their relationship to the world and see it from new perspectives; from high and low places; through energy and motion; in time and space.

Programs must help children appreciate ecological relationships, the natural order of things, and the need for peaceful coexistence with each other, their surroundings and, ultimately, the planet.

1   *Every type of child, no matter what level of ability, needs play opportunities.*

2   *Play settings should offer opportunities to learn about the physical world.*

3   *Play settings must be accessible to children with all forms of disability.*

d.   **Opportunities for fantasy play.**   The environment is a resource for imaginative and cooperative play, it provides the props and stage.   The richness of physical elements in the setting and their relationship to each other should arouse curiosity and trigger imaginative associations (Moore & Wong, in press).   If the environment is too literal, imagination will be limited; if too abstract, imaginations will not be fully stimulated.

e.   **Opportunities for social development.**   Settings must support positive interpersonal interaction and socialization, between able-bodied and disabled children, between different ethnic groups, between girls and boys, between children and adults (Moore & Wong, in press).

Children need opportunities for role playing, development of self-esteem, emotional development, and social communication skills.   Protected spaces must be available where small groups can withdraw from highly active equipment areas for quiet social play.

f.   **Playing should be fun.**   Smiling faces and laughter are the clearest indicators of a successful play setting.

These behavioral goals and objectives apply to all environments used by children.

2. SITE ANALYSIS

Every site is a special situation—in its own unique location in a particular community. External aspects (location, access, visibility, etc.) and internal aspects (size, shape, configuration, etc.) all influence site development, program administration, play opportunities and integration.

Every site should be analyzed for its appropriateness as a children's play area. Levels of analysis should expand from site, to neighborhood to regional context.

The park planner and designer may be faced with the task of evaluating an existing site or portion of a site for rehabilitation; a pre-selected site for new construction; or, several sites for selection and eventual development. In each case the process is the same: site features are inventoried and evaluated; climatic, biophysical and social contexts are assessed (Cunningham, 1984; Lynch & Hack, 1984; Moore & Wong, in press; Flood Park case example, Chapter 22; Rutledge & Molnar, 1986).

2.1 Design Programming and Analysis

Site analysis should occur at the same time that the design program is being prepared because each impacts the other with constraints and opportunities. An early analysis of the site will indicate its appropriateness for the proposed uses and indicate adjustments to the design program.

If the site designer or landscape architect is involved in the design programming, continuous reconciliation of the program will be required with site constraints, recreation program support and the available budget for development (Moore & Wong, in press).

2.2 Existing Conditions

A thorough inventory of the characteristics of each site should include, but not be limited to (Lynch & Hack, 1984; Rutledge & Molnar, 1986):

a. **Location.** Is the site located so as to serve the population of the neighborhood? Is it visible and attractive? Is it easy to get to by foot, by bike, by car, by transit?

b. **Site Function.** Each site must be judged for its fitness to accommodate the intended programs and facilities. The site must have ample space for the planned use and be amenable to development. The site should not require extensive, expensive reworking to function as a play environment.

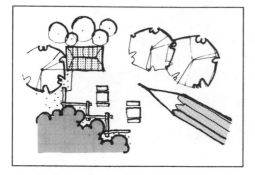

4   *Both external and internal aspects are important considerations in the site planning of play environments.*

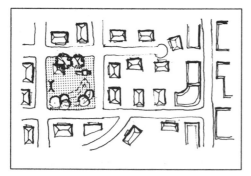

5   *What planning issues are raised by site location?*

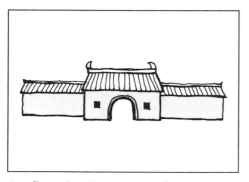

6   *Does the site have an existing use pattern which should be taken into account?*

c.   **Natural Features.** What are the characteristics of the topography? Vegetation? Are there any especially valuable amenities such as water or views? Are there any potential hazards such as bluffs or swamps? Are there toxic compounds in the soil? (Freeberg, 1983)

Children have a strong interest in playing in and learning from nature: streams (natural or created), hillsides, climbing trees, dirt mounds, leaf piles and so forth. Imported climbing rocks, wooded areas with trails, meadows, groves of trees and amphitheaters can be natural extensions of more formal play areas.

d.   **Utilities.** Is the site served by all utilities? Storm sewers?

e.   **Human and Cultural Features.** Is the site in an area that is frequently traveled? Are there areas nearby where people congregate? How have people traditionally used the site, how is it used now, especially by children? Are there particular features that are well-used and valued by existing users?

What is the character, scale and history of the neighborhood? Are there unusual design determinants such as special cultural or ethnic features to consider?

f.   **Existing Park Features.** If sited within a park, how does the proposed playground relate to the entire park area with its trees, bushes, paths, walls and drinking fountains. These must all be recognized as part of the child's play environment.

1)   **Topography** in or near the playground can provide active play space on slopes;

2)   **Landscaping and plantings** can provide screening, wind breaks, shade, shelter for retreat, protective barriers;

3)   **Shelters** located close to the playground area can facilitate observation of children from covered seating areas;

4)   **Storage** [close by] for equipment and play props is an asset close by;

5)   **Sports fields** are an asset, if located where the sideline activity will not interfere with the play area;

6)   **Restrooms** and **drinking fountains** located adjacent to the play area are essential. If possible, they should be for use by play area users only.

7) **Medical facilities** information should be provided close at hand, especially in unsupervised areas.

8) **Public telephones** are needed to provide an extra measure of security.

2.3 Community Context (Adapted from Canadian Council on Children and Youth, hereafter CCCY, 1980 *).

The opportunities and constraints of the local community should be fully recognized and used to advantage in the planning, design and management of play settings. The following srategies will help:

a. **Adapting to local conditions.** This document should be used as a set of guidelines, not prescriptions. Adjustments in how the guidelines should be applied and to what settings will vary to suit local conditions, demographic and social factors, legal requirements, and economic resources.

b. **Involving other programs.** While these guidelines focus primarily on playspace design, the physical aspect is only one part of the total provision for play opportunities. In any situation, physical planning should be undertaken in concert with other play programs to support maximum support of child development.

c. **Integrating with open space planning.** The planning of local play spaces must be integrated into comprehensive planning strategies for the whole community. Collaboration with departments such as public works, housing, education, and recreation will avoid duplication of effort as well as enhance opportunities for supporting child development.

d. **Collaborating with all agencies working on behalf of children.** No single individual person, organization, government department or level of government is likely to have all the resources and expertise to plan effectively for the full range of children's play opportunities. Efforts must be coordinated.

e. **Encouraging community participation.** Consultation and participation by community organizations, families and individuals helps contribute to successful planning for children's play. Local residents, child development experts and children should be included as members of the planning team. Incorporation of the ideas,

* A full listing of reference abbreviations is given at the beginning of the Bibliography, page 257.

of the play space a community effort. For children, it can become a significant learning experience. It is also an effective risk management strategy because it helps citizens understand and support children's developmental needs, including the need to take risks.

f.   **Facilitating children's involvement.** Children and youth are important contributors to the planning team and techniques are available to enable their genuine participation. Adult commitment to participation by young people in the planning and management of play spaces is the first critical step towards involvement. Young people's participation helps reduce their sense of alienation.

3. SITE DESIGN CRITERIA

Because each site, community, and planning process is different from the next, a wide margin of choice, interpretation and a combination of physical settings is needed to fit many different circumstances. The designer must be familiar with the particular characteristics of each situation.

The following criteria can help but are not sufficient by themselves to produce a design solution. They provide a framework for the designer's imagination and skill.

There are five key criteria for a good play environment (Adaptive Environments Center, hereafter AEC, 1980; CCCY, 1980; Canadian Central Mortgage and Housing Corporation, hereafter CMHC, 1980; Cooper Marcus, 1986; Los Angeles, 1987; Schneekloth, 1985; Seattle, 1986): accessibility, safe challenge, diversity and clarity, graduated challenge and flexibility; but there are many others of almost equal importance as described below.

a. **Accessibility.** Good places must be accessible to the intended users. This term implies that children can first of all get there safely; that it is integrated into the daily life of a child; that it is "barrier free," i.e., it has no or few physical barriers to its use; and further, that it is "psychologically accessible" (i.e. attractive and secure) and understandable to the children who use it.

Entrances mark the interface of site and community and should be designed to entice children into the site. A primary entrance should be designated while other secondary entrances may be less visible so children can "discover" them.

1) Play areas should be located so that potential contact between children and traffic is minimized (Beamish, 1980; Sandels, 1968).

2) Entrances to the park or playground should be clearly identified, visible from nearby housing and used to direct child pedestrians along safe routes to the park.

3) Parking areas and driving aisles must be separated from play areas by barriers. Parking area perimeters should be open and unobstructed to view.

4) Play areas should be accessible from main pathways through the park and routes to other use areas such as ballfields and picnic facilities.

5) Main pathways should be connected with main entrances, exits, meeting and working places to provide users with a clear mental image of the facility, especially children with orientation impairments.

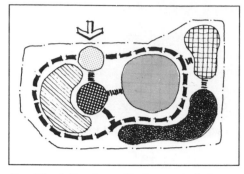

7   *Circulation is a critical aspect of site planning.*

8   *Play settings should include challenging environments and play elements.*

6) Fences, berms, plantings or other devices should be used to define playground areas, but not so strongly that they seem separated from the rest of the park.

7) Hard surface paths and bike paths should be separated from play areas.

8) Paths leading to restrooms and drinking fountains will inevitably carry bicycle traffic and must be separated from children's play areas.

9) Maintenance vehicles must have access to playground areas. Access ways must be at least 10 feet wide and be capable of supporting service vehicles.

b.   **Safe Challenge.** (Moore, G.T., et al., 1979; Seattle, 1986) Play areas should provide highly challenging settings with many different events for the physical development of the upper body, balance and coordination without exposing children to unnecessary hazards. This function is important because of the correlation between learning disorders and balance deficits. Coordination affects judgement about taking risks—the ability to visualize a movement before making it. Activities requiring full coordination should be supported.

A hazard is something a child does not see; a challenge is a risk the child can see and chooses to undertake or not. Children need to take risks to challenge their skills and courage. A risk free play area is neither possible nor desirable.

Injuries can and do occur from many different types of activities on playgrounds; falls cause the majority. Any fall can injure, particularly if the child strikes a hard surface (Boyce, et al., 1984; Langley, et al., 1981, 1982; Langley, 1984). Far more research is needed in order to understand the relationships between accidents and environment—both physical and social aspects.

To provide safe challenges, the following should be considered:

1) Ensure that settings which stimulate upper body strength like rings, turning bars, horizontal bars, climbing trees, swinging ropes and things to lift, are designed and positioned to promote mixed use by children with and without disabilities. Designs that protect children from common hazards, especially falling and collision, reduce the possibility of severe injury.

2) Balance settings which stimulate the inner ear such as tire swings, climbing surfaces, bridges, narrow rails or walls.

3)   Coordination and judgement settings such as horizontal ladders, stepping logs, climbers, tunnels, bannister slides.

c.   **Diversity and Clarity.** To meet their wide-ranging, ever changing needs, children need access to a diversity of play settings. To stimulate curiosity and exploration, environments can be novel and complex. Some aspects could change continually. Other aspects should be predictable to foster feelings of security.

9   Use of the natural environment adds more sensory variety.

Novelty and predictability will be balanced in an environment that presents a clear overall image to the user. Major areas, main access routes, principal play opportunities should be easily seen (which may differ for children with disabilities because of sensory or mobility impairments). Many minor "backwaters" should be designed, to be discovered over time.

Diverse play settings can liberate creative energy from children. A breadth of action and interaction distinguishes a play environment that is well designed and well managed, that always has something new to offer, yet at the same time is thought of as a familiar friend, a comfortable secure haven.

An aim of site design is to locate and juxtapose settings in such a way that the greatest variety of play activity patterns will be generated, producing the greatest possible range of interactions and relationships, while meeting the requirements of different ages, abilities and development stages.

d.   **Graduated Challenges** (Moore, G.T., et al., 1979; Seattle, 1986). Play settings should provide activities with a broad range of challenges and graduated levels of safe risk-taking to children of different ages and abilities.

Children should be invited to test their skills and build self-confidence. They should be able to reach, jump, climb, or slide to the level of their ability without frustration and should be able to withdraw from the activity without the risk of failure and humiliation.

1)   Each play event should be presented in several skill levels or levels of difficulty: steep, steeper and steepest.

2)   Each type of activity should have several levels of accomplishment: high, higher and highest.

3)   There should be places to enter and exit a setting at intermediate levels.

4)   Settings should be arranged so that the next level of challenge is apparent.

5) Challenges in each setting should not be related to heights, hazards and danger but to increasingly more difficult mastery of the body.

Settings do not have to be dangerous to be challenging. The important aspect of graduated challenges is that the challenge be "perceived" (Schneekloth, 1985). Therefore, construct physically challenging settings so that children read them as challenges, but in such a way that if they fail, they are not injured. For example:

1) Balance beams of varying widths are just as challenging 1 foot off the ground as 6 feet off the ground; it is their width that is critical. (The same is true of cargo nets and similar devices.)

2) High places are perceived as challenging regardless of the safety of their enclosure: the smaller the high place, the more dangerous it is perceived, even if well protected by edges and railings.

e. **Flexibility.** Physical elements that can be changed and moved around are needed. Children develop continuously, so their needs change as they learn and grow. To accommodate these changes, spaces must also have the ability to change. With careful planning, a space can allow for continual "tailoring" and not require costly or time-consuming renovations. Care must be taken to design flexible structures.

Play leaders should be trained to handle flexible space management. The environment should allow for easy rearrangement of elements for different programs and the addition or removal of special equipment for particular activities.

The needs of children with disabilities develop just as the needs of able-bodied children. Disabilities may be associated with other predictable conditions in individual children. A disease may be degenerative; a disabling condition may improve; or a child's physical and mental abilities may develop at different rates. The physical environment for all children must be planned with present and future adaptations in mind. Methods of supporting flexibility include:

1) Modular systems that can be moved around.

2) Mobile equipment such as inflatables, hoses, buckets, pulleys, ropes.

3) Play bases that can be set up, taken down and moved to a new location periodically.

4) Add-ons such as sheets that can be used to transform a play structure into a fire truck, spaceship, house, storefront, etc.

5)   All manner of natural objects and materials.

f.   **Defensible Space.** Play areas should be visible to both parents and children, although local values vary on this issue and should be assessed. There must be no area hidden from view which could encourage or harbor deviant or criminal behavior. This is especially important in unsupervised or partly supervised areas and less important in fully supervised areas (Cooper Marcus & Sarkissian, 1986).

1)   Boundaries of the play area should be defined but transparent. There should be no high, continuous, opaque barriers between nearby houses and the play area.

2)   Nearby housing or other places where adults gather should be used as the "eyes" of the neighborhood. Children's areas should be both visible and accessible (Cooper Marcus & Sarkissian, 1986).

3)   Large pieces of equipment might be placed toward the back of the site; other equipment might be either slightly recessed or raised to maintain visibility throughout the area.

4)   Spaces and equipment must be designed and placed to allow sight over, under and around. Private play spaces should be semi-enclosed with enough openings to see a child from any angle.

5)   Adults should have more than two directions of visibility into all play spaces; from the surrounding area and from the play area itself.

6)   Structures or vegetative barriers should be open for 2/3rds of their enclosure.

7)   Care must be taken to balance defensible space requirements with play value. At times, it is valuable for children to have at least an illusion of privacy.

8)   Tunnels, openings into or under a play space should be large enough for an adult and should have at least two means of egress.

g.   **Supervision.** The presence of adult playground supervisors allows for a much greater range of activities than at unsupervised areas. Activities which would be too hazardous, too difficult to maintain or too difficult to organize and equip without supervision can be planned if there are to be active recreational programs at the park. Play area designers should be aware of this potential and provide programmable space and facilities (Westland & Knight, 1982).

10   *Program support is a critical consideration in site planning and design.*

11   *Supervision is a critical aspect of site planning.*

h.   **Permanence.** Elements that remain fixed provide familiarity, security and identity (e.g., entrance features, benches, specimen trees, large rocks, play structures).

i.   **Change.** Elements that indicate changes in season (e.g., deciduous trees), weather (e.g., plants like bamboo that move in the wind, materials like sand that get wet when it rains) and the life of the community (e.g., bulletin boards).

j.   **Open-endedness.** One way to provide flexibility is with elements that users can manipulate and build onto for their own reasons (e.g., a corner of a play structure that can be draped with a blanket to make a "house," a low shelf where "mixtures" can be made from plant parts) (Moore, 1986 a,b).

k.   **Manipulability.** Some aspects of settings should allow children to manually change them to serve their own purposes (e.g., sand, dirt, water, vegetation and small toys) (Moore & Wong, in press).

l.   **Multisensory Stimulation.** Settings should expose users to the greatest range of colors, smells, textures, shapes, sizes, sounds, objects, materials, interactions, people, climate, time, space, movement and change. (See also Multisensory Cues, item w. below.)

m.   **Ambient Microclimate/Year-round Use.** Settings should protect users from excessive wind, rain, sun, shade and noise (protection from smog is also necessary in some locations) and provide for year-round bodily comfort. Trees, walls and shrubberies are important modifiers of climate (Moore & Wong, in press).

The play season for many play areas could be expanded to year-round use by consciously creating favorable microclimates and providing protection from adverse weather conditions. It is important to provide sunny areas, shady areas, wind buffers and dry spots. Cold climate play settings of snow and ice need careful consideration (Björklid, 1984/85; Thompsen & Borowieka, 1980). The features most appreciated by children are slopes suitable for sliding and sledding activities. Such features should be located to avoid potential conflict with other users. Flat areas are also desirable, that can be flooded and used for skating and other sliding games.

All play areas should be capable of year round use. While some special features, such as wading pools might not be used during the winter (although they may be flooded for skating and sledding activity in cold climates), other play elements will be. The special features that may be built with the supervised play area must be

12   *Microclimate modification is a critical aspect of site planning.*

13   *Play settings should be sunny.*

14   *Play settings should provide shade.*

15   *Play settings should protect children from cold winds.*

designed to withstand weather, vandalism and deterioration which can occur when supervisors are not present and during the off season.

1) Local climatic conditions should be taken into account when designing play areas. Best local climates for play area sites are usually on south or southeast slopes, near water and on upper or middle slopes rather than at their foot or crest.

2) Wind is generally quieter on the leeward rather than the windward side of a slope.

3) Wind speeds on the crest of a ridge may be 20% greater than on flat ground. Wind also tends to speed up around the sides of buildings.

4) Thick belts of shrubs or trees are effective wind breaks. They reduce wind velocities by more than 50% for a distance downwind of ten times their height and by 35% for twice that distance.

5) Structures can both block or channel winds or create unpleasant, gusty, "wind tunnel" effects.

6) Depending on climatic conditions, play areas and activities should be located to either avoid or take advantage of the shading effects of buildings and evergreen tree clusters.

7) Deciduous trees provide summer shade and sun in winter.

8) Proper drainage should help dry play areas quickly after rain.

n.   **Shelter.** There should be some shelter at every playground even though it might only be a place to get out of the rain like a covered picnic table.

Ideally, there should be a shelter house containing indoor play space combined with storage for equipment and play props.

1) Location. A shelter should be located near the center of action: a wading pool, playing fields or special play feature. It should be highly visible and have clear sight lines to all areas of the play setting; however, space for quiet activities should also be available, perhaps on the nonactive side of the shelter.

2) Storage. The shelter can be used to store maintenance equipment, chlorine and pool cleaning equipment, sports equipment, mobile play things and play props.

3)   Use. The shelter may be used as a place for children to "hang out," play indoor games, or for special events: plays, dances, community activities. In this sense it would function as a "clubhouse."

o.   **Social Interaction.** Settings that stimulate social development and support social relationships for different sized groups should be provided (e.g., bench and platform groupings, enclosed sitting areas, small shelters, play houses, domes, multiperson slides).

p.   **Design for All Ages.** Wherever possible, play areas should be designed for users of all age groups, although some separation because of incompatible activities may be necessary. Often, children's play areas lack facilities or accommodations for teenagers, parents or other adults. Providing facilities and accommodations for adults will encourage family use. Barrier-free design and good maintenance will encourage use by everyone. Facilities should include:

1)   Hard surfaced areas for court games and bike riding.

2)   Challenging equipment, especially if there is a supporting recreation program at the park.

3)   Picnic tables, barbecue stands, comfortable seating, lawn game areas and checkerboard tables.

4)   Specially designed areas for preschool children

q.   **Variety of Social Spaces** (Moore & Wong, in press; Seattle, 1986). A variety of spaces, from small to large, are necessary to support different sized groups of children engaged in different social activities:

1)   Small spaces for quiet play by one to five children.

These spaces can serve as "refuges" that allow individuals and small groups to withdraw from social interaction when desired (Kirkby, 1984).

2)   Private places supporting quiet exploration, that children can get into but adults cannot, under low platforms, on different levels and/or screened by vegetation.

Children, like adults, need time and space to be alone or in small groups. Make sure active, noisy areas are separated from quiet spaces.

3) Age-specific places as well as places where several age groups can play together.

Preschool children like to play in their own groups but in the company of older children; therefore, preschool areas should be included in spaces for older children.

4) Semi-enclosed spaces for group play led by adults.

5) Large grassy spaces for large group play.

6) Large group areas designed to facilitate gatherings of an entire class, a whole family, or a complete neighborhood for a wide range of activities.

7) Child-sized tables and benches.

By providing a variety of spatial settings—private, semiprivate, and public—the stage is set for a spectrum of personal and social experiences that together can contribute to full child development (AEC, 1980).

Children with disabilities often have limited opportunities for large group experiences. Environments which allow the experience of solitude as well as group activity can help children develop social skills and positive self-identities.

Where possible, leave space for wheelchairs to pull up for peer interaction, or for a hearing-impaired child to be close to a speaker or interpreter. Note: the idea is not to make a "parking space" for wheelchairs, but to provide enough space that they can move about easily.

r. **Variety of Spatial Experiences** (Moore, 1966, 1974; Seattle, 1986). Children need to learn spatial concepts such as over/under, in/out, up/down, right/left, depth and directionality and the limits of fingers, toes and head. They also need to measure the risk of jumping, reaching, and falling. To learn these concepts, children need a variety of spatial experiences.

1) High places such as knolls and towers from which to view activities.

2) Differently sized spaces to crawl in, under, over or through.

3) Environmental cues such as textures and shadows.

4) Opportunities to fall, jump or drop safely (for children with brittle bones, 6" may be too much).

16   *Play settings should provide a variety of spaces to facilitate social interaction and retreat.*

17   Children need to learn spatial concepts such as in/out, up/down and right/left.

18   Play settings should offer nest-like spaces for quiet retreat and observation.

19   Children sometimes need to get away from the action.

5)   A variety of fixed reference points for orientation.

6)   A variety of climbing experiences, up/down, in/out, over/under, etc.

s.   **Retreats and Breakaway Points** (Moore, G.T., et al., 1979; Seattle, 1986; Schneekloth, 1985). Although children need to interact with their peers, they also need to be alone, to get away and dream, to escape from external pressure. They need secluded spaces to engage in quiet cognitive, social and manipulative play, individually or in small groups. Nooks are required for solitary play and for watching others (Moore & Wong, in press).

At times all children feel an acute need for privacy, to retreat from too intense play or conflict, or when attempting a new activity that is discovered to be too difficult or otherwise unpleasant. Provision must be made for a child to contemplate an activity before deciding to do it and to leave before completing an activity without feeling failure, thus helping to maintain a positive self-concept.

An ideal retreat is neither too close nor too far from other children and provides privacy and the opportunity for observing the behavior of peers from a distance (Moore, 1979).

Escape opportunities prevent panic and provide encouragement for exploration by offering face-saving exits from unfavorable situations. Some groups can benefit by retreating from the larger population, thereby avoiding inappropriate comparison and conflict. There is some evidence that ethnic minorities play more easily when not outnumbered. The same may be true of disability groups. Children need places to test their own abilities without feeling that people are watching (the "fishbowl effect").

Provide more than one means of egress from challenging activities. For example, a ladder may have access to two platforms before reaching a top level. A platform may have both a slide and a ladder.

t.   **Visible Completion Points** (Moore, G.T., et al., 1979; Seattle, 1986). For encouragement and to avoid frustration, children need evidence of their success and accomplishments—milestones which tell them they are improving their skills. Play settings should provide:

1)   Clear stages of completion such as climbing platforms at different heights, viewed by all.

20   *Play settings should include visible completion points.*

2)   Positive signals at the point of completion or accomplishment such as something that can only be seen at or from the top; a bell to ring.

3)   Combinations of challenge and success scaled to children's capabilities.

u.   Spatial Orientation (Nordhaus, et al., 1984). Settings must contain appropriate signage (see Chap. 7, Sect. 3, Program/Site Information) and treat primary facilities such as restrooms, telephones and program headquarters as landmarks visible from pathways. A direct view of a facility is the simplest and most effective means of orientation. (This does not apply to everything on the site. Less important facilities and opportunities need to be "discovered" by the users. Too much openness and visibility can destroy the pleasure of exploration.)

Spatial orientation applies as well to inside-outside relationships. Siting and exposure to external landmarks can help users orient themselves to their surroundings.

v.   Landmarks/Visual Identity (Schneekloth, 1985; Seattle, 1986). Landmarks are key orienting devices used by all people to guide their movement through space. Because of their memorable form, or strategic location, landmarks tell us where we are in relationship to the whole.

Landmarks are elements that stand out strongly against their backgrounds because of their contrasting shape, silhouette, color, texture or size. They help establish the identity of a place (Lynch, 1961).

Landmarks can be very effective in helping children orient themselves in space, establish a sense of inhabiting their "own place," and acquire clear memories of their environment. These are valuable means for children to develop psychological independence (Moore, 1966, 1978b).

Therefore, provide easily recognizable objects and experiences (acoustic, tactile, visual, olfactory) such as play structures, trees, hills or ponds, which have known, permanent locations in the playground. Some should have a strong enough impact to provide an identifying image for the whole site.

Tall features from which children can view their surroundings and which can be seen from a distance are powerful landmarks (Moore, 1966).

Temporary landmarks such as flags and banners can be provided and, in some cases, made by children themselves.

21   *Play settings should help orient children and provide a strong sense of identity.*

w.   **Multisensory Cues** (AEC, 1980; Schneekloth, 1985).   A multisensory setting provides important cues for orientation and movement for children with a variety of special needs. The frequent repetition and reinforcement of cues can help capture attention and enable a child to cope with a strange environment. Sight, for example, can be reinforced by touch and sound.

The pairing or repetition of cues can reinforce information for all children. Different levels on a play structure, for example, can have a different flooring to cue children about how high they are off the ground; at the same time it can reinforce the visual cues of safety rails, color coding, etc. This further aids learning since one child can use the cue most easily learned and teach others.

22   *Play settings should be places of multisensory stimulation.*

Especially for children with sensory impairments, play settings should emphasize all the senses: taste, touch, sight, smell and hearing. Sites should be planned and settings designed to stimulate the development of all the senses.

Sounds. Sounds can be used as landmarks for visually and physically disabled children. Street lights, for example, can be coordinated with a pattern of sounds to allow the child to use an auditory cue for safe passage across the street.

Sounds are also important as a play phenomena. Children delight in producing sounds by striking things, it gives them a sense of interaction with the environment. Therefore, design settings to produce constant and patterned sounds (wind chimes, plants that make sounds like bamboo) to encourage children to rely on auditory sensations to determine their location.   Identify special areas with peculiar sounds. Giant musical instruments can be constructed (Sutton, 1985).

Visually, mentally and physically impaired children can use echoes to determine their location in an enclosed space. There are many ways to design echoes. A tunnel is a classic example that children love.

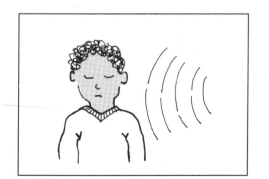

23   *Play settings should expose children to the acoustic environment.*

Settings should include sequences of solids and voids that reflect sound and give children locational cues. Use tunnels that have openings and closings at various places so that the experience of moving through an enclosed space becomes familiar. Paths with solids and voids along one edge can be used as sound cues for approaching intersections.

Movement and orientation skills are dependent to some extent on locating oneself with respect to the mass/void continuum in the environment. Sound is used as a major cue in this respect. Blind children also need practice in refining "facial vision," the ability to sense physical barriers, and to stop before running into doors

24 *Tunnels can have sequences of solids and voids.*

25 *Tactile sensations can be exciting experiences.*

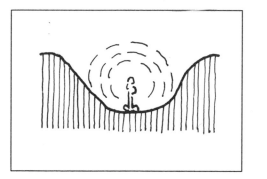

26 *Enclosed space.*

and walls. A combination of solids and voids on playgrounds can provide such experiences in a fun way.

Touch. Everyone uses touch to gather information. It tells children about changes and continuations in their environment. Unclear cues are obviously confusing and limit desires for exploration. Textures should be used to reinforce the kind of experience a child can expect: changes of texture where there is a change of activity or spatial relationship; different textures to designate different areas of the playground. Clearly, such treatments should be used consistently.

Sight. For the partially sighted child, visual tracking is an important learned skill for successful movement and orientation. For this, settings should have bright reflective colors that stimulate vision and help children move through space. Include graphics that help children practice visual tracking. At the same time, take care not to visually overload the setting for nonimpaired users.

Smell. Fragrant plant materials can help orientate visually impaired children, especially if used to reinforce other sensory cues.

x.   **Scale, Size, Shape, Enclosure and Continuity.** These are the basic dimensions of spatial design which must be varied, juxtaposed, contrasted and orchestrated to produce a range of spatial experience, suitable for different developmental and age requirements.

(**Scale** refers to the relative size of something; **size** refers to the actual dimensions; **shape** refers to the geometrical characteristics; **enclosure** is the sense of being contained by space; and **continuity** means the ability to move smoothly from point to point.)

y.   **Play Above Ground** (Moore, 1974b; Seattle, 1986). Children need to play and travel around above the ground plane in a challenging but safe manner, always with a choice of exits. Climbing is basic to development of gross motor skills, particularly body control, coordination of hands and feet, and for balancing on uneven, changing surfaces. Think of the spatial experience of children in all three dimensions.

Children are particularly attracted to moving up-and-down, as well as through space. Think of free-flowing activities such as swing ropes and safe trapeze-like experiences. Consider the "climb-ability" of all elements. Provide:

1)   A variety of safe climbing experiences: both rigid surfaces (platforms, ladders, rocks and trees); and flexible ones (cables, tires, nets).

27   Open space.

28   Play settings should provide opportunities to play above the ground plane.

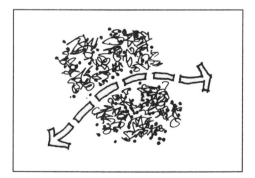

29   Play areas should be structured as a system of differentiated (separate-yet-connected) settings.

2)   Safe climbing and resting spots above the ground at many heights and levels.

3)   Space for small groups to play together above ground.

z.   **Differentiated Settings** (AEC, 1980; Moore & Wong, in press; Seattle, 1986). Different age groups use play spaces in different ways; some need private places within sight and hearing of their parents; others need places where different age groups mingle, learn mutually and enjoy each other's company.

Children achieve different developmental goals at different times of their lives and at different rates. Developmental stages have varying skill levels which require settings to be used in different ways. Settings should therefore vary in space, size and location, and be interconnected to give children choices between types of play.

Well-defined activity areas facilitate children's participation in all activities. The qualities of each space depend on the activities that go on there. Children who are easily distracted or have perceptual problems will benefit from clearly defined areas.

Children can recognize what activities are appropriate to certain spaces. Space dividers, to separate areas with different functions, can be as obvious as walls, or as subtle as changed lighting. Carefully chosen signs, color cues, changes in level, and varying textures communicate the functions of particular areas.

For the most part, settings should be differentiated in terms of size and physical character, rather than by age or some other social division. Social divisions are unrealistic and usually create more problems than they solve, with the following exceptions:

1)   Areas should be set aside for the exclusive use of parents and caregivers with very young children.

2)   Raised areas with shade and adequate seating for adults and older children to oversee small children.

Further recommendations regarding setting differentiation include:

1)   Locate settings for large-muscle activity and equipment away from settings for small-muscle manipulative play.

2)   Locate especially attractive high density activity areas with care, to avoid negative impacts on adjacent low density settings.

30 *Well-defined activity areas may help children recognize appropriate activities for certain spaces.*

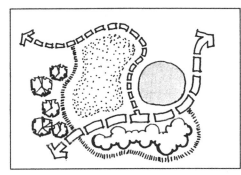

31 *Differentiation and linkage are critical considerations.*

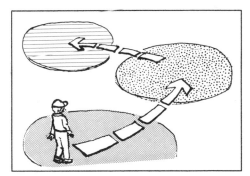

32 *Transition spaces allow children to move comfortably from one activity to another.*

3) Provide links between settings so that children can move easily from one to another and children of different abilities can see and interact with each other.

4) Differentiate between settings based on attributes such as:

- Types of play, either active or passive.
- Equipment size.
- Developmental task (quiet retreat, programmed, large muscle, etc.).
- Physical character (sand area, water play, moving equipment).
- Group size (single child, one to four children, six to ten and so on).

5) Identify settings by developmental goals rather than age groups (with the exception of separating toddlers and preschoolers). Provide links between developmental levels.

6) Within play areas, circulation should take a looping form and be used to define activity settings. Looping circulation assures no dead ends and allows children to progress readily from one setting to the next.

7) Circulation should encourage a developmental progression through graduated challenges. Links between settings of different levels of difficulty should be clear.

8) Avoid straight stretches of path that tempt children to run too fast, creating unsafe conditions.

9) All settings should be at least partly visible from circulation areas so children can easily choose where they want to go.

10) Main pathways should be clearly separated from main activity settings and related circulation.

11) Circulation routes should be wide and flat enough for wheelchairs and turnabouts and, where appropriate, for play activity and general milling-about. They should not overlap with activity settings that can be easily disrupted by noise and movement.

12) Transition spaces, when clearly defined, allow children to move comfortably from one activity to the next. Children who have difficulty relating to new environments—young children, shy children, or children who are autistic—need clearly demarcated transitional spaces. Without them, they may have trouble joining in and focusing on new activities.

Children using wheelchairs and other special equipment may need extra space for transfer and to park or store their equipment.

13) Boundaries of play settings should be clearly defined. This is important for supervision, and to make sure children know what is acceptable behavior within each setting, especially when it may be sharply different from adjacent settings. Knowing where you are is important for children's psychological security and their willingness to engage in new experiences (Schneekloth, 1985).

Edges are visually and tactually the most recognizable cue to differentiate settings. Even very small infants can see clearly defined edges as can many visually impaired children.

Accidents are more probable when objects, spaces, and activities are not clearly differentiated.

Define boundaries using objects and/or acoustic, tactile, visual and olfactory cues. Thus the sequence of settings and their relationship to the whole can be clearly perceived. Articulate edges by contrasting field/ground relationships through color, materials, spatial relationships and sun/shade patterns.

aa. **The "Edge" Effect.** To seek psychological and social comfort, children often prefer to gather around the edges of a space. The location of edges should be considered carefully in relation to other determinants such as orientation, activity pattern, access points, etc. Where appropriate, build social/play elements into edges—walls designed as places to sit, hide behind, climb on, walk along; nooks and crannies.

Edges are also significant habitats where plants and animals (and people) can find shelter, especially internal corners (the meeting point of edges).

Edges can be readily created in the interior of a site along setting boundaries—many times multiplying the edge effect—to support a complex pattern of interactions, particularly between people and plants.

33 *Play settings should contain well-defined activity areas and edges.*

bb. **Undefined Places** (Moore & Wong, in press; Schneekloth, 1985). Play settings can be used to stimulate creative and fantasy behavior. There is some evidence that undefined settings support fantasy play especially well (Hart, 1979; Moore, 1986c). In such settings, an undefined structure can become anything a child wishes, from a castle to a car.

34   *Open-ended, undefined spaces should be included in play settings.*

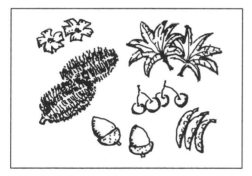

35   *People-plant interaction.*

36   *People-wildlife interaction.*

Avoid making play areas that are entirely made up of realistic play objects like trains. Some settings should be undefined in real world terms. If a platform is provided, be sure that it is not an explicit copy of a fort, so that the children can turn it into anything they want. A pile of rock, sand areas, geometric structures all provide the opportunity for imaginative play. Settings which have more than one use will be used longer and by more diverse age groups, and will provide more learning potential.

Settings and objects which are not obviously representative of a specific thing; e.g., rocketship, castle, animal, etc., allow the child to create his or her own fantasy play world. Undefined structures become whatever the child wants them to be, and the child will then create the story that goes with the imagined setting. "Let's pretend" games stimulate social interaction and help the child to experiment.

Military objects such as tanks and cannons and missiles have no place on playgrounds. They should be excluded entirely (IPA, 1977).

cc.   **People-Plant Interaction.** A variety of settings are needed where users can make close contact with vegetation including groundcovers, shrubs and trees (Moore & Wong, in press; see Chap. 13, Trees/Vegetation).

dd.   **Wildlife Habitats.** Shelter and food for small scale animal life—birds, small mammals, amphibians and reptiles, insects and other small organisms—must be provided. This can be on a permanent or temporary basis.

If natural habitats and features already exist on an undeveloped site, make sure they are conserved and integrated into the site plan.

Vegetation, rocks, logs, marshes and ponds can support the modest scale of wildlife that children find attractive, e.g., beetles, salamanders, snails, sowbugs, ants, fish, shrimp, worms, caterpillars, tadpoles, butterflies, spiders and so on.

ee.   **Domestic Animals.** Domestic and farmyard animals are important resources for children, and are especially helpful for integration (Children's Environments Quarterly, Vol. 1, No. 3, 1984; Handicapped Adventure Playground Association, hereafter HAPA, 1978; Shier, 1984). They require careful supervision and secure facilities for food and shelter. The City Farm concept is a viable idea here, as it stresses the needs of animals as well as children (Blue, 1986; Broadway, 1979; Schools Council, 1974a, b).

ff. **Mix of People-made and Natural Elements.** Children need exposure to the full range of settings and objects that represent contemporary culture and our biological inheritance.

gg. **Indoor-Outdoor Relationships.** A variety of transitions between buildings and the outdoors are recommended: terraces, decks, verandas, pagodas, etc. Adequate ramps are required (see Chap. 6, sect. 17) (Allen, 1968; CMHC, 1980).

hh. **Ease and Economy of Construction.** Playground budgets are always limited. Unnecessarily expensive features will mean cuts elsewhere. Playgrounds can be built in phases, as funds become available. The cost/play value benefit ratio should be carefully evaluated for all settings.

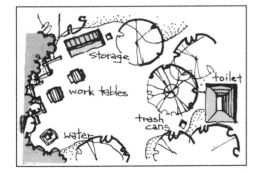

PART B :

Setting Design and Management

4. MANAGEMENT CRITERIA FOR PLAY SETTINGS

Eight criteria for managing play settings have been given particular emphasis throughout the guidelines.

4.1 Play Value

Play value is a measure of the developmental significance of a play setting, object or material as a stimulus for children's play. Critical questions include:

a. What are the play values and goals for integrated settings?

b. How are they communicated to users, designers, managers and manufacturers?

4.2 Programming Potential

Programming potential is a measure of the degree to which a given play setting, object or material can be used as a resource for creative program development. Critical questions include:

a. How can social and physical elements in a setting be extended to encourage a range of activity programming?

b. What qualities should be included in physical settings to make them more flexible as potential programming environments?

c. How can the program and environment be better esigned to accommodate each other?

d. Which environments and activities encourage integration of children with and without disabilities?

4.3 Play Leadership

Play leadership describes the role of those who enliven and inspire children to action, who support them, stimulate interest, encourage cooperation and integration and who help adapt play environments to accommodate all abilities. Critical questions include:

a. What are the roles and responsibilities of play leaders as facilitators and supervisors of children's activities?

b. What are their roles in risk management, safety and integration?

c. What constitutes effective training for play leaders?

37   *Every type of child, no matter what level of ability, needs play opportunities.*

38   *Play settings should offer opportunities to learn about the physical world.*

4.4   Safety

Safety embraces the broad concept of caring for the health and well-being of all children under all circumstances, recognizing that they are a powerless group in society. Children are dependent on adults to provide safe, appropriate high quality settings for their development; specifically, this means ensuring that children are not exposed to hazardous situations and that known dangers are removed from their environment. Critical questions include:

a.   What are accetable definitions of "safety," "risk," and "hazard" with respect to both physical and social aspects of play settings for children with and without disabilities?

b.   What do we actually know about these issues?

c.   How can we use the discussion of safety-related issues to increase awareness of the broader concepts of children's play including play value, child development and risk taking?

4.5   Risk Management

Risk management refers to management strategies and methods used to reduce the risk of accident, liability and lawsuit with respect to children's play settings. (Moreland, et al., 1985; see Chapter 25 for further details.) The critical question is how can we implement a comprehensive set of risk management strategies including:

a.   **Shared environmental control.**
Control over the physical environment is essential to the safety and security of children. Entrances to every play program space should be able to be monitored. Where the space is shared with other organized groups, staff should get to know each other and their children so that the monitoring task can be shared.

b.   **Defensible settings** (Newman, 1972).
Programmed activities can be dispensed into small group activity centers throughout the site. This decentralization of activity increases the possibility of informal surveillance of the whole site.

c.   **Shared site maintenance.**
Effective site maintenance is essential to the health and safety of children. For most sites this can be achieved most effectively as a shared responsibility of program staff and the parks and recreation or school department.

d. **High staffing/supervision ratios.**
    Clearly, the greater the ratio of trained staff to children the less likelihood of children getting into situations that could result in injury. The issue here is to ensure, through adequate training, that staff do not inadvertently block children from essential, nonhazardous risktaking activity.

e. **Staff and leadership training.**
    Professional training is an essential requirement for adequate risk managemant (and all other aspects of effective play programming). How and where such training should be delivered is a matter of current debate among the professions involved.

f. **Built-in risktaking within programs.**
    This strategy is an excellent means of providing safe yet challenging experiences for children. It reduces the risk of children seeking challenges in more hazardous settings.

g. **Allowance for spontaneous play within programs.**
    To ensure play opportunities covering the full range of developmental needs, spontaneous play must be allowed. However, staff must take care that hazardous situations are avoided.

h. **Community involvement.**
    By encouraging the participation of children's families and neighborhood residents in play programs, they will become more knowledgeable and positive towards the goals and objectives. The chance of a negative (litigious) reaction in the case of a mishap will thereby be reduced. Community-based management means parents and community members must take leading roles, such as sitting on the board of directors.

i. **Documentation, record-keeping and reporting.**
    As part of staff training, it is essential that everyone involved in a given play program follows standard record-keeping procedures and uses a pre-established documentation and reporting procedure in the case of an accident occurring.

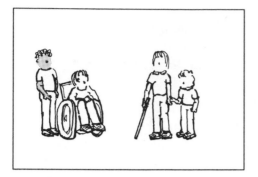

39   *Play settings must be accessible to children with all forms of disability.*

4.6   Accessibility

Accessibility is a measure of the degree to which users can experience all parts of an environment, recognizing that each will be more or less difficult for each individual. Critical questions include:

a.   What are the issues that hinder physical use, contact or sensory experience of particular elements or materials?

b.   Can all environments be physically designed for everyone? What role can managers play in facilitating access to settings and activity programs?

c.   What are the most effective management strategies for reducing psychological barriers to play settings (negative, uninformed attitudes towards children with disabilities, etc.)?

4.7   Integration

Integration is a measure of the degree to which children of different ages, sexes, ethnic and social groups and ability or disability interact socially and play together. Critical questions include:

a.   What is a reasonable definition of "integration" for programs and settings?

b.   What are some common sense-criteria for evaluating integration?

c.   What are the major barriers at the local level to achieving properly integrated programs and play settings?

d.   What is the role of play leadership in integration?

4.8   Management

Management refers to the systematic, rational processes, procedures and strategies used to allocate environmental resources to meet social goals. Included are policy, planning, participation, physical design, maintenance and budgetary activities. Critical questions include:

a.   What are the most effective strategies for management and maintenance of integrated settings and programs?

b.   How can their success be measured?

4.9   Play Setting Concept

The concept of play setting is used throughout this book as a means of integrating behavioral needs and physical requirements in design. Play setings are functional entities
that can be conveniently discussed and manipulated in the planning and design process
to meet the developmental objectives normally proposed for most public play environments. The detailed requirements of seventeen types of play setting (reflecing the importance of choice and diversity in the child's environment) are discussed in the chapters following this one. They range from entrance settings to storage settings.

5. ENTRANCES

Clearly defined entrances are important to orient, inform and introduce users to the site. Entrances are a critical transition zone between transportation vehicle and program, especially for children with disabilities and parents with disabilities. They are places where people can meet and talk, and are possible locations for displaying community information.

Planning Criteria

Play Value. Entrances are an important social space, where children and parents can socialize and where neighborhood contacts are made.

Programming. Entrances are an important information node and opportunity to advertise program details.

Play Leadership. Leaders need to recognize the program potential of entrance settings.

Safety. Moving cars or backing vehicles are a hazard. The chance of children running out in front of moving vehicles must be avoided by erecting barriers or by some other means. A warning sign on its own is insufficient (in English law a child is assumed to be unable to read, or if they can, not to realize the full implications of the warning).

Risk Management. Entrances are good locations for signs about risk and liability.

Accessibility. Ramps are mandatory for entrances not at grade.

Integration. Entrances provide good potential for integration. Everyone arriving and leaving has to pass through, linger and interact. Seating and shade must be adequate.

Management/Maintenance. Policies are required concerning public access and use of public space. Visibility of entrances and social support with benches, drinking fountains, etc., need careful consideration by site planners.

40   *Entrances should give a welcoming feeling to users and provide a multi-use zone for dropping-off, information and gathering.*

5.1   Functional Requirements (Barrier Free Environments, Inc., hereafter BFE, 1980)

The principal public entrance of a play facility is of fundamental importance, legally and emotionally, to people with and without disabilities.

The principal entrance must be linked by accessible walks to public transportation stops, passenger loading zones, accessible parking spaces, and public streets and sidewalks. A disabled person should be able to proceed independently from this entrance to all accessible spaces within the facility.

Entrances must be accessible and include drop-off and waiting zones.

5.1.1   Access (Kiewel, 1980)

a.   Provide grade-level or ramped walkways; stairs may be present but only in addition to the accessible walk.

b.   Use firm, continuous, nonslip walking surfaces.

c.   The walking surfaces should be kept free of leaves, ice, snow and debris by regular maintenance, weather protection or automatic snow melting equipment.

5.1.2   Drop-off Zones (Robinette, 1985)

Entrances are where children often get dropped off and picked up, usually by vehicle.

Wheelchairs, walkers and other equipment should also be accommodated. Requirements include:

11   *Drop-off zones should be provided close to play setting entrances.*

a.   Width of the drop-off zone should be a minimum of 12 feet wide to allow car doors to be fully opened for ease of access.

b.   Length of the zone should accommodate at least 2 cars, allowing 25 feet for each, and should have gradual access to the main road.

c.   Where the zone is at the same grade as the adjacent walk, bollards or some other suitable device should be used to separate the two functions. Where a curb exists and cannot be removed, one small 1:6 ramp per car should be provided to make the grade change.

d.   Signage should be provided to identify the drop-off zone and limit its defined use to a "pick-up/drop-off" function.

e.   Adequate lighting should be provided.

f.   Bollards:

1) Bollards are useful as traffic control devices as they allow for pedestrian access while halting vehicular access. They should be spaced a minimum of 3 feet apart to allow a wheelchair to pass.

2) Bollards can be useful for seats if they are at least 12 inches wide and between 18 and 24 inches high.

3) Bollards should be painted in a contrasting color to the paving around them. They should be well illuminated at night to minimize the risk of a person inadvertently walking into them.

5.1.3   Waiting Zones

(See also Gathering, Meeting, And Working Places, Chapter 20)

Entrances are places of coming and going, where people have a chance for a few words with each other and catch their breath, especially parents waiting to pick up their children.

a.   Waiting areas should be large enough to comfortably accommodate the average number of people normally using them (Robinette, 1985).

b.   Seating should be provided for the average number of daily users, with space also allotted to park wheelchairs, strollers and other wheeled vehicles (Robinette, 1985).

c.   Table(s) may also be justified to support social interaction and as a place to leave belongings.

d.   Bike racks must be provided.

e.   Litter receptacle(s) are needed.

f.   An overhead shelter or canopy should be used to minimize the effects of the weather. Care should be taken to locate vertical support posts out of the paths of pedestrians either using or passing near the shelter. If the shelter is enclosed, adequate space must be allotted for easy in and out movement (Robinette, 1985).

g.   Loading areas should be designed so that circulation from the waiting area is uncomplicated and over paved surfaces. The loading area itself should not have a curb that must be climbed. If a curb cannot be avoided, a 1:6 ramp will be necessary (Robinette, 1985).

42   *Bicycle stands should be installed at play setting entrances.*

43   *Bulletin boards should display program information at play setting entrances.*

5.1.4   Communications/Image

a.   Entrances should attract users and visitors, and give a positive first impression of the setting. They should present a welcoming, "please come again" feeling to people as they leave.

b.   Archways are a powerful welcoming element.

c.   Bulletin board(s) must be installed to advertise information about programs and related community events.

d.   Embellishments such as banners, flags, decorations and posters can be produced as a program activity and displayed temporarily.

6. PATHWAYS

Pathways provide accessibility and separate functionally different spaces; they enable users to move between and through elements and help them to orient in space. Pathways can be a recreational and play facility in and of themselves.

Planning Criteria

Play Value. Different types of paths support different types of activity depending on their design: circulation, wheeled-toy play, chase games, exploration activity, etc.

Programming Potential. Pathways provide potential for mobile activities.

Play Leadership. Leaders need to know how to use pathways for mobile games and interpretive activity.

Safety. Pathways must not be located near drop-offs; adequate lighting and guardrails are sometimes needed.

Risk Management. Pathways must be well maintained; major paths must be clearly defined and well lit.

Accessibility. Pathways require good surfaces and correct gradients. Within the overall park, a hierarchy of path difficulties can be provided ("Accessible," "Usable," "Difficult," Nordhaus, et al., 1984). Brochures, maps, etc., should be provided to allow users to make decisions on access and difficulty before venturing out.

Integration. Pathways stimulate cooperation and interaction during circulation. They support, interpretive or mobile games. Pathways get children to destinations where they can interact with each other.

Management/Maintenance. Policies are needed to allow multimodal use (pedestrians, wheelchairs, tricycles, bicycles, skateboards and other wheeled toys) as well as different levels of use.

6.1   Safe, Direct Primary Routes (AEC, 1980)

a.   Park areas containing playgrounds should be linked to residential neighborhoods, otherwise getting to the park can be difficult.

b.   A network of accessible routes needs to connect directly with entrances, extend across the site and connect main centers of activity. Six classes of pathways or trails have been developed by the U.S. Heritage, Conservation and Recreation Service, (Bunin, et al., 1980), and are described at the end if this section.

In planning accessible pathways, use site terrain to the best advantage. Secondary entrances that are nonprimary may be used if they are the best alternative and are made attractive. Appropriate placement of signs should indicate an alternate path or the location of a part of a facility. If the main route is inaccessible, a sign should guide people from there to the accessible route.

c.   Paths are the primary means for travel between activity areas and should be safe, accessible and convenient. (Bunin, et al., 1980)

d.   **Dimensions** (AEC, 1980). Pathways must have an adequately wide, continuous, even surface; they must be as level as possible. Overhead clearance to 8 feet 6 inches under tree limbs, signs, etc., is especially important for blind people.

Primary routes must be wide enough (9—10 feet) for wheelchairs to pass each other in opposite directions. Baby strollers must be accommodated (Los Angeles, 1987).

Other pathway design specifications include:

1)   A width no less than 3 feet, except at doorways.

2)   No changes in level that exceed 1/2 inch (thresholds, doormats, heaved pavement).

3)   A maximum slope of 8.3% (no steeper than 1 inch of rise per foot of length) for a maximum allowable distance of 30 feet. 0—4% is desirable for longer distances:

   •   0—1% is level.
   •   2—4% is moderate.
   •   5—7% is steep.
   •   7% is impossible.

44   Minimum 6 feet 8 inches clearance for blind access.

45   Minimum width of 4—5 feet is recommended.

46   *Wheelchairs need 5 feet 4 inches turning space adjacent to benches.*

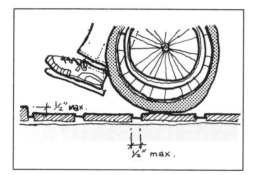

47   *Pathways should not have joints greater than 1/2 inch or changes in level greater than 1/2 inch.*

48   *Slopes: 5% easy; 6.25% accessible; 8.35% difficult.*

Level of difficulty depends on percent slope and length. A 1:12 (8.3%) slope is the California state guideline for urban areas but 1:15 or 1:20 is much preferred (Zirpolo, 1987; Cangemi, 1987). 1:12 not recommended for trails.

4)   A nonslip surface;

5)   No cross slope (from side to side of path) steeper than 2%, 1% is preferred (Zirpolo, 1987).

6)   Landings at tops, bottoms and at turns.

7)   Resting places at intervals no greater than 200 feet.

8)   Handrails on both sides; double handrails at two heights are preferable.

9)   Slope, cross slope and surfacing dictate levels of pathway accessibility (detailed later in this section).

e.   Children travel in straight lines in active play, and will do so unless diverted by substantial barriers or an especially desirable feature.

f.   A ramp in excess of the maximum slope may be the only solution where there is no room to build a ramp to the appropriate length. Only in the case of a small ramp, as at a threshold (up to 3 feet), could the incline be usable with a slope of 12.5% (1:8). Since steep ramps are dangerous for pedestrians as well as for people in wheelchairs, stairs must be provided also. (For further information see National Center for a Barrier-Free Environment, hereafter NCBFE, Access Information Bulletin "Ramps, Stairs & Floor Treatments.")

g.   **Third Dimension.** Some paths should lift users above grade to provide "overviews" of the setting. Bridges are an excellent solution (Robinette, 1985).

Minimum "roll-under" height for wheelchairs is 38 inches.

h.   **Bicycles.** Large or full-size bicycles present a hazard on main pathways (skateboards and roller skates sometimes, too). Without direct supervision they are difficult to exclude, even with regulatory signs. The risk should be recognized by all caretakers in the play setting.

In a large setting, a separate bikeway path should be constructed along primary circulation routes. Bike racks should be provided.

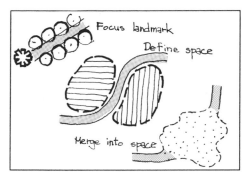

49 *Pathways should be used as a major structuring element in site design.*

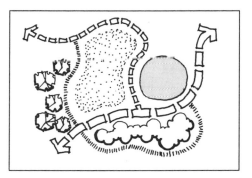

50 *A variety of pathway choices should be available.*

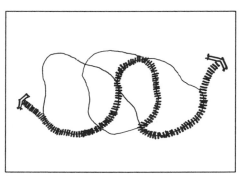

51 *Pathway layout should follow the principle of intersecting circles.*

6.2   The Flow of Play Activity (adapted from Seattle, 1986)

In diverse play settings, children's play activity takes on a complex, mobile form, especially when play props are freely available in the setting.

a.   Much mobile activity happens away from the main pathways. Play settings should allow for activities to ebb and flow continuously with multiple branching and decision points.

b.   Alternative choices of direction and activity should be visible.

c.   Because some children are easily distracted by too many choices, some subsettings should be visually separated.

d.   Branching should happen horizontally, vertically and in a combination of directions.

6.3   Choice of Route

a.   **Variety.** Play areas should contain a variety of different types of paths, other than primary circulation routes, to accommodate hiking, triking, biking, interpretive activities, hide and chase games, and to meet the varied needs of children.

b.   **Indirect.** Some paths should be planned as indirect, informal routes, where children can explore the setting, away from the main centers of activity. Some paths should be designed to reveal surprise, spatial contrast, sequential exposure to a wide variety of experiences, artifacts, views, etc.

c.   **"Intersecting Circles".** Minor paths should be laid out on the principle of "intersecting circles," to accommodate continuity of movement and provide complex settings for hide-and-chase games. Dead ends and bottleneck situations where users might collide should be avoided.

6.4   Wheeled toys

a.   Major paths should accommodate appropriate wheeled toys (see Chapter 15 for details). They are an important means for physically disabled children to achieve independence and an important stimulus for integration between children.

52 *Special self-contained tricycle circuits should be provided.*

b.   Special, circular, self-contained routes should be provided for tricycles and small bicycles to avoid potential hazards and conflicts with pedestrian users.

6.5   Related Facilities

a.   Sitting areas should be provided at regular intervals on main paths, in suitable locations.

b.   **Rest Areas and Shelter** (Nordhaus, et al., 1984).

1)   Level 1: Accessible.

5 feet by 5 feet (minimum) level space for resting every 200 feet; seating and shelter every 1/8 mile.

2)   Level 2: Useable.

5 feet by 5 feet (min.) level space for resting every 400 feet; seating and shelter every 1/4 mile.

3)   Level 3: Difficult.

Level resting space every 1/4 mile, maximum; rest areas should be closer for paths steeper than 1:20.

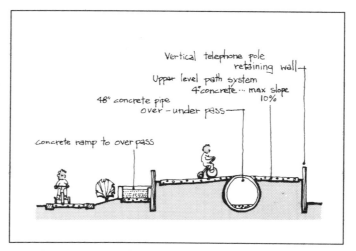

53 *Peech Playground gives tricycles their own domain.*

c.   **Gates and Doorways** (Nordhaus, et al., 1984). Gates and doorways must have a clear opening width of 32 inches. A clear approach space must be provided.

6.6   Surface Treatment Definitions

Pathway surfaces should be selected according to the following criteria: slip resistance, accessibility, impact absorption, stability/rigidity, durability, maintainability and aesthetics.

Mobility-impaired persons need stable, firm, flat, nonslip, antiskid surfaces, as defined below (Kiewel, 1980).

a.   **Stable:** Surfaces that do not move unpredictably when subjected to pedestrian traffic. Examples of surfaces that are not stable are: loose gravel or sand, carpet or sheet flooring that is not bonded to its backing or the floor and that may bubble, pucker or ripple when stressed.

b.   **Firm:** Surfaces that are highly resilient to deformation under concentrated loads. The bearing surface of a crutch or cane tip and the area of contact of wheelchair tires are considerably smaller than the net area of the average person's shoeprint. Therefore, surfaces need to be very resilient before they "feel" sound and can effectively support a person's mobility.

c.   **Flat:** Surfaces without abrupt changes in level and without irregularities. Surfaces that are not flat pose problems for people with shuffling gaits and for some people who use crutches or canes. There are two principal concerns here:

1)   Certain tile or textured floor patterns can, when wet from maintenance or inclement weather, become a hazardous "sliding track" for crutch or cane tips and cause falls. Crutch and cane tips themselves can bring ice, snow, or rain indoors on their "treads."

2)   Surface jointing patterns can create a "washboard" ride for wheelchair users, which is uncomfortable and potentially harmful. Joints between pavers or materials must be tight, shallow (if not flush) and preferably short, so that their potential as agents of falls and fatigue are minimized.

d.   **Nonslip, slip resistant,** and **antiskid** describe the elusive opposite of "slippery." There has been considerable research on this topic, dating back to at least 1924, but it has focused on able-bodied people in "normal" straight-line walking.

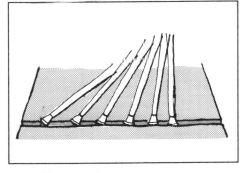

54   *Sliding track.*

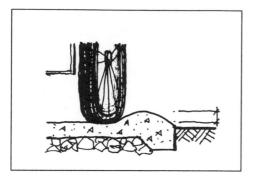

55 *Edge treatments stop wheelchairs from running off pathways.*

6.7   Edges and Curbs (Seattle, 1986)

a.   Curbs may present a tripping hazard; therefore, only provide a raised edge where there is a hazard on the other side of the path. Better still, locate paths where edges are not required.

b.   Prevent abrupt or protruding edges or grade changes along paths and on informal paved areas where bicycles, trikes, wheelchairs, gurneys or other wheeled conveyances are likely.

c.   Provide a minimum 3 feet radius for inside and outside corners on curved walks to minimize wear on plantings at corners.

d.   Where edging is omitted along asphalt surfaces, use a rolled edge having a taper of 30—45 degrees.

6.8   Warning Textures (Nordhaus, et al., 1984)

a.   Changes in texture and material may be used as a tactile warning of hazards and dangerous locations for people with severe visual impairments. However, this technique is not commonly used, and people may not recognize it. If warning textures are used at a site, they must be used consistently throughout. Partial or inconsistent use may be dangerous. Care must be taken not to create trip hazards for running children.

b.   Warning textures should begin at least 36 inches before a hazard is encountered.

c.   Textures should be 1/16 to 1/8 inch high. The texture and pattern should contrast strongly with the pathway.

d.   Materials with different noise and resiliency characteristics are more detectable than changes of texture alone. Warnings should be reinforced by contrasts in lighting value (light/dark).

e.   Changes in pathway texture may also be used to indicate a point of interest, seating area, sign location, etc. Textures used for communication must be used consistently throughout the site.

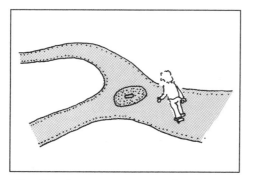

56 *Tactile treatments at path edges and intersections help blind persons.*

f.   Tactile warnings on the walking surface should be provided at locations potentially hazardous to people with severe visual impairments, such as crosswalks at roads, stairs, water areas, etc. Noise devices are required at busy street crossings. Such devices are educational for nondisabled users.

6.9   Levels of Accessibility (Nordhaus, et al., 1984)

Accessibility requirements must accommodate mixed ability groups, such as an able-bodied child with a disabled parent.

Three levels of accessibility have been defined which present a more realistic prediction of degree of difficulty for wheelchair and physically impaired users. Note, however, that levels will vary according to standards of maintenance.

a.   Level 1: Accessible.

Hard surface with light texture. Vertical joints less than 1/4 inch. Horizontal joints less than 1/2 inch. Use gratings only if necessary, with openings less than 1/2 inch perpendicular to the direction of travel.

b.   Level 2: Usable.

Firm surface with moderate texture. Vertical joints and texture less than 3/8 inch. Horizontal joints and grating openings less than 1.2 inches.

c.   Level 3: Difficult.

Passable in a wheelchair.

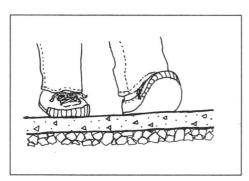

57   Concrete.

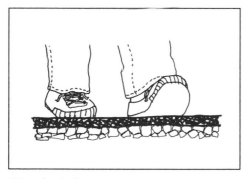

58   Asphalt.

6.10   Pathway Surfaces (Bunin, et al., 1980)

In large part, the surface of a path determines its accessibility. Balancing topography with the need to provide a wide range of pathway accessibility, one can choose from a variety of pathway surfaces. In order of decreasing accessibility, possible choices include: concrete; asphalt; wooden planking (over wet, fragile or sandy areas); solidly packed, fine crushed rock; well compacted pea gravel; bound wood chips; coarse gravel; rock; unbound wood chips; and sand. By using surfaces (adapted to regional climatic variations) in combination with other features such as slope, pathway width and rest areas, a large and extremely varied constituency of users can be satisfied.

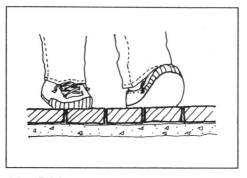

59   Brick.

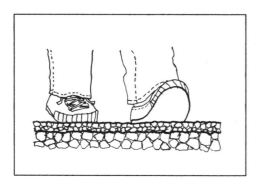

60   Crushed stone.

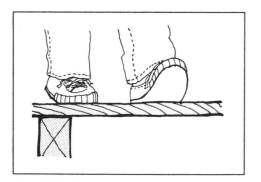

61   Wood decking.

a.   **Concrete** (Nordhaus, et al., 1984). Concrete must be poured on a well prepared base that is clean and free of debris. Finishes should have a light texture, such as a broom finish, so that the surface will not be slippery when wet. The texture should drain water off the pathway so it does not stand or freeze.

b.   **Asphalt** (Nordhaus, et al., 1984). Asphalt pathways may be used if they are carefully constructed and maintained. Typical construction should include:

1)   Subgrade cleaned and cleared to a depth of 6 inches below finished grade, compacted to 95%. A soil sterilizer may be utilized to control weed growth.

2)   4-inch base of course aggregate, compacted to 95%.

3)   Primer coat.

4)   2-inch surface course of hot mix bituminous concrete, compacted to 95% density. An epoxy finish, coated with sand may be used to give a natural appearance and reduce softening problems in hot climates.

5)   Slope to drain.

Asphalt surfaces may become soft in very hot climates, causing difficulty for people in wheelchairs and should not be used in very hot, sunny locations.

Maintenance is important so that the pathway is not degraded by weeds, cracks or erosion.

c.   **Pavers on Concrete** (Nordhaus, et al., 1984). Brick, tile or concrete pavers, set on a properly constructed concrete base can provide a Level 1 pathway surface. Joints between pavers must meet the requirements of the designated Level of Accessibility.

d.   **Crushed Stone and Decomposed Granite** (Nordhaus, et al., 1984). Crushed stone can form an accessible surface if it is correctly designed and constructed, and adapted to regional climatic conditions.

1)   Subgrade cleaned and cleared to a depth of 6 inches below finished grade, compacted to 95% density. The use of a soil sterilizer is recommended.

2)   4-inch base course, 3/4 inch crushed stone, compacted to 95% density. A binder of 2—3% Portland cement with water and gravel may be used.

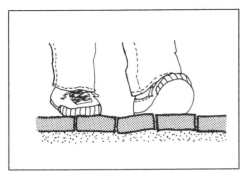

62   Pavers on sand.

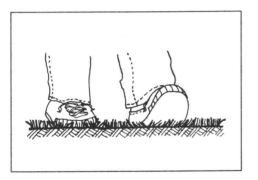

63   Grass.

64   Untreated soil.

3)   2-inch surfacing course of crusher fines, rolled and compacted to 95% density. Cement binder recommended.

4)   Maintenance is essential to ensure a consistent surface.

e.   **Wood Decking** (Nordhaus, et al., 1984). Wood decking may be used as a pathway and flooring surface for all levels of accessibility, providing joints meet the requirements of the Level. Warpage and movement of the material must also be controlled.

f.   **Pavers on Sand** (Nordhaus, et al., 1984). Brick, tile, concrete or other paving materials set in sand are not recommended for Level 1. Winter heaving and movement of the material over time may cause unacceptable irregularities. They may be suitable for Level 2 or 3 if properly installed.

g.   **Grass (Turf)** (Nordhaus, et al., 1984). A grass surface can be passable as a Level 2 or 3 surface if level and well maintained.

h.   **Untreated Soil** (Nordhaus, et al., 1984). Untreated soil is highly variable. Some situations may be acceptable for Level 2 or 3 if level and maintained. Soil is likely to change significantly due to precipitation, erosion, wear, etc.

i.   **Gravel** (Nordhaus, et al., 1984). Loose gravel is not recommended. It can be very difficult for a person in a wheelchair or with walking aides. Packed gravel may be suitable for Level 3.

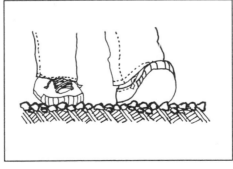

65   Gravel.   *66   Wood chips.*

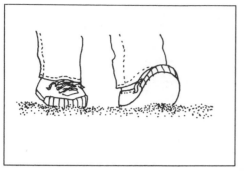

67   *Sand.*

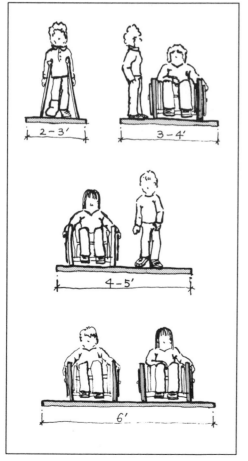

68   *Width dimensions.*

j.   **Wood chips.** Small gauge chips make an attractive surfacing material. They have a pleasant smell. When well compacted on a level subsurface, the surface is accessible at Level 2, otherwise Level 3 is more likely. On the negative side, wood chips are splintery (especially when freshly ground) and have a high bacteria count.

k.   **Sand.** Sand is not recommended for pathway surfacing.

6.11   Width (Nordhaus, et al., 1984)

Three feet minimum width is recommended for single wheelchair, or 4 feet for a wheelchair and pedestrian can pass. 5 feet minimum width is recommended for 2 wheelchairs to pass. If the width is less than 5 feet, provide a 5 foot level passing area every 200 feet.

6.12   Visually Impaired Specifications (Nordhaus, et al., 1984): Research is needed to develop more specific guidelines in this area, However, some overall considerations are:

a.   **Detectable Area.** The Detectable Area is the area of space within which a visually impaired person, using a cane, can detect an obstacle.

b.   **Obstacles.** No obstacle may overhang the edge of a pathway by more than 4 inches if the bottom of the obstacle is more than 27 inches above the walking surface.

c.   **Tactile Warnings.** Tactile warnings on the walking surface should be provided at locations that are potentially dangerous to people with severe visual impairments, such as crosswalks at roads, stairs, water areas, etc.

6.13   Treatment Definitions (Kiewel, 1980)

a.   **Abrupt changes in level:** A net change in the height of a walking surface of between 1/4-inch and 1-1/4 inches, at an angle of more than 45 degrees to the horizontal. Abrupt changes in level must be avoided in pathways.

b.   **Change in elevation:** A net change in the height of a walking surface in excess of 1-1/4 inches, regardless of the angle at the edge of the change. Changes in elevation must also be avoided in pathway design, or ramps must be provided as an alternative route.

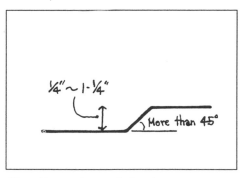

69   *Abrupt change in level.*

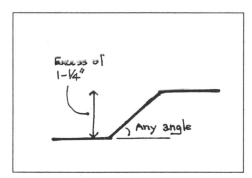

70   *Change in elevation.*

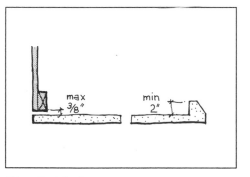

71   *Crutch stops.*

c.   **Crutch stop:** A low curb or rail along the edge of a ramp or wall, designed to stop crutch or cane tips from sliding off the surface.

6.14   **Components** (Nordhaus, et al., 1984)

a.   **Curbs and Railings**

Curbs and railings should be provided according to the requirements for different levels of accessibility:

Accessible	Usable	Difficult
Provide a 2-inch high curb at the edge of paths that slope at the side. Provide a 42-inch high railing at hazardous pathway edges.	Provide a 2-inch high curb and 42-inch high railing at difficult and dangerous locations.	Provide curbing at difficult and dangerous locations.

Be aware that children can use curb and railing structures as play features.

b.   **Pathway Edge**

Accessible	Usable
Provide a distinctive edge on at least one side of the pathway as a "shoreline" for visually impaired people who use canes. A curb 2 inches high is preferred.	Provide a distinct change of material at the edge of the pathway.

6.15   **Steps and Stairways** (Kiewel, 1980)

One of the most frequent misconceptions regarding accessible design is that stair design has nothing to do with accessibility. There are, however, people with disabilities who actually prefer to use stairs. Therefore, step or stair design is critical to the safe and efficient use of the built environment.

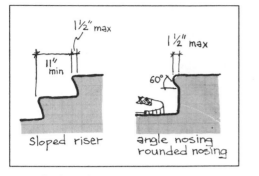

72   Stair nosings.

73   Acceptable handrail designs.

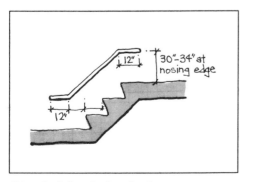

74   Stair handrail projections.

Besides nonslip treads, there are three basic components of accessible stairway design:

a. **Risers.** The physical existence of risers is important for two groups of people. People wearing prosthetic or orthotic devices on their legs often use the riser face to guide their leg(s) up the step. Other people with impaired coordination, who use crutches or canes, place their crutches against the riser of a step above them for balance as they maneuver up the stairway.

b. **Nosings.** Open riser stairs represent the worst kind of nosing design, that is, the stair with the greatest tripping hazard. Poured sloped-riser stairs provide the best nosing design, that is, the stair with the least tripping hazard.

The most accessible step has a riser that slopes out to meet the leading edge of the tread. The nosing should be shallow (preferably less than 1 inch) and either be beveled at 60 degrees or more from the horizontal, or rounded to minimize its potential to trip. In no case would open riser or square nosing steps be acceptable if they were one of the redundant systems, or the only system, providing access between distinct levels of a facility.

These principles should apply to any exit stair that is designed to be used in the up direction, regardless of the lack of accessibility to that level. Since exit stairs are designed for use in emergencies, every caution should be taken to ensure their safety. These accessibility parameters would be safety considerations in an upward emergency exit situation.

c. **Handrails.** It is critical that stairways have handrails on both sides. People who have had strokes, amputations of a hand or arm, or who have hemiparisis from disease or accident will have only one hand to use the handrail. Handrails must be available on both sides so that no matter which direction the person is going, he or she will always have a handrail on the "good" side.

Handrail projections are also important. Wherever possible, the handrail should extend at its angle of descent for the distance of one tread length before leveling off. This is to provide the person using the handrail with consistent support all the way to the stair landing. The handrail at the upper landing need not continue at the angle of ascent, but should project horizontally to the upper landing at least 12 inches to provide continuous support.

Handrails must be designed to fit the human hand for maximum grip. The preferred shape is round, which enables the hand to almost close.

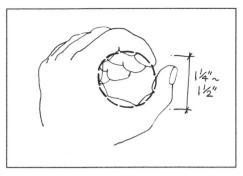

75   Hand grip dimensions.

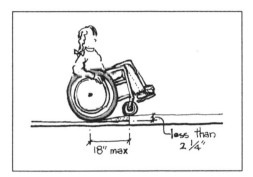

76   Low-rise thresholds.

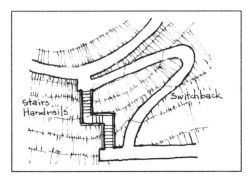

77   Switchbacks.

6.16   Ramps (Ruddy, 1981)

The single most significant aspect of ramp design is slope selection. A recent study completed by Syracuse University for the revision of the ANSI A117.1 specifications show that 44 percent of the wheelchair users tested could not traverse a 30-inch rise in elevation at the currently acceptable slope of 1:12, while all persons tested could negotiate at least a 24-inch change in elevation at a slope of 1:20. (Note: The test ramp was not long enough to test rises in excess of 24 inches at the 1:20 slope.)

Another example is the "high door threshold." If a 2-inch threshold is ramped at a slope of 1:12, the threshold will project 2 feet beyond the doorway. In many cases, the wheelchair user will have three, possibly four, wheels on the inclined surface while trying to manipulate the door latch hardware. A 2-1/4 inch rise has the same relationship to the large wheel of the chair as a 1/2-inch rise has to the smaller "caster" wheel. It is desirable to bevel such a rise so that (a) only one pair of wheels is on the incline at a time, and (b) the large tires can negotiate the rise in one push.

Note: An 18 inch travel distance (the thrust of the average, single arm-push) represents approximately one-fourth of the circumference of the large tire of a standard chair. Changes in elevation of less than 2-1/4 inches (if encountered in remodeling situations) should therefore be beveled at slopes between 1:17 and 1:8 to eliminate the need to have the entire chair on a slope at one time.

Landings provided for ramps should conform to ANSI A117.1 (1980) Section 4.8.4 specifications. Landings should be as wide as the full width of the ramp; have a 6 feet minimum depth at the bottom landing; have a 5 feet minimum depth at the top landing; and have a 5 feet minimum depth at all other landings. Cross slopes, which are usually for drainage, and which run perpendicular to the major direction of pedestrian traffic, are quite common on sidewalks. Persons in wheelchairs traveling on inclined surfaces planned as accessible paths cannot tolerate cross slopes. Even on essentially level surfaces where cross slopes are required, care should be taken to balance the distances of right-hand and left-hand slopes.

The integration of ramps with conventional or central circulation systems is important. People with mobility impairments generally use considerably more energy than their able-bodied people. The integration of ramps with regular circulation systems means that

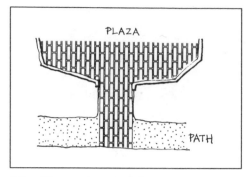

78   *Change in materials.*

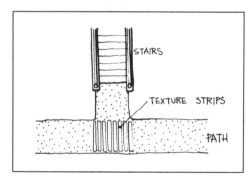

79   *Change in texture.*

they are not required to travel extra distances, or divorce themselves from the main traffic in order to gain accessible paths of travel.

Another consideration, especially in northern states, is exterior versus interior ramps. Many northern states have established codes that require 1:20 maximum slopes for exterior uses. This is because of the increased problems of inclement weather. Snow, ice, frost, etc., can significantly reduce the safety of a ramp. To alleviate this problem, some states (e.g., Minnesota and Michigan) have distinguished between interior sloped walking surfaces (ramps) and exterior sloped walking surfaces (walks). They have also set different interior and exterior standards (1:12 interior, 1:20 exterior).

Handrails for ramps should be designed to conform to the cross section parameters discussed for stairs. Rampway railings, however, need not continue to ascend or descend beyond the inclined surfaces, but should project horizontally at least 12 inches beyond the inclined surface over the landings. For additional requirements for specific applications, check Section 4.8.5 of the ANSI A117.1 (1980) specifications.

Another safety feature which is often needed for ramps, raised walks, or landings is the crutch stop. Curbs or rails designed to provide breaking action for crutch or cane tips and wheelchair casters, must have a minimum height of 2 inches, and cannot have weep holes or gaps that exceed the design parameters for grate or grille openings (see also Section 4.8.7 of ANSI A117.1 1980).

6.17   Pathway Development (Bunin, et al., 1980)

In designing and developing pathways, the following standards should be applied:

a.   If ramps or switchbacks are needed, provide stairs for a more direct alternate route.

b.   Stairs should have rounded nosings.

c.   Treads should be a minimum of 11 inches from nosing to nosing. Risers should be no higher than 7 inches and no less than 4 inches.

d.   Cross slope of pathways should be just enough to provide drainage (1—2%).

e.   Expansion joints should be less than 1/2 inch.

f.   Gratings for storm drainage should be placed off of pathways. Where they do occur, openings should be less than 1/2 inch.

g. Prune tree branches overhanging pathway to a height of 8 feet 6 inches.

h. If pruning will damage or detract from tree, consider rerouting path around it.

i. Use separate texture and color cues to indicate:

1) High risk areas such as a steep embankment, steps or intersections

2) Functional changes such as seating areas, fountains or plazas.

j. Tactile cues alert the blind as well as the sighted who are approaching an area of concern or interest.

k. Keep in mind that differential surface settling, if it occurs, must be less than 1/2-inch.

l. Differentiate color of material when a change in level occurs. Otherwise, the visually impaired may overlook stairs, ramps or steps.

m. Bold patterns or colors may be disorienting over a continuous surface.

7. SIGNAGE

Signs that can communicate to people of all abilities are vital. They ensure good orientation, direct traffic flow, satisfy requirements of effective risk management and provide information about site and programs.

The need for signs depends on the size of the play setting. Play settings should not be oversigned. Signs should be designed in the spirit of play.

A realistic assumption is that children (and people who's native tongue is not English) cannot read verbal signs or if they can the implications of the message are not fully understood. Hence the need to emphasize graphic signs, especially those child-oriented and child-designed. International characters and standards should be used as much as possible.

Planning Criteria

Play Value. Signs can be designed as play objects or sometimes become unintended play objects.

Programming. Signs provide permanent interpretive information about site. Temporary signs can advertise special events and add to the sites aesthetic appeal.

Play Leadership. Responsibility for using and managing temporary signs should be shared by play leaders and park maintenance staff.

Safety. Signs alert users to the special features of equipment, improve users' sense of security and reduce the risk of getting lost or feeling lost.

Accessibility. Appropriate heights, depths, colors, pictographs and tactile qualities can be used to communicate information to all types of users.

Risk Management. Signs provide information about appropriate use of equipment and facilities.

Integration. Signs must communicate an image of "ALL users welcome."

Management/Maintenance. A clean, readable, up-to-date, secure sign system is essential. Signs should be designed as part of the total design concept, not as an afterthought. Signs should be attractive and consistent with the overall aesthetic style.

80   *Informational signs.*

81   *Directional signs.*

82   *Identification signs.*

7.1   **Types of Signs**

a.   **Informational Signs** present general information in words and graphics (for those who cannot read) about the organization of a site or access network and the availability and location of facilities.

Informational signs placed at the entry to a site should identify and locate accessible facilities, describe the level of accessibility of the site and indicate where additional assistance may be obtained (Nordhaus, et al., 1984).

Entry signs should convey a welcoming attitude to the user, and emphasize support rather than restriction of activity. However, it may also be important to communicate safety rules as a risk management strategy.

b.   **Directional Signs** present information that indicates direction to a space or facility, change in route or confirmation of correct direction. They usually include an arrow. They are located at entry and all decision points (Robinette, 1985).

"You are here" signs help people find their way around. They should be oriented in the same direction as the visitor and show prominent landmarks within view.

Directional signs should be systematically placed on the site to direct visitors to appropriate pathways and facilities including:

1)   Signs at site entry, indicating direction of parking and facilities.

2)   Signs at parking areas, identifying access to pathways and direction to facilities.

3)   Signs at all decision points along a pathway.

Signs should be visible from pathways and within reach for touch reading. Indications of direction must be clear.

c.   **Identification signs** present information in both words and pictographs indicating specific features or facilities.

Identification signs should be placed at all accessible facilities and pathways. The signs should:

1)   Visibly and unambiguously identify the facility from the approaching pathway.

83   Regulatory sign.

84   Signs must be readable by children and adults with senses other than vision.

85   Raised letters are better than Braille signs.

2)   Indicate the level of accessibility of the facility ("accessible," "usable," "difficult").

3)   Use both letters and standard pictograph symbols (Nordhaus, et al., 1984).

d.   **Regulatory Signs** present notification of rules, requirements, warnings and restrictions and are used for traffic delineation and control.

7.2   General Guidelines for Readability (Bunin, et al., 1980)

A good series of signs means that the whole setting becomes accessible. Nighttime illumination should be considered.

Signs should be "readable" by senses other than vision, such as touch or hearing. Raised lettering and symbols convey information to people reading with either hands or eyes. For the visually impaired, however, a sighted guide or audio tape device is often a more effective way to convey information at zoos, nature centers, museums and other recreation areas. Raised letters are preferred since many visually impaired people, especially the partially sighted, do not read Braille. In general, however, more research and development is required on types of signs that will accommodate people with visual impairments.

When words are used, what is being "taught" to disabled people must be taken into account. Signs can have a strong positive (or negative) educative value for parents and children.

Design considerations include:

a.   Place signs logically, within easy range of vision and reach, at main intersections and nodal points.

b.   Keep signs free of obstructing vegetation and buildings.

c.   Place signs so that they cannot be inadvertently walked into.

d.   Place signs at a comfortable height for children and seated or standing adults. Use consistent mounting height and location.

e.   Use light colored letters or symbols on a dark background for maximum readability. Use bright, noticeable colors with a matte finish.

f.   Many visually impaired people can read signs by touch if designed correctly. Raised characters should be at least 5/8 inch (16mm) high, but no higher than 2 in-

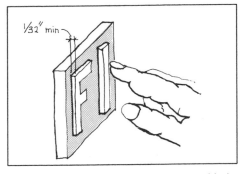

86 *Raised letters should contrast with the background.*

87 *Pictographs should be used in addition to written information.*

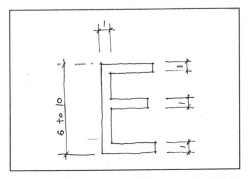

88 *Stroke width to height ratio 1:6 to 1:10.*

ches (50mm) and raised at least 1/32 inch (0.8 mm) off the background to be legible to blind or partly sighted persons.

g. Use standard letters without serifs and Arabic numerals (see Specifications for Letter Character Size and Shape).

h. Recognize predominant foreign language groups in multilingual signs where necessary. Use precise, clear instructions and direct, concise language.

i. Pictographs should be used in addition to written information. Use simple, high contrast, bold, clear graphics. Symbols must be understandable as well as visible. Use standard symbols such as those used by the U.S. Department of Transportation for ease of recognition.

Regular street signs can be used for "Stop," Yield," etc., which also have an educational advantage.

j. Where possible, consider using signs which engage children in cause-effect learning, e.g., pressing a button gives a verbal response. Allow children to make their own signs in supervised play areas, as part of play programs.

k. **Specifications for Letter Character Size and Shape**

1) **Character Height:** The height of a character should be a function of the distance the viewer is from the character. The Canadian System for determining character height is shown below. This table is only a guide; final size should be determined by field tests.

Pedestrian		Vehicular		
Character x height, inches	Reading distance, feet	Character x height, inches	Reading distance, feet	Traffic speed, mph
0.20	10	2.00	100	10—20
0.24	12	2.40	120	10—20
0.32	16	3.20	160	20—30
0.40	20	4.00	200	20—30
0.48	24	4.80	240	40—60
0.60	30	6.00	300	40—60
0.80	40	8.00	400	40—60
1.00	50			
1.20	60			
1.60	80			

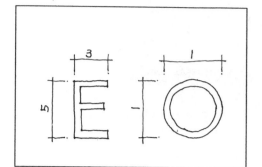

89 *Character height to width ratio 3:5 to 1:1.*

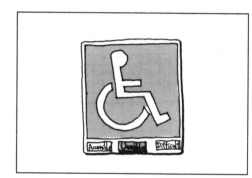

90 *International symbol of accessibility with "level" indicated. Recommended dimensions: viewed from 60 ft. or less— 4-1/2" x 4-1/2"; from more than 60 ft.— 8-1/2" x 8-1/2".*

2) **Character Proportions:** A character's proportions should also assist in the legibility and readability of a sign. The ANSI Standard A117.1 (1980) calls for a character width to height ratio of between 3:5 and 1:1 and a stroke width height ratio of between 1:5 and 1:10. These dimensions, when used with a matte finish and a high contrast between the color of the character and its background, can increase readability.

1. **The international symbol** of accessibility is a standard symbol which indicates that a facility or route is fully accessible. The symbol should not be modified, nor should extraneous elements be added. Supplemental signs and symbols which indicate level of accessibility, or direction, or identify a facility may be used in combination with the symbol of accessibility.

The international symbol of accessibility may be displayed as a white figure on a blue background or as a blue figure on a white background with a blue border (Nordhaus, et al., 1984).

The color should match the blue of international road signs indicating hospitals and parking.

The wheelchair figure should always face right unless it is used as a directional sign pointing to the left.

The width of the border should be equal to the stroke width of the figure.

Good quality, vandal resistant, weather resistant materials should be used.

The symbol of accessibility should be used to:

1) **Identify accessible parking spaces.** Each space should be marked with a vertical signpost or a symbol painted on the pavement. Each group of spaces should have at least one signpost.

2) **Indicate beginning of pathways.** Use symbol and level of accessibility signs.

3) **Indicate accessible facilities.** Use sensibly and with discretion to convey areas and facilities that are not obviously accessible to the user, or situations where the level of accessibility is unclear. In heavily vegetated areas, for example, users may need details of accessibility before venturing forward.

7.3   Program/Site Information

a.   Provide interpretive signs for parents and teachers at the entry of all playgrounds that indicate special features or opportunities offered by the area; for example, a water play area.

Parents need to know whether a site is fully or only partially accessible.

b.   Provide signs on individual items of play equipment that inform parents and caregivers about special features or opportunities. Signs can show how spaces and facilities can be used for creative play, for example, making a "house" by draping a sheet over a play structure or branch of a tree.

91   Signage should be designed as an information system directing and explaining to users the opportunities of the site.

8. FENCES/ENCLOSURES

Fences are a primary means of defining, protecting, separating and creating activity settings. They perform a crucial function in vegetation management of protecting resources from severe impact. If used inappropriately, they can also restrict play opportunities unnecessarily and cut children off from the environment (in a park, for example), or create play "ghettos".

Planning Criteria

Play Value. If used correctly, fences provide a sense of security, enclosure and support for activities.

Programming. Fences provide physical support and places to hang or attach objects, strings, etc. They are useful for defining play areas.

Play Leadership. Fences can help improve supervision and create defensible space (Newman, 1972).

Safety. Fences are important safety devices; they can define zones of legal responsibility, but can become hazardous if used unintentionally as climbing structures.

Risk Management. Attention must be paid to climbing risks inherent in fences. Gateways must be clearly observable by staff.

Accessibility. Entrances must be clearly visible and wide enough for wheelchair passage (at least 3 feet 6 inches).

Integration. Fences should not be used to separate children in such a way that unintentioned segregation results, especially between disabled and nondisabled children.

Management/Maintenance. Policy for location and modification of fences with respect to vegetation management should be developed. Fences should be kept in good repair.

8.1   Design Considerations

Fences have a primary function of directing pedestrian movement, enclosing and/or defining activity areas and protecting vegetation.

Locking sites at night is very often ineffective or causes more problems than it solves. Children still climb over fences, and liability is still an issue because the playground can be legally considered an "attractive nuisance." Only very high fences will keep able-bodied children out of an area. Fences will get climbed and can present a hazard unless an easier means of access is provided.

Play experiences should be incorporated into fencing design where appropriate; for example, with peek-a-boo holes, chalking surfaces, child-created mosaic walls and murals. Think of fences as a positive design element integrated with other elements like play equipment, or as a play element in their own right (walls to walk along, for instance).

Fencing and barrier systems should reflect the physical structure of the site and the pattern of movement and activity within it. In the case of vegetated areas, the barrier system should reinforce the spatial structure of the maturing landscape. When designing fences the following criteria should be considered:

92   *Barriers can be designed as play elements in their own right.*

a.   **Height** should be sufficient to stop direct forward movement. Children's midchest height is about right. For young children this means that a single rail is often sufficient, but it is not a good solution for someone with a cane (the single rail cannot be detected and a blind person may fall over the rail). For higher fences, a double rail is necessary—otherwise, small children will scoot under. A second rail also increases climbability. Some fences should be set low or multirailed so they can be sat on. The top rail should be set at a good "leaning height" (this varies according to age). Rails must be 38 inches high for wheelchairs to roll under.

b.   **Visual Privacy/ Visual Access.** The transparency of a fence should relate to what is on the other side. If it is planting, then the fence should be as unobtrusive as possible so visual contact is unimpaired. If privacy is important, the fence should be more solid.

It is often a good idea to let planting grow through the fencing which increases the strength of both the fencing and the plants.

93   *Fences make good places to "hang out."*

c.   **Spatial Definition/Visual Interest.** A major function of barriers is to differentiate and modulate interrelationships between people and vegetation, and to define main pathways and social spaces within vegetated areas.

94 *Barriers can define different degrees of privacy.*

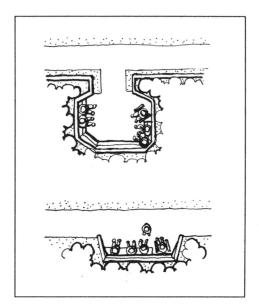

95 *Fences can be used to define gathering places.*

The definition of potential social space should always be borne in mind when designing fencing. Straight-line fencing is boring and antisocial. All manner of nooks, perches and hangouts can be formed by modifying fence lines.

d. **Degree of Protection/Permanence.** Longevity requirements of barriers used for different purposes vary considerably. Temporary protection of plantings may be needed only for a few months; at the other extreme, permanent definition of vegetation and activity zones is usually required. Construction of all permanent fences must be robust. Chain link fencing is an effective low maintenance fencing medium. Welded mesh is better. Both require aesthetic enhancement with plantings or other applied materials or surfaces.

1) Use vinyl coated mesh for chain link fencing around children's play areas (Seattle, 1986).

2) Wood fencing should be used in approved locations only, taking into consideration visibility and design details which prevent decomposition (Seattle, 1986).

e. **Multiprotection Techniques.** To protect vegetation, barriers of differing degrees of permanence can often be used as successive "lines of defense." The objective is *not* to keep children out of planted areas, but to reduce impact so that planted areas have a better chance of survival. Main planting areas can be enclosed by a permanent barrier, behind which shorter-term, less obtrusive protection can be provided according to the growth, protection and aesthetic needs of specific plants. Individual plant stakes provide a further degree of protection.

f. **Aesthetic Appearance.** In public play areas, fences and barriers must be attractive. Shrub plantings, ground covers and vines can be used to camouflage unsightly fences.

96 *Fences can define intimate social corners.*

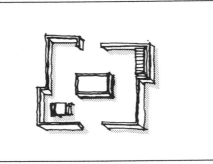

97 *Fencing should enclose specific settings.*

98 *Sturdy, temporary fencing protects new plants.*

99 *Fencing also protects plants from "running through" behavior.*

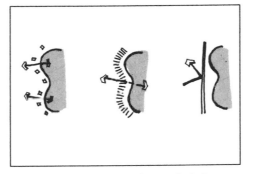

100 *Fences can provide varied degrees of protection and penetration of planted areas.*

101 *Fences can support vines and shrubs which can hide unattractive qualities.*

102 *Peep holes, color and varied textures, solids and voids make fences attractive play settings.*

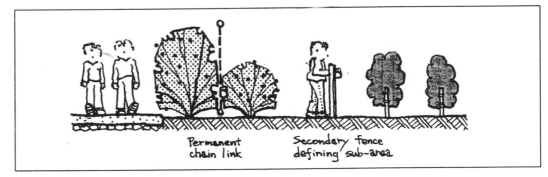

Permanent chain link

Secondary fence defining sub-area

103 *"Lines of Defense."*

9. MANUFACTURED PLAY EQUIPMENT SETTINGS

Most equipment settings stimulate large muscle activity and kinesthetic experience, but they can also support areas of child development, other than physical. Equipment can provide opportunities to experience height and serve as landmarks to assist orientation and wayfinding. They may also become rendezvous spots. They stimulate social interaction, and provide hideaways in hiding and chasing games. Small, semi-enclosed spaces support fantasy and dramatic play. Seating encourages social play. Properly selected equipment can support the development of creativity and cooperation, especially structures that incorporate sand and water play. Equipment settings must be designed as part of a comprehensive multipurpose play environment. Isolated pieces of equipment are ineffective on their own.

Systematic maintenance is essential (Fair Play for Children, hereafter FPC, n.d.; Root, 1983; Simm, 1985).

Planning Criteria

Play Value. Equipment can support large muscle, psychomotor coordination and social interaction, fantasy and dramatic play.

Programming Potential. Play structures can be converted to other temporary uses like stage settings; loose parts can be strung from and attached to the equipment; backdrops and banners can be supported; temporary structures can be added.

Safety. A variety of issues have been well-documented (Root, 1983; Simm, 1985; U.S. Consumer Products Safety Council, hereafter CPSC, 1981): falls, entrapment, protrusions, collisions, splinters. Loose clothing, scarves and cords on clothes present a potential of strangulation if caught on equipment.

Play Leadership. Trained supervision is necessary; leaders must know how to adapt equipment to other program purposes.

Risk Management. Equipment should be properly sited over appropriate fall-absorbing surfaces. A systematic safety inspection program must be developed and put into effect. Procedures and standards for equipment purchase and installation must be developed. Site and program supervision standards are required. Accident and incident records must be kept. Parents and care givers must be warned about the dangers of loose clothing and extreme weather's affects on equipment.

Accessibility. Equipment must be designed for children, not wheelchairs. Off and on places should always be marked both visually and tactually. The most significant aspect of making a piece of equipment accessible is to understand that children with disabilities need many of the same challenges as able-bodied children.

Integration. There is potential here, especially when programmed with other activities. Play settings should be exciting and attractive for parents as well as children—adults accompany children to the park or playground more often today than in the past.

Management Issues. Strict policies and standards are needed. A safety inspection schedule is mandatory. The CPSC Guidelines (1982) provide an important base, but they are limited. Their scope needs to be broadened. Play settings should be re-evaluated and renovated periodically, about every five years, and this should be allowed for in the budget. Manufacturers' catalogs should be used as part of a community education process to broaden and deepen the understanding of play by decisionmakers.

9.1   Design Criteria for Manufactured Equipment

9.1.1   Safety

a.   **Hazard versus Challenge.** A serious issue in play environment design is that challenge for the child is being eroded by adult concerns (sometimes unfounded) about liability and risk of suit. Children will use equipment in all possible ways, regardless of original design intent. Since the idea of play is to explore the potential of any play setting, children will test its use beyond the limits of their ability—that is how they discover their limits.

The testing process teaches children new skills. Good play setting design allows for such tests and anticipates the consequences of this normal behavior. Children will run up slides, and they will jump out of swings. Play setting designers must understand this and adjust the environment so that misjudgements by children are not injurious. Playgrounds must be places where it is safe to stretch the limits of ability without the risk of serious injury.

A hazard is the unforeseen consequence of a child's inability to handle a given challenge. It can result from a poorly designed feature which children see but do not comprehend its behavioral implications, such as insufficiently high guard rails and nonlevel surfaces at slide entries. A hazard can also result from poor maintenance (rather than design) as something something children cannot see, like broken glass in sand.

A challenge is something the child can see and chooses to attempt. The playground designer's responsibility is to maximize challenge and minimize hazard.

1)   Play structure designs and play events selected shall be accompanied by a description of developmental opportunities and a list of appropriate uses.

2)   Manufacturers should provide lists of typical maintenance procedures with each piece of equipment in the support documentation provided to playground supervisors for preventive maintenance.

3)   There is a need for reliable information on accidents. Manufacturers only hear about big law suits. Consumers need information related to safety in everyday use.

104   *To what extent is it necessary or realistic to separate play settings for different ages?*

105   *Children will use equipment in novel ways regardless of original design intent.*

b.   **Separation of Play Areas for Different Age Groups: Is this realistic?**

As they get older, children need to repeat similar experiences at larger scales. Mixed age groups of siblings and friends need to play in the same general vicinity. Children with disabilities may wish to play with their peers. This means that physical age separations should be minimized.

Separations should normally be based on developmental needs, activity characteristics (separation of noisy or large-muscle activity, for example) and environmental requirements (separation of water play areas, for example) rather than age .

Separate areas for very young children (three years and under) are required. Their needs should be given special attention to supply developmentally appropriate and challenging settings such as wet sand areas, clatter bridges, low platforms and level changes, low wide slides and a variety of textures. Physical barriers may be needed to facilitate supervision.

Insufficient research has been conducted to indicate the advisability of age separation and under what conditions it might be appropriate and successful. Accident reports and claim records show that very young children have been gravely injured while playing on equipment intended for older children, sometimes while the parents are actually facilitating their play. Similarly, accidents can occur when older children use equipment designed for toddlers.

So-called tot lots may act as a safety valve, allowing young children to retreat. But additional research is needed to verify the effects of siting, enclosure, supervision and parent involvement.

c.   **A Range of Play Opportunities.** Equipment should be designed to provide a wide range of behavioral options for children of varying abilities.

d.   **Chemical Pollutants.** Environmental contaminants are a special problem around children. Diagnosis and treatment is difficult because individual responses to disease vary. Symptoms for the same exposure often range from flu-like, to allergy-like, to behavioral reactions.

Unfortunately, a surprising number of playgrounds are located on former industrial sites or land fills. Many are adjacent to major highways with associated high levels of wind borne asbestos, lead and rubber (Freedberg, 1983).

106   Every reasonable effort must be taken to keep toxic substances out of play settings.

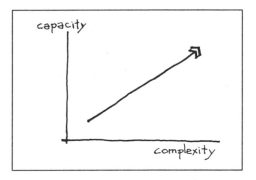

107   Capacity of equipment increases with complexity.

Park management practices sometimes include weed abatement and insect control measures which introduce significant levels of contamination. Occasionally entire playgrounds are heavily sprayed with no effort made to restrict access while the chemicals are active.

Some communities (e.g., Berkeley, California) have laws and integrated pest management programs that severely limit the use of herbicides and pesticides in public areas.

The chemicals of greatest concern are those which are recognized as toxins and carcinogens. Most petroleum products, asbestos, reactive metals, and some agricultural/industrial by-products fall into this group. The wisest policy might be to remove all materials from the children's environment which have not been proven safe.

1)   Every effort must be made to reduce chemical contamination of play areas (see National Playing Fields Association, hereafter NPFA, 1983, for a discussion of the working definition of "reasonably foreseen," as developed in the English courts).

2)   Playgrounds with detectable levels of chemicals, whether permanently or temporarily present, must provide notification and restrict access to the public. Lead level in paint is also a concern.

9.1.3   Play Value

a.   **Options.** Research has shown that a diversity of settings stimulates a wide range of play activity and supports the needs of a broad variety of children at all levels of development (Moore, 1966, 1974a,b, 1978b, 1980; Rothenburg, et al., 1974).

Playgrounds that are insufficiently diverse are often underutilized (Gold, 1972). Although traditional equipment settings are appealing to many children (Moore, 1978b), a broad diversity of settings is necessary to maintain interest and to provide developmental challenges for all children. Successful playgrounds usually have a high manipulative factor (Moore, in press). Even a well-designed, multi-event structure with many options still provides only one type of play setting and is not equivalent to a multi-setting playground.

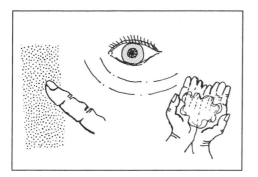

108 *Play structures need to stimulate all the child's senses*

109 *Play structures should support crawling.*

b. **Sensory Variety.** Play structure settings present a good opportunity to provide sensory stimulation and discrimination. Children can be exposed to qualities of processed materials in a structured sensory experience over which the designer has considerable control. These materials can be intentionally manipulated to increase access (Playing and Learning in Adaptable Environments, Inc., hereafter PLAE, 1981—87). Primary dimensions are heat, light, resiliency, texture, color and sound:

- hot—cool—cold
- light—shade—dark
- color

- rough—smooth
- hard—soft
- noisy—quiet

Sensorially diverse environments stimulate more complex patterns of activity, for a greater number of children.

c. **Spatial Complexity.** Developmental potential is increased by emphasizing the third dimension and continuity of movement. In this way, children can learn spatial concepts such as over-under, in-out, up-down, right-left, spatial depth and directionality; they can realize the limits of their own fingers, toes, head and body; they can measure the risk of jumping, reaching and falling (Seattle, 1986).

Play equipment should be designed to support the maximum potential for creative physical action by all children.

d. **Large Muscle Activity.** Some play structures have a primary purpose to accommodate large muscle activities from which complex patterns of activity are built up (Moore, 1974b). Individually and in combination, activities vary according to the physical characteristics of the structure and the psychosocial characteristics of the users. The following are most desirable:

- climbing
- swinging
- bouncing
- balancing
- jumping
- crawling
- hopping
- skipping
- creeping

- sliding
- rolling
- lifting
- pushing
- pulling
- knee walking
- hand over hand
- hanging by arms
- twirling/spinning

e.   **Movement.** Children love movement and derive great pleasure from the stimulation of their kinesthetic senses.

1)   Build a variety of movement as an end in itself into manufactured equipment settings.

2)   Provide interactive play equipment which responds to children's input.

The "up-down," third dimension stimulates a special sense of movement through space and encourages dramatic play. It is a basic dimension in spatial perception ("I am higher than you." "I can see you, you can't see me").

Children with physical disabilities have few opportunities to get "above the action." Equipment should be designed to allow a child with a physical disability the opportunity to slide, crawl, tumble or pull themselves up to an "overview" position (Shaw, 1980). Wheelchair access onto equipment in public settings may be unsafe. Making equipment accessible to a wheelchair also makes it accessible to bikes, skates, skateboards and other wheeled toys.

•   Safe, accessible "overviews" should be built into equipment settings where feasible.

110   Play settings should emphasize linkage and flow.

f.   **Linkage and Flow.** Psychomotor activity involves children in mastering the flow of their own bodies through space, in a continuous sequence of movement. Continuity of physical support is very important; it enables the child to make a variety of "play circuits" through the play environment (Moore, G.T., et al., 1979).

•   Each main "play circuit" should provide a range of choice of "subcircuits" to maintain interest and to avoid the potential boredom of "one way to go" systems.

Early playground designs provided many separate play events to avoid competition and crowding. But this idea failed to recognize that children play in small groups. More recent concepts of linkage and concern for traffic flow have highlighted the use of decks and other linking devices such as balance beams to create flexible traffic flow patterns.

111   Multilevel, pyramidal structures provide a graduated challenge and reduce fall distance.

Where the accent is on movement and large muscle activity, linked equipment settings are normally preferable to isolated pieces (Moore, 1974b).

However, where a manufactured equipment setting is provided to support quiet social activity, it should be separated from the main cluster of equipment.

112 *Play equipment should support jumping.*

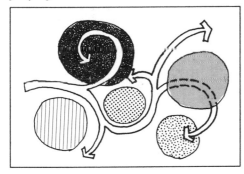

113 *An effective play structure emphasizes sensory variety and many psychomotor opportunities.*

114 *Effective play structures emphasize three-dimensional movement, variations in complexity and continuity of play experience.*

g.   Motor Challenge. Equipment settings must be designed with a low risk of serious injury (children will always suffer minor bumps, bruises and grazes wherever they play). The most important design parameters are "distance of fall" and "resiliency of landing surface." Safety surfaces will not stop accidents, only reduce the severity of injury.

Where possible, equipment should be designed with only a few feet of sheer drop to ground level. In Section 9.11.4, the recommended maximum climber height is specified as 64 inches. In multilevel structures, drop distances can be reduced by using a pyramidal form with intermediate decks or other components such as nets and ramps.

Since falls from a height have been established as a major playground hazard, characteristics other than height must be found to provide appropriate challenges to children.

1)   New and traditional equipment settings should provide physical challenges not based on height, including upper body movement and balance.

2)   Challenges should be "graduated" (Moore, G.T., et al., 1979). Upper body development activities, for example, would include turning bars, chinning bars, parallel bars, ring treks, and track rides, in addition to traditional elements such as horizontal ladders.

3)   For greater accessibility, provide graduated challenges at varying heights (PLAE, 1981—87).

h.   Differentiation. Refuges away from the main currents of activity are needed by some children. Small tributary spaces should be designed into equipment settings to increase the variety of activity options.

•   Differentiate equipment settings to provide tributary and refuge spaces to accommodate activities for all children.

9.1.4   U.S. Consumer Products Safety Commission (CPSC)

CPSC Compliance

The CPSC *Handbooks for Public Playground Safety,* Volumes I and II, were the result of an extensive investigation with the active participation of both the public and equipment manufacturers. As such, they represent the current "standard of care" in a legal sense.

Unfortunately, the CPSC looked narrowly at the issue of safety. Their mandate did not extend to the problems of accessibility and integration, nor were they concerned with maximizing the developmental benefits for all children. These Guidelines are based on the CPSC work but also address these additional areas in an attempt to promote better environments and to resolve a number of problems and conflicts which have surfaced in the intervening years since 1978.

Playground and play equipment shall conform to the CPSC Guidelines:

a. **Entrapment—Opening Size.** The language in the CPSC documents is not especially clear in regard to opening size. Manufacturers have adopted a simple formula:

- Openings must be smaller than three inches and larger than seven.

This effectively meets the CPSC requirement with an additional safety factor.

b. **Entrapment—Opening Shape.** The current industry trend is to remove acute angles wherever possible. Where this is unavoidable a fillet is used to prevent entrapment. The CPSC Guideline states that:

- Vertical angles formed by adjacent surfaces on the boundary of an accessible opening should exceed 55 degrees.

This standard is generally in line with official standards in other countries, as published by Kompan, 1984. Both the CPSC Guidelines and the British Standard, BS 3042:1971, require the use of standardized "probes" to test potential entrapments (CPSC, 1981; Simm, 1985).

c. **Protrusions.** The CPSC guideline allows objects to protrude from structures so long as they are of a minimum size and length. Most manufacturers now exceed these guidelines and have removed nearly all protrusions.

- Play equipment which exceeds the CPSC guidelines for protrusions is preferred. As a general rule *all* nuts and bolts should be recessed, fitted with tamper-proof locks and the holes plugged.

d. **Signs.** The CPSC looked at the issue of warning signs and found the issue too complex for a guideline. They do, however, suggest color coding equipment for the degree of difficulty. Substantial research is required on this issue before any guidance can be offered. For instance, "red for danger" may well encourage rather than inhibit hazardous activity, if children interpret such signs as a challenge.

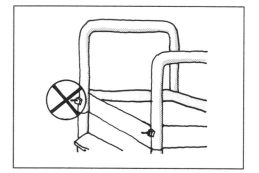

115 All nuts and bolts should be recessed, fitted with tamper-proof locks and the holes plugged.

In the years since the publication of the CPSC Guidelines, several liability cases have established the requirement for warning signs on the basis of the public's right to be informed of hazards. Currently there is no generally accepted language for such signs. Compounding the problem, many users may not read English or may not read at all. Therefore:

- Play equipment shall have both verbal and graphic playground safety signs (see Signage, Chapter 7, Section 3, Program/Site Information).

9.1.5   Specific Population Requirements

a.   **Vision Impaired.** Children with vision impairments must be able to "read" the environment to be able to use it. To assist them, provide the following (Schneekloth & Day, 1980; Schneekloth, 1979):

116 Use two- or three-dimensional representations of the equipment as part of a mapping system.

1)   Use two- or three-dimensional representations of the equipment as part of a mapping system to teach the child or adult how the equipment looks and where it is located.

2)   When practical and necessary for safety, equipment should have guide rails.

3)   All means of entering or leaving a piece of equipment should be indicated by a change in texture and/or material on the rail and/or floor. Care should be taken that this does not create a trip hazard for children who may be running and assume they are on a level surface.

4)   Areas of entry and exit should happen only after some distinct physical movement has been initiated, i.e., turning a corner, stepping up or down.

5)   Orient swings away from main circulation. Swings should be separated from the rest of the play area. The common practice of attaching swings to one end of a multiplay structure should be discouraged.

6)   Surfacing materials should change at the junction of safety zones and circulation pathways. The change should be distinct and preferably standardized.

7)   All edges of equipment settings must be well defined.

b.   **Motor Impaired.** In addition to the grip enhancements and the concept of graduated challenge, children with motor impairments benefit especially from soft settings. Play events such as nets and resilient surfaces are particularly appealing and beneficial.

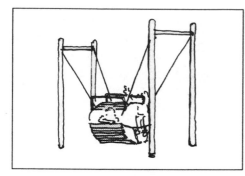

117 *Equipment should be designed to accommodate wheelchairs in such a way that out-of-chair activity is encouraged.*

118 *Grab bars or pulls should be located at corners or positioned to help children enter new play events or to get from one level to another.*

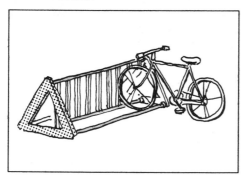

119 *Bike racks.*

c. **Nonambulatory.** Children in wheelchairs like to play in equipment settings as much as their non-wheelchair peers do. Manufacturers should be urged to make equipment accessible so that wheelchairs can come adjacent to or penetrate it. Equipment should be designed to accommodate wheelchair users in such a way that out-of-chair activity is encouraged.

To improve accessibility to nonambulatory users, equipment should have the following (further research is needed to fully confirm and elaborate these requirements):

1) Rails at two different heights (1 foot and 2 feet).

2) Grab bars or pulls should be located at corners or positioned to help children enter new play events or to get from one level to another.

3) Platforms should be made of cool, nonabrasive, nonsplintering material comfortable for crawling or knee walking. Care should be taken to see that this does not create a difficult maintenance problem, however.

4) Transfer areas should be provided at several entry points.

5) Wheelchair parking spots should be provided to encourage children and caretakers to use accessible equipment.

6) Seats on equipment should be varied to allow for different seating positions or styles.

Bicycle control. Creating playgrounds with good access for wheelchairs also supports access for bikes (and skateboards and roller skates). Simple "No Bikes" signs are unlikely to fully discourage them and the potential hazard they represent. One solution is to provide attractive bike riding facilities elsewhere in the playground.

• Install bike racks and "no bike" signs at playground entrances, with "thank you" signs next to bike racks. This would make the "no bikes" rule abundantly clear and encourage adults within the play area to exercise supervision.

d. **Hearing Impaired.** Children with hearing loss comprise one of the largest child disability groups. The major issue with hearing loss is communication with playmates and supervising adults.

120 *Supervision of hearing disabled disable children is improved when sight lines within the playground are clear.*

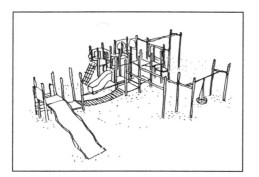

121 *Play equipment with many ways on and off.*

Supervision of hearing disabled children is improved when sight lines within the playground are clear, especially for settings such as benches, entrances and gathering areas.

1) Children with hearing impairments are more dependent on visual cues; therefore make all information properly visible. Alert all children to potential hazards.

2) Each element of the equipment setting should be easily visible from any other. However, a balance must be struck so that possibilities for exploration and discovery are retained.

3) Play equipment must be configured so that children with hearing loss can see potential hazards and other children playing on the equipment.

4) Vibrations or materials which cause vibrations can be used to warn of others on the equipment. However, it can also cause metal fatigue, especially at weld points.

e. **Cognitive Delays.** The major issue when equipment settings are designed for children with cognitive delays is orientation. Equipment elements must be visually understandable, not confusing. There are a number of ways to help orientation by using color, texture and shape. Throughout the play area, these orientation cues should remain consistent.

Children with developmental impairments sometimes find it easy to climb to some portion of a piece of equipment but then become fearful and unable to proceed. They discover that backing down is also too frightening and are left stranded like a kitten up a tree. This situation is more likely to be avoided by using the linkage concept in equipment setting design.

Level of cognitive delay and age will determine level of risk awareness.

1) Climbing equipment should not contain free fall distances higher than what can be matched by the impact absorbency rating on the chosen fall absorbing material.

2) Free fall distances should not exceed the absorption of the safety surface, measured in terms of a severity index.

3) Elevated equipment should have more than one means of exit. For example, more than one set of stairs should be provided to permit an adult to climb up

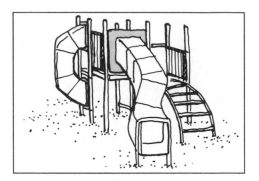

122 *Equipment should reinforce concepts of up and down, in and out.*

123 *Children with psychological, emotional and behavioral problems are the most difficult to accommodate and integrate.*

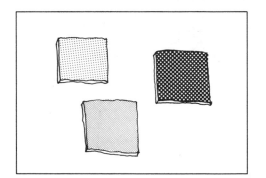

124 *It is often assumed that children respond to primary colors. This assumption may have no basis in fact.*

or a child to easily climb down when there is a line of other users restricting the way (see Section 11.2 for more discussion of slides).

4) Equipment should reinforce concepts of up and down, in and out, to teach control over the environment and to help orientation. This can be done by a carefully worked out system of tubes, squares and crawl-through shapes.

f.   **Behavioral Disability.** Children with psychological, emotional and behavioral disabilities need an environment that is well structured and focused. Interaction with other children is sometimes difficult.

Children with behavior disabilities and their caregivers benefit from carefully designed enclosed settings which help to safely retain children.

Diverse, linked settings reduce the need for turn-taking and competition and contribute to a more successful play experience for these children. More research is needed on this issue, but, in general, develop diverse, linked equipment settings that are well enclosed and easy to supervise.

g.   **Allergies and other Environmental Disabilities.** Some children have extreme sensitivity to certain plants, synthetic environmental pollutants, noise, etc. Known aggravations of these disabilities must be avoided in play settings.

h.   **Multiple Impairments.** Special consideration must be given to the needs of children with more than one impairment. For children who are severely impaired, watching, or "vicarious play," may become the major form of interaction, so places to sit and observe in the middle of the action may be especially important.

9.1.6   Appearance Considerations

a.   **Color.** It is generally believed that children respond best to primary colors, although little research exists to support this assertion.

There is insufficient research about children's response to color.

b.   **Theme.** Making slides look like rocket ships and climbers look like castles is based on the assumption that they will support and stimulate fantasy play more strongly. But these are adult ideas that have little grounding in research.

The issue is whether figurative expressions have developmental value. Certainly they attract young children, especially if the expression is taken from nature.

125 Most "thematic" elements have a pronounced effect.

126 Equipment settings should allow the child and/or playleader the opportunity to program them for a variety of dramatic purposes.

However, children will tire of such a diet day after day. Nonthematic equipment is more adaptable for informal as well as programmed activity (PLAE, 1981—87).

The effect of theme equipment is different for different ages and closely matches developmental ages and stages. For most ages, the more abstract the thematic representation the more supportive the setting is for the imagination (Moore & Wong, in press).

However, modest "thematic" elements can have a pronounced imaginative effect. A simple "steering wheel" fixed on a piece of equipment will be enough to turn it into a "fire truck," locomotive," "space ship," wagon train," etc. (Moore & Wong, in press).

Thematic elements provide strong visual identity and clear landmarks in play settings (see subsection c. below).

1) Equipment should be designed to allow for a variety of fantasy play opportunities.

2) Equipment settings should allow the child and/or play leader the opportunity to program them for a variety of dramatic play experiences.

3) Since the impact diminishes rapidly, thematic equipment is best suited for large "magnet" playgrounds in community parks which are not visited by the same children frequently.

4) In school and neighborhood parks which are used daily by the same children, thematic equipment has a lower priority; however, it can still provide strong identity.

c. **Visual Identity.** Because play structures are usually centrally sited, it is important that they have a strong visual identity. This identity can be expressed in abstract or figurative terms.

An advantage of figurative expression is that it gives visual identity to a setting and is therefore an aid in orientation and recognition. It provides a sense of belonging (Moore, 1978b; Moore, G.T., et al., 1979). Child interviews suggest that a visit to a playground with significant visual impact creates a lasting impression (Moore, 1986c).

127 *Play structures should have strong identity and expression.*

The meaning and psychological impact of visual expression will be increased if the community, especially the children, participates in designing and executing the work.

1)   Strong visual identity should be designed into equipment settings, using both figurative and nonfigurative means.

2)   The local community should participate in deciding on the visual expression and identity of play settings.

9.1.7   Scale

Few items of manufactured equipment are scaled to the needs of very small children. Research needs to be conducted on this issue, for instance, an evaluation of the impact of "monumental" play environments that are much larger than the children using them.

•   Equipment should be based on anthropometric data and conform to the physical size of children.

9.2   Maintenance

The need for carefully planned and professionally administered maintenance programs has become a critical aspect of public play provision (Root, 1983; Simm, 1985), especially for risk management.

9.2.1   Inspection Program

There is considerable variance in the frequency of playground inspections across the nation. Not only do similar municipalities with similar conditions have quite dissimilar standards but equipment manufacturers also differ greatly in their recommendations. A basic inspection program should include these components:

1)   Daily to weekly (depending on site usage) visual review of the play environment, inspecting for hazards as specified in an approved checklist. For example, some cities have instituted daily inspections of equipment such as Washington, D.C., Los Angeles and Daly City, California).

128 *Daily and monthly inspection is a critical aspect of maintenance.*

129 *Rotten structural wooden members can be vary hazardous.*

2) Monthly to three times monthly (depending on site usage) recorded inspection by a trained operative using an approved checklist (FPC/NPFA, N.D.; Root, 1983).

3) Bi-annual to annual (depending on site usage) "tear down" inspection to examine features such as bearings and footings for deterioration as detailed in manufacturer's specifications and on approved checklists.

4) A comprehensive maintenance program (NPFA, 1983) including staff training, provision of inspection checklists, prompt repair of discovered problems, follow-up quality assurance and detailed documentation.

9.3   Installation

a.   Footings. The tops of playground equipment footings must be covered by safety surfacing to the same specifications as the rest of the play area. The top edges of the footing must be smoothed with a two-inch radius. Frame members should rest on a well drained bottom of gravel to prevent encasement of posts and subsequent deterioration.

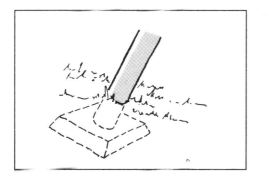

130 *The tops of playground equipment footings must be covered by safety surfacing.*

b.   Installation Instructions. Most manufacturers supply detailed installation instructions with their equipment. Problems arise when installers do not (or cannot) read these documents, or do not receive them. Companies which rely heavily on export trade have begun to use purely graphic instructions. Not only does such an approach resolve translation problems but it also provides appropriate guidance for the nonreading installer.

1) Check the quality and quantity of material supplied before installation. The supplier should include a parts list against which quantities are checked.

2) Check that suppliers provide appropriate installation instructions and that these are followed precisely. Retain these documents in the project file.

c.   Factory Support. Ideally, factory representatives should inspect final installations of play equipment for compliance with manufacturers' standards.

• Request factory inspection of installation and documentation of compliance with factory specification. Note, these may be different to those of the CPSC. Get a letter from the manufacturer stating the equipment has been installed to factory specifications.

9.4   Surfacing

See Ground Covers/Surfacing, Chapter 11.

9.5   Drainage

Drainage is the most frequently overlooked aspect of playground installation. In most sites, few investments have better cost/benefit ratios than improved drainage. Even locations where rain is infrequent can have mud problems due to irrigation.

131 *Good drainage around structural supports is essential.*

At the same time wet sand and mud are important play materials and opportunities for wet sand and mud play should be encouraged in appropriate locations. Such play opportunities should be deliberately designed into the playground rather than left to chance. Careful design of the drainage system is one way of providing temporary water and mud play opportunities (Moore & Wong, in press).

1)   Install positive drainage, utilizing French drains or similar systems for best results.

2)   The site must be practically level if loose material such as sand is to remain in place (unless there are effective retaining features). Locations under swings and at the end of slides (because they tend to become the lowest points) need the most active drainage.

9.6   Retainers and Edge Detailing

(See also Pathways, Chapter 6, Section 6.7, Edges and Curbs)

132 *Swings need a well-protected fall- and use-zone.*

a.   **Border Setback and Materials.** The minimum setback from low, non-moving equipment to border is six feet; most park departments require eight feet, which is preferred.

Certain equipment, such as swings, require special fall- and use-zones. British Standard 5696 (1979) has some notes on minimum use zones. More investigations of this issue are needed, considering the impact which conservative specifications impose on the amount of space and additional costs.

Edging, curbing or other containment is required around play areas filled with loose surface materials. Few elements of the playground have more visual impact than the retainers of loose surfacing materials. Care in the installation of the retainer will enhance the environmental appearance and have a positive impact on maintenance requirements.

Wood used for this application must be treated for ground contact. A nontreated wood cap may be advisable. Concrete edges should likewise have a wood cap to help reduce the possibility of broken glass.

133   *Edges can be designed for sitting.*

Loose material can be retained by a grass covered berm. This is an effective solution, provided that care is taken with details so that mowing can be accomplished with standard practices and that proper drainage occurs. Designers in the UK are finding that a 600mm (2 ft) pit with drainage works well without underlay or side walls.

Be certain that adequate fall zones (as specified by supplier, for instance) exist around all play equipment.

Pay special attention to the surface material retainer for visual impact and maintenance requirements.

b.   **Height Differential.** The height of the surface material barrier should be determined by two factors: the ability to retain loose material and the creation of a potential trip hazard. Logically, the higher the barrier the better the retention of loose material. Eight inches will normally contain all but intentionally thrown material, although no research findings are available on this issue.

c.   **Trip hazards.** Trip hazards exist in both directions, in and out of play areas. If the ground cover is added over existing grade, which greatly simplifies drainage requirements, then the approach height should be a minimum of 16 inches, 8 inches for loose material and 8 inches for retaining. Such a detail presents little trip hazard since it must be intentionally climbed. A minor problem exists on exit since the child may be unaware of the additional 8-inch differential. An 8-inch pit with an additional 8-inch barrier presents the same obstacle entering and exiting. A 16-inch pit presents an obstacle in the exit direction. Clearly, falling into sand is less of a concern than exit falls onto concrete. When surrounded by grass, any of the above combinations are acceptable. When surrounded by concrete the 16-inch pit may present a minor trip hazard. Note, however, that no research has been done on this question.

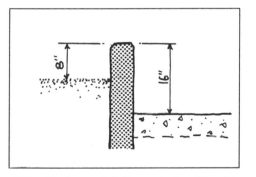

134   *Such a detail presents little trip hazard since it must be intentionally climbed.*

d.   **Transition Zones Around Equipment Areas.** The area around the surface material retainer, extending out about five feet, is an area where significant future maintenance will occur.

Material thrown out of the retainer will be deposited here and should be anticipated. A popular solution is a five foot pathway of decomposed compacted

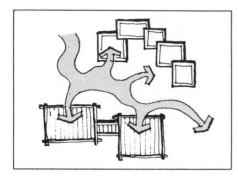

135 *Access "corridors" are required in play settings with rubber matting covering fall zones.*

136 *Wheelchair parking place next to a transfer zone.*

granite surrounding the play area. When a hard surface such as concrete is used for such a path the ejected material can act as roller bearings and create a significant fall hazard.

e.   **Accessibility.** The single most vexing problem in making playgrounds accessible is the paradox of providing a hard surface for wheelchairs, cane users and walkers, and providing a soft surface to protect against falls. To resolve this question an examination of detailed needs is required. Three broad categories of individuals have difficulty navigating soft fall surfacing;

1)   Ambulatory but disabled, i.e., those using walkers, canes, braces or crutches.

2)   Wheelchair users with transfer skills.

3)   Wheelchair users without transfer skills.

All three categories require access corridors into the play area, preferably at several locations. Where paths enter the fall zone of the play equipment they must be covered with rubber mats. Children who can dismount their wheelchairs will require space to stow their chairs out of the traffic and fall zone, yet keeping them close at hand. Children without transfer skills will require sufficient mobility within the play environment to maintain social contact with playmates.

Provide access corridors for all play environment users but be certain that access corridors do not present a fall hazard.

9.7   **Structural Considerations**

a.   **Testing.** The CPSC recommends thorough testing of play equipment and a number of testing procedures. Manufacturers are not, however, required by law to perform these tests. Currently, consumers cannot discover which products have been tested or the results of those that have been tested. Documentation should be required on any testing performed on play equipment to be purchased.

b.   **Modularity.** Modular systems use a few simple parts which combine to make complex structures. Such structures can be added to and modified as new product or safety trends emerge. Currently, many products in a wide variety of materials use modular parts. Such systems offer designers more flexibility and more possibilities for adapting play structures for all children. Additional railings, adjustment of deck heights and other modifications are easily accomplished.

•   Select equipment composed of simple modular parts.

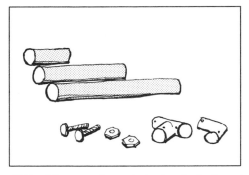

137 *Play equipment is best designed with modular parts.*

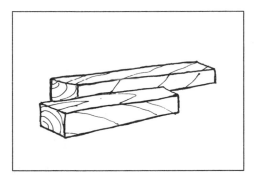

138 *Wood.*

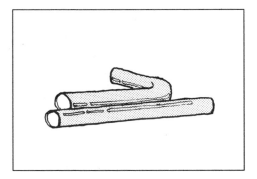

139 *Metal.*

9.8   Materials

a.   **Wood.** The first play equipment was wooden. This was replaced with steel equipment around the turn of the century. Wood was reintroduced in the 1960's, reflecting the mood of the times. The late 1970's saw the introduction of composite systems using a wide variety of materials.

1)   Ensure that wood play structures are properly treated to avoid wood rot and infestation.

2)   A major concern with wood is that it is subject to insect invasion and rot when in contact with soil. Currently, copper arsenate is the treatment of choice for in-ground wood provided that the treated surface is low in residual arsenic salts (4% solution is typical). Apply sealers or coatings over wood to more fully protect.

3)   Inspect treated wood to ensure that no arsenigens are still present on the surface.

4)   Insist on complete documentation of treatment materials and residual arsenigens. Follow proper handling procedures.

b.   **Metal.** While wood has gained some popularity over the past two decades, metal still predominates as the basic material for play equipment frames. Steel offers high strength and ease of fabrication. Steel is subject to rust, however. To solve this problem most steel is galvanized and painted. Structural tubing is used for most fabrication. However, because tubing is not galvanized on the inside, rust can be a concern. Proper footings will reduce water accumulation in pipes in many installations and this removes most of the problem. Some manufacturers attempt to solve the interior rust question by using water pipe, but this material is not fabricated for structural use and must be used in the heaviest gauges in order to approximate the strength of structural tubing.

Determination of life expectancy is a factor in specifying metal treatments. It is possible to treat and maintain metal to last 25 years (assuming one wants a setting to last this long).

Aluminum frames have recently been introduced with only slightly higher costs. While aluminum does not have the strength of steel, its superior resistance to rust makes it an attractive choice.

- Make a careful determination of site requirements for each playground and its life expectancy. Locations without significant standing water problems can use use steel effectively, provided the manufacturer's footing details are followed precisely. Wet and coastal installations should consider aluminum frames.

c. **Plastics.** Hundreds of different types of plastic are currently available. Some of these have found durable application on play equipment. Chief among these is high density polyethylene which is used for rotational molded slides, panels and spring-mounted animals. It can also be used in injection molds as a "structural foam" and has been employed for spiral slides and deck planks.

Polyvinyl chloride (PVC) has recently been used to apply a soft coating to chain and decks (see below).

Fiberglass is used for decorative elements but has low impact resistance and thus is not recommended for unsupervised play settings.

In general, the use of plastics increases the visual appeal of environments by offering a great range of color and form. The lack of heat build up, rounded edges and softness are generally positive play values.

d. **Rope and Chain.** Flexible elements like cargo nets are appealing to children. Such devices require frequent inspection and replacement when used on public playgrounds because of their low durability. Chain is sometimes substituted for rope. Unfortunately chain is harsh and can produce pinch points. Vinyl coating, a recent technical innovation, can greatly improve the quality. Another newly developed composite material, wire cable woven within polypropylene rope, provides flexibility and durability.

- Use durable materials such as vinyl coated chain or cable/rope for "cargo net" play settings.

140   *Rope and chain.*

141   Vandal resistant play equipment.

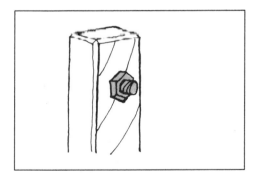

142   Eliminate dangerous protrusions.

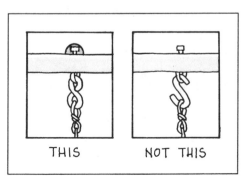

143   Joints with bearings, not simple metat-to-metal "S" hook attachments.

9.9   Hardware

a.   **Vandal Resistant Hardware.** The goal of vandal resistance has been long sought by playground manufacturers. Most current solutions involve the use of fastening devices using special tools which may be supplied by the manufacturer. These fasteners should be free of protrusions which could cause injury.

In addition, thread treatments are also used to keep fasteners in place. Old fashioned hex head bolts should be avoided both for vandal resistance and safety. It was once common practice to field spot weld hex head fasteners and then paint with "cold galvanize" to achieve acceptable levels of durability. Most modern equipment is powder coated and will be damaged by welding. Nails should not be used to hold together play equipment.

• Determine that the fasteners used on play equipment are vandal resistant and protrusion free.

b.   **Protrusions.** The guidelines for protrusions established by the CPSC specified the maximum allowable protrusion. Many recently developed equipment systems are free of any protrusion which might cause injury. Because these new systems tend to be modular, a review for protrusion of the basic frame is straight forward. More variation is possible in attached play events.

1)   To fully determine the protrusion standards of a total system, buyers should make a field inspection of actual installations whenever possible.

2)   In no case should an object protrude more than its diameter (e.g., a 1/2 inch bolt not more than 1/2 inch).

c.   **Moving Joints.** Moving joints are one of the most troublesome maintenance features on playgrounds. Modern nylon bearings perform significantly better than traditional roller bearings or bronze bushings. But despite much improvement, any bearing will eventually fail. For this reason all moving joints must be disassembled periodically to inspect for wear. As sealed joints cannot be disassembled, replacement records must be kept. There are many moving joints on play equipment which are not immediately obvious, such as the connection of rings to their support beam and chain events to fixed structures.

1)   The manufacturer should supply all such joints with bearings, not simple metal-to-metal "S" hooks.

2)   Determine the quality of the bearings used in all moving joints and chain connections to fixed structures and the ease with which they can be maintained and inspected.

9.10   Finishes

Significant advances in equipment finishes have been made in recent years. While rust resistant galvanized finishes are still commonplace, "powder coating" has replaced nearly all other paints. Powder coating is an electrostatic process which applies epoxy, nylon or polyester plastic as a very fine dry powder which is then oven cured and bonded to the surface of steel or aluminim. Powder coating is the most durable choice of finishes where many color options are important to the consumer. Efforts have been made, when using steel, to powder coat over the galvanizing. This helps provide extra protection from harsh environmental conditions. The additional protection should be weighed against increased costs.

9.11   Play Events

9.11.1 Enclosure

To the extent that play structures also function as social places, enclosure is important. It supports the many "chase" and "hide-and-seek" games that children always adapt to play structures. Enclosure is essential for safety, e.g., in a multideck structure where a high deck is adjacent to a low deck.

144 Enclosed spaces in play structures support games and restful interaction.

a.   **Nonclimbable Enclosure Height.** The CPSC recommends that all platforms above 30 inches be surrounded by "nonclimbable" protective barriers at least 38 inches in height. In practice, this specification has created confusion as various manufacturers try to determine what is "nonclimbable".

For the most part, the industry agrees that horizontal rungs constitute a "climbable" barrier since these are generally constructed in the same manner as ladders. Vertical rungs are preferable, provided they meet entrapment specifications. Some companies simply wall in the opening completely. Such a barrier may indeed be nonclimbable but it also greatly inhibits supervision.

Three designs which seem to meet the CPSC guideline and provide for supervision without creating entrapments are vertical wooden slats or metal rails with 3 to 4 inch spaces, panels with cutouts covered with clear plastic and wire mesh panels.

- Be certain that platform enclosures are at least 38 inches in height and present no entrapments or footholds for climbing.

b. **Children with Motor Impairments** may require additional railing details to support their movement through the play environment. Prior to the issuance of the CPSC Guidelines this was accomplished by having two parallel banisters. This solution may no longer be allowable because it conflicts with the CPSC's "non-climbable" requirement. A re-examination of this requirement may be needed.

Basically, the need for additional support for ambulation occurs where there are changes in surface, activity or elevation. Such transition points can be improved with the addition of vertical grips and thereby provide the needed security while complying with the CPSC Guidelines.

145   Children with motor impairments may require additional railing details.

1) Specify vertical grips at changes in surface, activity or elevation.

2) Provide continuous hand grips at one and two feet from the base of the platform.

9.11.2 Slides

Slides are a popular item, especially when integrated into varied play settings. They need to conform to the developmental needs of children. Slides for toddlers should have different dimensions to those for older children. Safety features need careful consideration.

a. **Slide Heights.** Falls are the number one playground hazard and can be reduced considerably with the installation of high quality impact absorbing surface materials and height reduction. Ideally, slides should be restricted to 64 inches in overall vertical fall distance or may be higher if installed on slopes. If slide heights are greater than 4 feet, access decks should be properly enclosed with a 38" non-climbable enclosure.

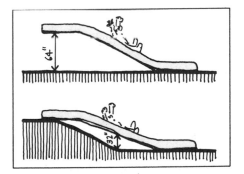

146   Slide heights.

1) Restrict freestanding slides to 64 inches vertical fall height or to limits defined by the test results of the safety surfacing material installed, whichever is the smaller.

2)   To guide slide height decisions, charts should be developed to describe the relationships between distance of fall, surface resiliency and severity of potential injury.

b.   **Slide Gradient.** While standards in other countries may differ, the current U.S. CPSC guideline states that "the average incline of the sliding surface shall not exceed 30 degrees."

Wave slides may have portions which are steeper so long as the total slope requirement is not exceeded.

c.   **Slide Chute Side Rails.** The CPSC guideline for slide rail height is 2 1/2 inches but in other countries it is much greater. England requires 6 inches but also allows a steeper angle of descent. A disadvantage of standard slides is that they prevent adults sliding down with a child between their legs. Wide slides solve this problem and offer the advantage of group play experience; however, they are sometimes threatening to young or disabled children.

1)   Slide side rails must be a minimum of 2 1/2 inches above the slide surface.

2)   For accessibility and integration, paired slides are preferable to wide slides.

d.   **Slide Exit Zones.** The CPSC requires that slide exit zones be a minimum of 16 inches long, with a height between 9 and 15 inches. This specification is based on the assumption that children will use equipment in the prescribed manner. Several objections to this guideline have been raised.

Prior to CPSC, some slides where available with shorter exit regions placed directly at surface level with the advantages that, a) children were prevented from falling back on the exit lip of the slide, b) children tended to move out of the path of following players more quickly, and c) better exit transitions were provided for nonambulatory children. More research is needed on the preferred height of slide exits. The British Standard, BS5696 (1979), is a useful reference.

•   **Accessibility.** Slide exit regions require special adaptations to provide for nonambulatory users. Such modifications may be different from the CPSC Guidelines.

Note! Many disabled children and those 18 months and younger frequently lack sufficient trunk strength and control to remain upright while sliding. In motion they fall supine and may injure their head and/or neck on exiting a slide which is raised above the surface.

147   Slides: design of the exit needs carefully consideration.

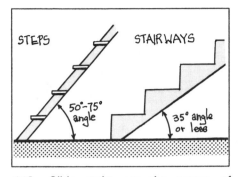

148 *Slide stairs are the source of numerous accidents.*

149 *Access for non-ambulatory children can be facilitated if there are steps alongside the slide.*

e.   Freestanding Slides.   Decades of slide use by millions of children have demonstrated both the popularity of slides and their hazards. The vast majority of the slide accidents occur in three areas. Slide stairs are the source of numerous accidents. Very young children find themselves fearful of progressing and unable to climb down. Older children often use stairs for horseplay. The slide entrance area is often used for king-of-the-mountain games. The top section of the slide chute, where sliding children collide with children running up the slide, is also a problem.

The risk of injury from these ancillary behaviors is reduced significantly when slides are attached to composite play structures, where decks replace stairs, or are installed on mounds.

CPSC guideline 11.3.2.4 requires closed stair treads on traditionally configured slides. Such closed treads fill with sand and create a slip hazard. A better plan would be to use small holes (too small to catch fingers but large enough to let grains of sand through without clogging).

1)   Free standing slides should be avoided, unless the steps are fully enclosed.

2)   Check that stairs are fuly enclosed and not sand traps and therefore slip hazards.

e.   Slide Entry Areas.   When standard narrow slides are attached to play structure decks, railings or loops are used to facilitate entrance and reduce the possibility of falling. For many years a single rail has been the standard solution. This introduces the possibility of skin-the-cat type actions as part of the child's entrance movements. Solutions to this problem use a double rail or a vinyl coated chain across the entryway. Whatever solution is adopted, the child's transition from deck to slide must occur without significant exposure to falling.

Access for nonambulatory children with transfer skills can be facilitated if there is a large smooth platform at the end of the slide, 16 inches above a paved surface. The design includes a cleated ramp parallel to the slide for access to the deck or steps along the side of the slide. Such a configuration provides a fully accessible (for the intended population) slide experience and does not introduce significant new hazards.

•   Ensure that slides have devices which provide transition security at their entrance and that such devices do not introduce new hazards.

f.   **Slide Materials.** For the past twenty years stainless steel has been the material of choice for slide surfaces.

Stainless steel, while very durable, is not without problems. The most significant is the tendency to cause second degree burns. To minimize this problem it is recommended slides be installed pointing in a northerly direction. While this technique is somewhat effective in reducing burns, it greatly reduces design and configuration options. Alternatively, slides must be provided with adequate shading.

A second problem with low grade stainless steel is that when it fails it tends to expose razor sharp edges.

Plastic slides solve problems of heat and sharp edges of stainless steel. When first introduced, plastic slides were made of fiberglass. While these slides accomplished the goal of adding color and reducing burns they proved to be flammable and subject to impact fracture.

Currently, high density polyethylene slides solve the durability problem and add an element of permanent color. They will melt if a fire is built around them, although they are not in themselves combustible. If they are not well made, they can be light sensitive and can be damaged by sand and by heavy objects being thrown against them.

- Evaluate carefully the possible replacement of stainless steel slides with polyethylene slides.

g.   **Variety and Challenge of Slides.** Modern equipment settings have many innovative slide designs (wave, spiral, wide, tunnel, banister, even slides with rollers) in addition to standard narrow slides.

Roller slides should be purchased with caution. While being extremely interesting to children, they have a number of unique characteristics. While normally not a pinch hazard, roller slides tend to induce "surf riding" play. Thus, roller slides from 4 foot decks are preferred. They are not recommended for schools.

Roller slides should not use ball bearings and cannot be installed over pea gravel. The best resilient material under roller slides is rubber matting.

Creating play settings with several different types of slides makes the playground more interesting, developmentally more challenging, and safer, since children can select the types of slides best suited for their own skill levels.

- Play settings should have many different types of slides.

150 Slides should be varied and challenging.

151 *Select slides with lap joints rather than butt joints.*

h. **Slide Joints and Seams.** The seams which occur in the construction and/or assembiy of slides are important. Butt seams, those which do not overlap, offer a significantly greater chance for foreign objects to become lodged in the cracks and protrude into the sliding regions.

- Use one-piece slides where possible. Otherwise, select slides with lap joints rather than butt joints to avoid foreign objects being inserted into the chute area.

9.11.3 Swings

Swings can take a variety of forms, depending on the method of suspension, type of seat, length of arc, character of takeoff and landing, etc. The traditional double-hung swing (with a reinforced vinyl seat) is still probably the most popular piece of play equipment ever invented (Moore, 1986c, 1978b).

Several types of swings are possible: "triple-hung" auto tires are a well tried idea. The suspension hardware is a crucial detail and should be a high quality manufactured item.

a. **Swing Height.** Swings should be suspended from a variety of heights to cater to different age groups and to provide a range of movement. Don't assume that small swings will always be used by small kids. Big kids often enjoy the quicker "period" of small swings; therefore, they should be made just as robust as big swings.

While high swings appeal to children, the danger involved both from falls and collisions makes high swings unacceptable in public facilities. Research is needed on this issue, to determine relationships between height, swing throw, jumping-off distances, distance between suspensions, and size and shape of fall zone. Height limits are necessary to minimize the dangers of swing use and falls by children who climb to the swing beam.

b. **Swing Seats.** Most swing injuries result from a swinging child hitting another in its path. Even empty swing seats with significant mass and/or sharp edges can cause injury when thrown. The minimum requirement for swing seats is the CPSC guideline for impact and protrusion.

1) Accessible swings must have a back and side support or a hole/indentation (as in a tire swing with a cloth or webbed bottom) for the child's backside.

152   *Swings should be isolated from other play equipment.*

153   *Tire swings require a large, clear area.*

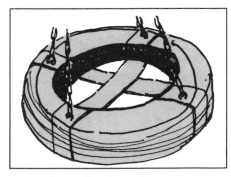

154   *Accessible tire swing.*

2)   Remove all swing seats except the rubber belt type and triple-hung auto tire. If reinforced, belt seats should not allow sharp edges to be exposed. Swing seats for special applications are allowed so long as they conform to the CPSC Guidelines.

c.   **Isolation and Traffic Flow Barriers.** Because swings can act as battering rams and small children commonly walk into the swing use zone, swings should be isolated from other play equipment. They should not be combined with multiplay structures.

Additional protection can be afforded if a traffic flow barrier surrounds the swings. Such a barrier should not become a play event itself (e.g. a turning bar). Entrances to the swing zone should be located so as to maximize visibility, i.e. if there is a logical "front," such as a view of the playground itself, this should be the location of the entrance.

•   Locate swings in their own enclosure separate from the rest of the playground.

d.   **Swing Setbacks.** Setback guidelines for swings vary considerably. A commonly used measurement equals twice the height of the swing cross arm or sixteen feet front and back.

1)   The minimum setback requirement for swings is two times the height of the swing beam from any edge or obstacle. For tot and tire swings with low beams this distance can be reduced slightly.

2)   Swing areas should be defined by distinct differences in ground texture.

e.   **Tire Swings.** Tire swing hangers are one of the most critical hardware items used on playground equipment. This is due to the stresses which are applied when multiple children utilize this activity at the same time. The amount of weight and centrifugal force which can be applied during normal use warrant extensive testing by manufacturers. Failure of these hangers is potentially catastrophic. Two types of hanger design are available: ball joint and universal joint. Each has their advantages and disadvantages.

Ball joints are a clean design and present no pinch points. A shortcoming of these joints has been their limited degree of motion which causes wear and eventual failure. Tire swings require about 170 degrees of freedom and most ball joints provide only 145 degrees. Universal joints are not prone to such limitations. They do, however, present pinch points. Commonly, these are covered with a protective

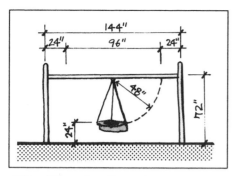

155 *Tire swing dimensions.*

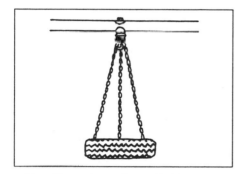

156 *Tire swing universal joint.*

157 *"Tarzan" ropes are popular, but not recommended in public playgrounds.*

boot and, if well designed and maintained, provide satisfactory protection from pinching. New hanger designs are under development.

The other common failure of tire swings results from movement of the mounting hardware. Permanent positive attachment of the bearing to the beam is essential.

Tire swings, since they move in all directions, require a beam support span which is two times the swing length plus 4 feet. A twelve foot span, common for this type of swing, would therefore be limited to 48 inches length of support chains and have a horizontal member height of 72 inches.

1) Tire swings are easily made accessible by strapping webbing to the bottom or inserting plasticized canvas in the hole and bolting it in, thus creating a "nest."

2) Tire swings should consist of beams at 72 inches, with universal joint bearings protected by a boot securely attached to the beam.

f.   **"Tarzan" ropes.** Although popular, swing ropes are not recommended in public playgrounds unless exemplary inspection and maintenance procedures are available. Close supervision is necessary. Ropes should be removed when supervision is not available.

1) Tarzan-type, freestanding swing ropes should be installed only under the strictest conditions of maintenance and supervision. They should be removable by playground staff.

g.   **Swing Accessibility.** Unless stabilized, swings are hard to get into at transfer points. A challenge for manufacturers is to design a swing into which a child in a wheelchair can transfer effectively, paying particular attention to: positioning, visibility and security.

Currently, no adequate solution has been developed for independent nonambulatory access to swings. Seats need to be 16 inches off the ground rather than the customary 18—24 inches but more research is needed on this issue. Exerglide is a make of swing that can be operated without lower body movement, however upper body strength must be robust. Wheelchair swings are not recommended for public play settings.

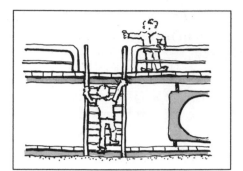

158 *Play structures should support climbing.*

9.11.4 Climbers

a.   **Climber Heights.** As noted in several other guideline categories, height limitation is one of the best means of reducing injuries from falls. In the case of slides, some height is absolutely required for the equipment to perform its function.

Climbers on the other hand do not require heights above 56 inches to be fully challenging. The height of a climber should be based on four factors:

1)   Type and quality of the fall absorbing surface.

2)   Location.

3)   User group.

4)   Ability to maintain the equipment and surfacing.

Climbers, including ladders, are attached to play structures to achieve proper traffic flow patterns. But even in these applications the child never needs to be exposed to a fall greater than 56 inches; the European standard is 2 m (6 ft 6 in); U.K. is 2.5 m (8 ft 2 in). Tunnel climbers and net climbers are designed to reduce the total drop to which a child is exposed. Equipment height should be partially determined by the degree to which the surfacing can protect the child from a severe injury due to a fall.

b.   **Climber Rung Size.** Consensus among manufacturers favors 3/4 inch minimum to 1 1/2 inch maximum. The range is intended to allow proper grip for differing age groups. If playgrounds are to be made safe for all children then one rail size should be selected. Rails from 1 inch to 1 1/4 inch are acceptable.

•   Rails and grips on climbers should be between 1 inch and 1 1/4 inches in diameter.

c.   **Climber Obstruction Free Fall Zones.** Wherever possible, all play equipment, and especially climbing apparatus, should present an obstruction-free fall zone. For example, arch climbers are preferred over cube climbers.

•   "Free fall" climbers are required except in those rare circumstances where a climber connects with a deck above 48 inches and the climber, such as a net, is used as an intermediary fall protection device.

d.   **Climber Variety and Flexibility.** As with other play events, climbers will provide more benefits with greater safety if they are presented in several types to provide

159   *Play equipment should support balancing, both static and dynamic.*

160   *The most effective balance activities are slightly elevated above grade.*

161   *Play equipment should provide for differing levels of skill.*

for graduated challenge. Of particular importance is the provision of flexible climbers, such as nets, which require dynamic balance instead of simple static balance.

- Ensure that a variety of climbers is included in each play environment. Flexible climbers have additional developmental benefits.

9.11.5 Balance Events

a.   **Static Versus Dynamic Balance.** Child development specialists point out that, except for children under four, dynamic balance (balance on surfaces which move) has more developmental value than static balances such as beams.

Such activities can be incorporated into playgrounds through the use of cable, clatter, chain/log bridges, rolling barrels, or spring platforms.

Suspended balance events like cable walks and nets place very large loads on play structures which must be carefully engineered to accommodate these stresses.

- Include dynamic balance activities in equipment settings.

b.   **Balance Height.** The most effective balance activities are slightly elevated above grade. In most cases 24 inches is sufficient.

- Balance activities should not be greater than 24 inches in height.

c.   **Balance Linkage.** Balance activities are more frequently used when they link parts of the playground. Because of their low height and minimum fall potential, they may be used to link play structures with surrounding walkways (Moore, 1974b; Moore & Wong, in press).

1)   Balance activities should be used as linkages.

2)   To make balance activities accessible to children with visual and motor impairments provide at least some events with guide rails and grips at pull-up (transfer) places (PLAE, 1981—87).

9.11.6 Upper Body Events

a.   **Graduated Challenge.** Examples of upper body events include turning bars, chinning bars, horizontal ladders, ring treks and track rides. Safety in the use of upper body development equipment is promoted by the use of many different events with differing levels of skill.

   •   Include upper body development events with graduated skill
        levels in each equipment setting.

b.   **Linkage and Size of Upper Body Events.** Upper body events such as ladders and treks stimulate more use when they are used to link parts of the play environment because they become part of the flow of children's games. Grouping these events also encourages children to demonstrate their abilities to each other.

   Horizontal ladders are used with less conflict if they are wide enough for more than one child. For children from three to five, a ladder (6 feet long) with a 5 degree incline aids learning. For older children spans of 12 feet are appropriate.

   •   Upper body events should be used to link sections of the play environment
        and should be sized to challenge children of various abilities.

c.   **Mount-Dismount on Upper Body Events.** The mount and dismount of upper body development devices such as ladders and treks is important. Children often approach the dismount in a fatigued state and must be able to dismount with ease and security.

   Two methods are currently used to accomplish this goal: rails or loops, and decks. No evidence is available as to the superiority of either approach. In either case, however, the last handhold should not be placed directly above the dismount rail or deck, but should be inset by 8 or more inches to prevent children from falling onto the rail or deck.

   •   Upper body development equipment must have appropriate, easily used
        mount/dismount features.

d.   **Grip Size for Upper Body Events**

   (see Section 9.11.4b, Climber Rung Size, for discussion of this topic)

e.   **Height of Upper Body Events.** Determining the proper height of upper body events is another area where the use of the equipment is in conflict with safety considerations. Horizontal ladders are not too much of a fall hazard. When placed at

162   Child going hand-over-hand along a climber.

80 inches they are high enough to be used effectively by most children and are still low enough that should a child fall from the top onto appropriate safety surfacing, the chance of serious injury is not too high.

Ring treks and track rides require at least an additional foot of elevation to accommodate the hanging ring handles. This places them at 92 inches which will exceed the fall absorbing ability of all but the very best surfacing. Using these conservative heights for installation guides, children taller than 60 inches will have to fold their legs somewhat to keep from dragging their feet. While this makes use of equipment awkward, such knee bending requires additional skill and strength from these older and larger children and is thus not entirely negative.

1) The height of horizontal ladders should be limited to 80 inches. Events may exceed this height by as much as 12 inches when installed over 6 inches of chopped tire or 12 inches of uniform round sand.

2) Ladders can be lowered to make them accessible for young children and children in wheelchairs with upper body strength, but choosing an appropriate ground surface for both fall cushioning and wheelchair access is important (PLAE, 1981—87).

9.11.7 Spinning Equipment

Children are attracted by the circular movement of merry-go-rounds and other forms of spinning equipment. The safety issues, however, are substantial.

a. **Size and Speed of Spinning Equipment.** Injuries on spinning equipment (merry-go-rounds or whirls) consist largely of falls against or under the moving equipment and are made more serious by its size and mass. One of the most common accidents occurs when young children attempt to dismount while older children (and even adults !) are spinning the whirls. The most obvious means of reducing these injuries is to limit the size of whirls. A four foot diameter whirl will hold four children and is much less likely to cause serious injury.

Several manufacturers now supply speed limiters on larger whirls. While not as effective as limiting size, they may reduce accidents.

• Limit the size of whirls to 48 inches.

b. **Surfacing of Spinning Equipment.** The use of whirls causes loose material to be pushed away all around their base exposing the underside for possible entrap-

163 *Children are attracted by spinning play equipment.*

ment. Some installers attempt to solve this problem by mounting the units over rubber matting. If the matting is sufficiently resilient and properly maintained, this may be an acceptable practice.

- Be certain that rotating equipment is installed in such a manner that children cannot become entrapped underneath.

c.   **Design Requirements of Spinning Equipment.** A too frequent injury on whirls is finger loss caused by the gap between the central support post and the whirl—the result of poor maintenance. Newer designs shroud this connection so that even with negligent maintenance no finger entrapment occurs.

For many years whirls where fabricated from pipe and had open centers. Such designs have proven extremely hazardous as children become easily entrapped.

- Remove whirls with open frameworks. Ensure that the equipment is properly maintained and that the bearings do not present possible finger entrapment.

9.11.8 Rocking/Spring-mounted Equipment

Children respond dramatically to opportunities for bouncing and rocking.

a.   **Appropriate Age Group.** Spring-mounted animals are especially appealing to children five and under. They should therefore be included in areas designed for tot play. Because this equipment is intended for young children it is important for them to be able to hold on without falling. Grip size of 3/4 inch and ample foot rests are recommended.

Designs which contain, and correctly position and support the child are preferred so long as they are not too heavy for small children to activate (which is the case with some vehicle theme designs).

Conventional seesaws, while providing support for cooperative play and remaining popular with children, present a significant chance for back injury and crush points. They are not recommended, except for spring-loaded seesaws which have solved some of these problems. More research is required on this issue.

1)   Include rocking spring-mounted animals within play areas for tots.

2)   Rocking equipment should contain the child as much as possible.

3)   Spring-loaded seesaws are permissible. Conventional seesaws are not recommended.

164   Play equipment should support bouncing activities.

165 *Young children love to ride "springing" animals.*

166 *Equipment settings resembling interpretive stations are desirable additions.*

b.   Spring Performance on Rocking Equipment. Springs designed for use on playgrounds must meet a difficult criteria; they must be soft enough for small children to move yet strong enough to avoid damage when used inappropriately by large children.

9.11.9   Manufactured Inflatables.

Inflatables have a great potential for use by children with and without disabilities. They can be used by people of all ages and abilities either in integrated settings or in specific programs for the physically, mentally or emotionally challenged. Inflatables are mobile and can be used as the basis for a mobile play environment in parks, playgrounds, recreation centers and during summer programs.

Select units with welded construction as opposed to stitching so they are strong enough to be used by adults as well as children. Welded construction eliminates the need for protective covers when water or other liquids being introduced onto the structures.

More research and development needs to conducted in this area of equipment.

9.11.10 Interpretive Play Equipment

Equipment settings that are more like interpretive stations that stress environmental education and hands-on experience rather than physical education are desirable as additions to conventional play equipment. They are especially appropriate in settings with trained play leadership and have a broader potential for the integration of children with disabilities. The concept also extends the developmental potential of public playgrounds.

9.12   Documentation

Play equipment manufacturers' promotional materials, catalogs and installation documents accompanying specific pieces should be improved as sources of information for prospective users. Many catalogs could be more informative with respect to the criteria used in the CPSC Guidelines and the Play For All Guidelines. Safety could be more visibly promoted. Inspection schedules should be included. Manufacturers' catalogs can become significant vehicles for public education.

9.13   Documentation Checklist

The following list itemizes most of the documentation required for a comprehensive playground risk management program. While every attempt has been made to be as complete as possible, the specific program may require additional information. Not every site needs documentation as this as indicated by this list.   Final determination of the proper files to keep, the information they contain, and the length of time they should be retained must be made by each agency and organization in light of its unique needs.

a.   **Assessment**

1)   Site inspection for conformance to CPSC Guidelines.

2)   Environmental inventory with unusual feature identification, e.g. open bodies of water.

3)   Activities and program descriptions.

4)   User profiles.

5)   Community needs assessment results.

b.   **Design**

1)   Project goals.

2)   Names and roles of individuals involved in developing the project.

3)   Designer qualifications.

4)   Equipment specification requirements.

5)   Manufacturer's catalogs.

6)   Site layout (conforming to master plan) and installation details.

7)   Public (playground task force) and administrative review process with written approvals.

c.   **Purchase**

1)   Purchasing agent's procedures and qualifications.

2)   Manufacturer's guarantee.

3)   Permitted and actual deviation from specification.

4)   Purchase orders.

5)   Verification of correct shipment.

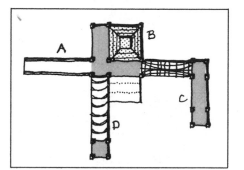

167   Site layout and installation details.

168   Site inspection.

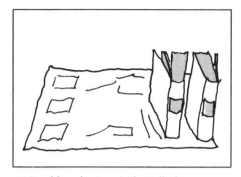

169 *Manufacturer's installation manual.*

d.   **Installation**

  1)   Installer qualifications and insurance.

  2)   Provisions for on-site safety of workers and public during construction.

  3)   Manufacturer's installation manual.

  4)   Manufacturer's verification of proper installation.

e.   **Supervision**

  1)   Adult/child ratio guidelines.

  2)   Manufacturer's use guidelines.

  3)   Student and/or community safety awareness program.

  4)   Warning signs.

  5)   Accident monitoring and systematic review.

f.   **Maintenance**

  1)   Post-installation design review.

  2)   Daily or weekly inspections.

  3)   In-depth inspections.

  4)   Equipment amortization schedule.

9.14   Prototypical Language For Purchase Documents And Criteria For Purchasing

To be considered for purchase, all vendors of play equipment shall provide the following:

a.   **A Certificate of Insurance** for both products and general liability of not less than 500,000 dollars. The issuing underwriter shall be AA rated.

b.   **A Manufacturer's Certification of Compliance** with the Consumer Products Safety Commission's Playground Equipment Guidelines.

c.   **Structural and Materials Specifications** with complete details and performance specification on all connection hardware, materials and structural components.

d.   **Site Inspection.** Purchaser shall be provided a clearly detailed checklist by manufacturer for on site verification that the equipment has been installed according to manufacturer's specifications. This checklist should be filled out by the vendor or a qualified equal.

After receiving this completed document, the manufacturer will issue a Warranty Validation Certificate to the owner. Special care should be taken to ensure adequate fall absorbing materials and appropriate minimum setbacks from equipment are maintained.

e.   **Warranty.** The minimum required warranty is one year on materials and workmanship. In addition, a special ten-year **Post and Deck Integrity Warranty** is also required.

f.   **Maintenance Schedule,** provided by the manufacturer, shall estimate the frequency with which inspection and maintenance should be performed in relationship to time and use.

g.   **Use and Safety Information,** including a manual listing appropriate activities for each play feature. For school site installations, lesson plans for increasing student and staff safety awareness and encouraging proper use shall also be provided. Specific hazards and consequent potential injury, if any, shall be identified.

h.   **Equipment.** Where applicable, all integrated play structures shall be modular in nature, that is, their framework shall be composed of similar elements which can be configured in a variety of ways. Expansion and modification can be easily accomplished.

i.   **Materials.** Different consideration include:

1)   **Attachment Hardware.** There shall be a minimum number of types of attaching hardware. All hardware shall be of a vandal resistant type. Hex-head type bolts are not acceptable. Bolts and nuts must have vandal-resistent fastening methods. Nails should never be used to secure play equipment.

2)   **Posts.** Posts shall be steel, aluminum, wood or plastic. All posts should be warranted for ten years.

3)   **Decks.** Decks shall be retained without exposed hardware. Nails are not permitted. Metal decks are permissible if vinyl clad.

4)   **Plastics.** All plastics shall be high grade polyethylene, polyvinyl chloride or polycarbonate. They shall be stabilized against ultraviolet light degradation. They shall be self-extinguishing.

5) **Chain and Cable.** All chain or cable on climbing structures shall be covered with a durable plastic coating which is cut resistant. Joints shall be smooth and free of burrs.

6) **Wood Treatment.** All wood shall be treated with copper arsenate. The manufacturer shall certify that wood treatment complies with the C-17 standard of the American Wood Preservers Institute and is free of residual chemicals. Coating or sealer may also need to be applied.

Checks may not exceed 18 inches in length or 1/8 inch in width when received. Wood may not check after installation for a period of one year to a check dimension of 24 inches in length and 3/16 inch.

7) **Metal Treatment.** Touch up scratches in posts. Paint shall be supplied by the manufacturer. (Be aware that dents can affect the integrity of posts.)

j. **Population Capacity.** The maximum number of users for each play activity and for the overall environment should be specified. This population estimate shall be adjusted to consider developmental characteristics and use by both same age and mixed age groups.

k. **An Inventory of Educational Benefits** shall detail the specific learning experiences provided by the apparatus.

l. **Cushion Material and Setbacks.** The minimum cushion area shall be illustrated in a plan view drawing of the play equipment. Specific detail shall be provided as to the manufacturers recommendation for type and depth of fall absorbing materials in accordance with the standards set forth by the Consumer Products Safety Commission and ASTM Standard F08.52.

m. **Installation Manual.** The installation instructions shall be complete in all details and provided prior to purchase. The minimum required information shall include the site layout process, order of assembly, footing requirements, list of parts by subsection or component and estimated construction hours required.

10. MULTIPURPOSE GAME SETTINGS

To support team sports, large group games, places for traditional games and ball play, flat open spaces are required (NPFA, 1985). For wheelchair use they need to be hard-surfaced; otherwise, turf is the best surface.

Planning Criteria

Play Value. Game areas support activities which promote cooperation, team spirit and large muscle development.

Programming. A high level of expertise is required to program game areas appropriately for all children.

Play Leadership. Ensure that leaders balance sports and team games with other program opportunities. Encourage training in cooperative games.

Safety. Do not locate hard surfaces near fixed equipment from which children could fall. Recognize that pedestrian falls onto hard surfaces are one of the most common forms of minor injury. Hurts from falls and collisions are common and difficult to avoid.

Risk Management. Safe, well maintained ancillary equipment is required. Ensure that children and parents have a knowledge of the rules. Prepare settings so that accidents can be dealt with expeditiously: telephone, transport, emergency procedures, first aid supplies and staff training.

Accessibility. Partial shade is required for adequate comfort. Viewing areas for spectators, parents, and disabled children should be fully accessible.

Integration. Cooperative games (Orlick, 1978 & 1982; Orlick and Botterill, 1975) have more potential for integration than traditional sports. Modifications of mainstream sports can also be tried. Besides the inherent pleasure generated for disabled children by activities such as bowling, swimming, basketball and football, major enjoyment is derived from their recognition that the nonhandicapped world also enjoys these activities. The children feel they are part of the larger whole and not "different." However, some design modifications are necessary (HUD, 1978).

Management/Maintenance. Policy is needed to specify who is allowed to play on teams. An important issue is that ball game areas are underused compared to the space they occupy, and are not often used by girls (Moore, 1978b).

10.1 Places to Run (Schneekloth, 1985)

Children need to run. For the child with visual or physical impairments, opportunities are often limited to certain areas and times when adult supervision is available. Therefore, safe places to run without supervision need to be provided. Running lanes, rope guides or other devices can be provided to make running possible for specific disabilities. Runs for wheelchairs can be installed. Appropriate running surfaces need to be provided (see Chapter 6, Pathways, and Chapter 11, Groundcovers/Surfacing).

10.2 Court Games

Supervised play areas can provide more challenging games (volleyball, basketball, racquetball, tetherball and badminton). They require hard surfaced areas, special equipment stored at the site and, perhaps, leadership and supervision for some age groups.

10.3 Hard-surfaced play areas

There may be some hard-surfaced areas for less structured activities: bike rodeos, skateboarding and roller-skating In Glasgow, Scotland, a BMX/roller-skate/skateboard facility was developed as a shallow hard-surfaced bowl about 45 feet wide, with a side-to-center fall of about 12 inches, and a central drainage vent. It is surrounded on three sides by seating and shrub planting (P. Heseltine, correspondence).

10.4 Ball Play Areas

Ball play is a universally popular play activity, ranging from simple informal games that can be played alone or with one or two others (Moore & Wong, in press), to organized team sports. Important considerations when designing ball play areas include:

a. **Time-sharing.** Ball games go through "seasons," climatically and culturally. Ad hoc, informal games are usually different from organized team games. This means that various ball play areas can be superimposed on each other to create a "time-shared" space, particularly basketball, handball and kickball areas (Moore & Wong, in press).

b. **Irregular Boundary.** Beyond the actual pitch size, there is no reason to make ball-play settings rectangular in shape. An irregular boundary adds to the visual interest of the space and makes it look less monofunctional. If the boundary has "depth" (e.g. vegetation rather than a hard line of chain link fence), other uses are more likely to be encouraged.

170   *Ball walls are an important addition to ball play areas.*

171   *Multipurpose asphalted games areas can include formal ball courts, places for spectators and areas for community activity. Shade is especially important for children with disabilities.*

172   *Lowered basketball hoops allow use by children in wheelchairs.*

c.   **Half-size courts.** Most basketball games use only about one-third of a regular court. Demand for full-size courts is much less than for half-courts, which are also easier to incorporate into an irregular layout.

d.   **Adjacent Ball Walls.** In addition to an asphalted ground surface, the most important ball-playing accoutrements are walls; and in contrast to asphalt, there never seem to be enough. The best way to get ball play to happen in some places rather than others is via the strategic location of "strike-out" walls and other dividing walls. Ideally, several walls should be provided, with one or two curved ones to add interest. They should be high enough to stop fly balls (10—12 feet high). They make terrific surfaces for art work such as murals (Moore & Wong, in press).

e.   **Multipurpose.** Ball playing areas can also accommodate other functions requiring large spaces, such as community events and festivals. Design considerations like microclimate, visual appearance, shady sitting places, trash cans, etc., should be carefully considered.

Multipurpose games areas should contain rectangular ball-playing pitches, but may also have an irregular outer boundary of "ball walls" and places to sit and watch the game, read a book and meet friends. Trees for shade and climatic control and additional vegetation for reducing visual impact should also be provided. They should be designed as places where people can hang out, rest or converse (See "Kickabout Areas" NPFA, 1977).

10.5   **Game Ideas** (CMHC, 1977)

a.   **Basketball Hoops.** Basketball hoops lower than the standard 10 feet height allows those in wheelchairs and young children to enjoy the game. Some designs allow hoop heights to be adjusted.

b.   **Ping-pong.** Outdoor ping-pong tables need protection from the wind; sometimes solid fencing is used if the area is too exposed. Bats and balls must be provided at the site. Ping-pong is a school age, teen and adult game that takes up little space and develops skills and team play.

c.   **Badminton and Volleyball.** Badminton and volleyball do not need fancy court surfaces or even regulation dimensions, only a relatively flat surface. These games are enjoyed by all ages.

173   *Box hockey.*

d.   **Box Hockey** (CMHC, 1977). This simple game is very popular in Sweden and is perfect for school-age children; it is also a space saver. It can be played with four as well as two. The hockey stick needs to have a shorter foot for maneuverability. Swedes use a round stick more like a cane with a curve at the striking end. The object is to get the puck out of the opponent's end through one of the holes in the middle board and the goal hole.

e.   **Tetherball.** This is a game for school-age children that does not take up too much space. Children can develop their own rules or use standard ones.

11. GROUND COVERS/SURFACING

Both soft and hard play surfaces are needed to support different types of play activity. Safety surfaces are mandatory under all manufactured equipment. For children to have contact with nature, and to provide habitat for small animals, a choice of natural ground covers should be provided.

Ground covers and surfaces include: organic materials such as bark nuggets and wood chips; inorganic materials such as asphalt, concrete, and other, smooth, resilient surfaces; and soft, impact absorbing surfaces like sand and pea gravel. They also include: turf; un-mown, rough areas of wild grasses and plants; carefully managed rough areas suitable for use by crawling infants; and nonaccessible erosion control areas.

Planning Criteria

Play Value. Soft surfaces help promote and extend social interaction. Hard surfaces are necessary for ease of access and for activities like ballplay.

Programming. Soft surfaces and natural ground covers are a source of play props and sensory stimulation. Hard surfaces are necessary for particular games.

Play Leadership. Leaders need knowledge of how to use various surfaces.

Safety. Should meet the under 200g's CPSC impact attenuation standard and the ASTM standards when those become available in 1988 (see sections 11.3 and 11.4 for further details). Avoid allergenic, toxic, hurtful, spikey varieties of plants.

Risk Management. Fall-absorbing surfaces must be installed in all equipment settings. Careful maintenance is required for all surfaces.

Accessibility. Long grass is difficult to wheel through and difficult to walk through for people with balance problems. Hard-surface pathways are needed.

Integration. The potential for supporting integration varies from surface to surface.

Management/Maintenance. Fall absorbing surfaces for equipment settings. Many new safety surfaces are coming onto the market. They need to be carefully evaluated against the ASTM standards to be published in 1988.

11.1   Natural Ground Covers

Ground covers are a smaller scale form of vegetation than trees and shrubs which also create small ecosystems. Ground covers are more manipulable for children but also more vulnerable and more prone to wear.

Some species change according to the season, which enhances the sense of the passage of time. Some species attract small insects, which is another attraction and source of excitement for children.

A clump of shrubs can become an intimate, enclosed place for children. A place surrounded by flowers is a source of fantasy play (Moore, 1986b). Flowers can be used to create a happy mood. Raised flower beds enhance the sense of enclosure and close the distance between childrens' eyes and the flowers.

Circulation considerations are important to avoid unnecessary erosion and the need for replanting.

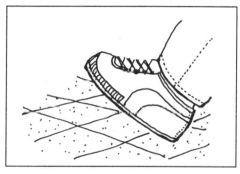

174 *Appropriate surfacing materials should be chosen according to use patterns.*

11.2   Surfacing Materials under Play Equipment (See also Pathway surfaces, Chapter 6, Section 10)

From all corners of the country, park and recreation personnel and school administrators have recognized the fact quoted by CPSC (1981) that approximately 70% of all playground injuries are due to falls from equipment to unsafe surfaces. Adequate surfacing under equipment is an essential safety requirement. The principal standard of adequacy is the "under 200g's impact attenuation" standard conducted according to ASTM F-355/86 (Standard Test Method for Shock-Absorbing Properties of Play Surface Systems and Materials, 1986). Consumers should require that manufacturers supply the results of such tests conducted by an independant laboratory before specifying a given safety surface. ASTM will publish further standards in 1988.

Surfacing is a critical aspect of manufactured equipment settings. A number of alternative treatments are available. Each has positive and negative points. Most surfaces are costly. All require regular maintenance, some more frequently than others.

Surfacing under equipment and other play areas such as ball fields and game courts should be selected according to the following criteria: durability, toxicity, allergenicity, slip resistance, all-weather use, climatic zone, durability, maintenance, aesthetics, accessibility and the impact absorbency rating for each location.

175 *Surfacing materials need careful consideration.*

A diverse use of surface materials provides more opportunities for play by the widest number of users.

11.2.1 Organic materials

Organic Materials, such as pine bark mini-nuggets, pine bark mulch, shredded hardwood bark and cocoa shell mulch, etc., share the following characteristics (CPSC, 1981):

a.   Cushioning properties depend on the air trapped within and between individual particles. In rainy weather, or during periods of high humidity, these materials absorb moisture and tend to compact, thereby losing the trapped air necessary for protective cushioning.

b.   With the passage of time, they decompose, are pulverized, become less cushioning and need to be replaced.

c.   When wet and exposed to freezing temperatures, they freeze and lose their cushioning protection.

d.   When wet, they provide an ideal condition for microorganism growth which might allow transmission of communicable diseases.

e.   Wind blows these materials, reducing the thickness necessary for adequate cushioning.

f.   They are gradually displaced by the playing action of children, thereby reducing the thickness of protective layers in vital fall areas.

g.   They harbor and conceal various insects (invariably harmless learning opportunities), animal excrement and other trash such as broken glass, nails, pencils and other sharp objects that can cause puncture and cutting wounds.

h.   With use, they may combine with dirt and other foreign materials resulting in a loss of cushioning properties.

i.   They may be deliberately removed (stolen) for use as mulch by residents.

j.   They are susceptable to burning.

k.   Generally, these materials require replacement and continuous maintenance such as leveling, grading and sifting to remove foreign matter in order to remain effective as cushioning materials.

l.   Wooden equipment installed in organic surfaced areas will tend to have more problems with post deterioration than with inorganic surfacing materials.

m.   A major benefit of wood-based fall cushions when compared to inorganic materials such as sand is that they are less abrasive when tracked into buildings.

n.   When used to surface informal play, circulation and social areas not under equipment, several of the above reservations that relate to reduction in impact absorbency no longer apply. Under these conditions, organic materials provide a viable, wear resistant alternative to grass. They also provide children with useful "props" to support dramatic play.

Common Organic Surfacing Materials:

a.   **Bark Nuggets.** The principal wood product used for surfacing under play equipment is bark nuggets from 1/2 inch to 1 inch screen size. Its fall absorbing characteristic is due primarily to its compressibility.

On the negative side, bark nuggets tend to retain water and decompose over time. Their softness allows them to abrade which accelerates this process. Thus, in time, the nuggets are reduced to a soil-like composition. Some children are allergic to bark dust. When dry, it blows in their eyes.

Bark nuggets can get thrown around. This makes the play setting look untidy, and is hazardous and uncomfortable for pedestrians and ball players on adjacent hard surfaces. Bark nuggets are difficult for wheelchairs to wheel through and may be inaccessible for those with balance problems.

The initial cost of bark and its maintenance requirements make it an expensive alternative. Sawdust is occasionally used as a less expensive substitute but it decomposes very rapidly and is not recommended.

b.   **Wood Chips.** Wood chips are in many ways preferable to bark nuggets as a surfacing material. Once matted down, wood chips provide a wheelchair accessible surface. Wood chips are readily available from Parks Departments or tree servicing companies, from "chippers" used in tree pruning operations. Chips come in different sizes. The smallest chips work best.

Suitability depends on the source. Coniferous chips are the best because the chips are not so splintery as hardwood, when first spread. Pine scent is an added attraction and the pine needles help to make a soft "mat". Softer hardwoods such as sycamore do almost as well.

When wood chips are first put down they are spikey and splintery, but these characteristics disappear with wear and weathering, and the chips soon "mat" into a comfortable play surface. They have good drainage, and provide an excellent habitat for insects. Children like to explore this microcosmic world for both living organisms and other "finds" like coins, bottle tops, and small plastic toys. Wood chips are much easier than bark nuggets or sand to police for broken glass, and do not attract cats and dogs. There are also manufactured wood chip products.

1)   Maintain a minimum of 12 inches of bark nuggets or wood chips in equipment areas, and a minimum of 4 inches in nonequipment areas.

2)   Use chips rather than bark nuggets except where the initial abrasiveness of chips will be a problem.

176 *Grass provides a soft, but not resilient, play surface.*

c.   **Grass/Turf** (Mason, 1982). Grass is the most common plant found in play environments throughout the world. It is a living thing, however, and can take only so much wear and tear before it dies.

Grass is used in one of three situations:

•   Sport playing surfaces.
•   Unstructured recreation areas.
•   Surfaces on mounds and slopes.

It is not suitable as a fall absorbing surface under equipment.

Turf normally contains a mixture of plants (not always grasses—clover is also common). There are two types of plants: tussock forming and creeping. Creeping plants have a far greater power to rejuvenate, and thus are always an advantage in heavily used turf. (See "Grass Seed Mixtures for Children's Play Areas." NPFA, 1986.)

Another important consideration is the width of leaf and stem. Plants with wide leaves and stems make a less smooth surface than the very fine leaved. However, wide leaved plants are more hard wearing than the fine leaved. The best playing surfaces are made from grass sown on sand fed from below.

1)   Different types of grasses have different abilities to withstand wear.

2)   Different grasses have different abilities to regrow after being damaged.

3)   Some grasses have a dormant period when they turn brown.

4)   Grass requires more work to maintain it in reasonable condition than do nonliving surfaces.

5)   Grass turns to mud in wet weather if an unsuitable variety of grass is used or equipment is not moved regularly.

6)   Grass is soft and cool to look at and is relatively soft (but still firm) to play on.

7)   Grass is difficult for wheelchairs to move through over a long distance (10—15 feet). It is not suitable for an accessible playing field.

11.2.2 Inorganic Materials

Inorganic materials can be loose or compact. Loose materials (e.g., sand, pea gravel, blue stone dust, blue sandstone, crushed stone, etc.) share the following characteristics (CPSC, 1981):

a.   They can be blown or thrown into children's eyes.

b.   They can be displaced by the playing action of children, thereby reducing the thickness of protective layers in vital fall areas.

c.   They can harbor and conceal various insects, animal excrement and other trash such as broken glass, nails, pencils and other sharp objects that can cause puncture and cutting wounds.

d.   With use, these materials may be combined with dirt and other foreign materials, resulting in a loss of cushioning properties.

e.   With increasing amounts of moisture, sand becomes cohesive and less cushioning. When thoroughly wet, sand reacts as a rigid material when impacted from any direction.

f.   When wet and exposed to freezing temperatures, these materials will freeze and lose their cushioning protection.

g.   Pea gravel is difficult to walk on and impossible to roll through.

h.   Generally, these materials require replacement and regular maintenance such as leveling, grading and sifting to remove foreign matter in order to remain attractive as cushioning materials.

Compact inorganic materials include rubber matting, synthetic turf on asphalt base, etc. Many share the following characteristics:

a.   They often must be used on almost level uniform surfaces, and are therefore difficult to lay.

b.   They may be subject to vandalism damage (defaced, ignited, cut, etc.).

Common Inorganic Surfacing Materials:

a.   **Sand and pea gravel.** These materials are most frequently chosen for fall cushioning under play equipment. Since they have no compressibility, their impact absorbing characteristics are due to their ability to deform to the shape of the falling child. They spread the area of impact while increasing its duration (a slow, large area impact is less injurious than a narrow quick impact).

177 *Sand with rounded particles 1/16—3/16 inch in diameter is a good fall surface.*

Sand is preferable and more popular than gravel as an impact absorbing surface, and has been used throughout North America and Europe for many years (Los Angeles, 1987). Particles must be round in shape and as uniform in size as possible. Particles 1/32 inch or less will be significantly affected by the surface tension of water and tend to bind together when wet.

Particles larger than 3/8 inch have sufficient mass to cause serious eye injury when thrown. Sand of the type required is produced by interaction with water and exists in river and ocean deposits. It is sometimes known as washed river bed sand, grain, or bird's eye sand.

The species of original stone affects the longevity of sand. Hard sand will last longer than sand composed of soft stone particles. Because of the weight of sand, the major cost is transportation.

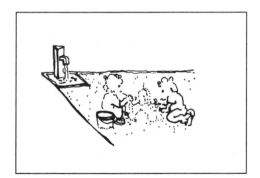

178 *Sand is the most responsive, malleable ground surface, but wheelchair access is problematic.*

1)   Maintain a minimum of 12 inches of sand.

2)   Select sand composed of hard round particles between 1/16 inch and 3/16 inch diameter.

3)   Institute a maintenance program appropriate to each play area.

If sand is used as a surface under play equipment, additional sand areas must be provided for sand play. Sand under and around equipment cannot serve both purposes. If additional sand areas are not provided, children will play in traffic areas, a potentially hazardous situation, and the products of their sand play will get stomped on, causing much frustration and unnecessary social conflict.

If sand is used as the primary fall absorbing surface, then it should be used in combination with manufactured resilient surfaces to provide access to the equipment.

b.   **Decomposed Granite.** This material provides a good all-weather surface for picnic areas, pathways and around trees. It should not be used under play equipment.

c.   **Rubber Surfaces/Synthetic Compact Materials.**

Rubber surfaces have been used on playgrounds for decades. The traditional form is a one-inch thick interlocking mat with a waffle pattern on the underside. CPSC tests showed that it performed satisfactorily for falls less than four feet in height. More recently, other rubber surfaces have come onto the market that meet CPSC tests up to heights of eleven feet.

Chopped tire, installed to a six inch depth, significantly out-performs other fall absorbing materials. Like sand and bark nuggets, it will spread outside its containment barrier. To prevent this, some suppliers add a flexible plastic binder. The material retains most of its fall attenuating characteristics but the surface tends to deteriorate with wear and is subject to vandalism. To counteract this, a skin of the binder material or artificial grass is added. Such composite materials are available up to three inches thick, affording protection up to a ten-foot fall.

These manufactured surfaces provide for wheelchair access and should be used on pathways which come within the fall zone of an equipment setting.

A major drawback of chopped tire and similar composite materials, with and without binders, is their flammability.

When purchasing these materials, there are a number of factors to take into consideration:

1)   Does a drop onto this surface from the height of the highest deck on your play structure result in a G-force rating of less than 200 G's?

2)   Does the surface allow for water drainage?

3)   Is it slip-resistant?

4)   What are the installation requirements?

5)   What are the maintenance requirements?

6)   Can it be easily cleaned?

7) Will it look attractive and complement the appearance of your playground equipment?

8) Is the surface durable and capable of withstanding extremes of temperature, frost, vandalism, etc?

9) Is it easily repaired?

10) What is the warranty and estimated life of the surfacing material?

d. **Concrete/Asphalt** (Mason, 1982).

These are very hard surfaces to fall on, and therefore cannot be used under equipment. They are necessary for activities such as ball play in situations where turf surfaces are impractical. They are very accessible to wheel chairs and are easy to maintain and to keep free of broken glass.

Asphalt must be laid to a fixed solid timber or concrete edge or it will crack and become broken around the edges.

e. **Artificial Grass.**

An expensive material, suitable for general play and games areas, artificial grass must be laid on a hard, smooth, flat surface. It can be damaged easily by fire. It should not be used under play equipment.

f. **Other Propietary Surfacings.**

New or improved manufactured surfacings are continually appearing on the market. They vary greatly in suitability for different play settings and climatic conditions.

11.3 Surfacing Standards.

Standards are currently being developed by the American Standards Testing Association (ASTM). However, there are none to date and consumers are limited to information provided by vendors and manufacturers. Manufacturers should back up surfacing products with tests conducted by independant laboratories showing that the surfacing meets the under 200g's criterion when tested according to ASTM F–355/86. The results should be made available to consumers.

11.4   Testing on the Site.

The ability to protect a child from a catastrophic injury from a fall is directly related to the distance of the fall and a suitable fall absorbing surfacing. The only way to truly know if the fall absorbing surface is within the 200 G force rating accepted by the CPSC is to test on site. Up until now this has been unrealistic due to cost.

Paul Hogan has developed a head form that can be dropped from any height onto a surface to determine the G force of a fall. It is called Max G SRT, Surface Resiliency Tester. The Max G will provide managers of children's playgrounds immediate feedback about fall absorbing surfaces and the necessary maintenance action which should be taken. For more information, contact Paul Hogan, Playground Clearinghouse, Inc., 36 Sycamore Lane, Phoenixville, PA 19460.

SUMMARY OF SURFACING MATERIALS FOR USE UNDER PLAY EQUIPMENT

MATERIAL	FALL ABSORBING CHARACTERISTICS	ADVANTAGES	ISSUES TO CONSIDER
I. ORGANIC LOOSE MATERIAL (pine bark, bark nuggets, shredded bark, cocoa shell mulch, etc.)	Air trapped within loose materials provides a cushioning effect. An adequate depth of material must be provided to have this effect.	Low initial cost. Ease of installation. Attractive. Less abrasive than sand. Good drainage. Does not attract cats and dogs.	Environmental conditions can reduce fall absorbancy. Susceptibility to burning. Ideal for microorganism growth when wet. Increased problems with wood post deterioration. Can get thrown around. Concealed animal excrement and sharp objects.
A. Bark Nuggets	As above.	Bark nuggets from 1/2—1 inch screen size are a principal wood product used for surfacing under play equipment.	Softness accelerates its decomposition process. Some children are allergic to bark dust. Initial cost and maintenance requirements make it an expensive alternative.
B. Wood Chips	As above. Chips come in different sizes; the smallest chips work best.	Preferable to bark nuggets: lower cost, ease of maintenance. Easier to police for broken glass. Readily available.	Suitability depends on the wood source (see page 113).

RECOMMENDED DEPTH	MAINTENANCE REQUIREMENTS	ACCESSIBILITY	PLAY VALUE	COST
10—12 inches (Depends on Equipment Height)	Requires replacement and continuous maintenance to maintain approprate depth and remove foreign matter.	See specific materials.	Provides useful "props" to support dramatic play. Children can manipulate the material itself. Some types of organic loose materials increase playground accessibility for individuals with disabilities.	See specific materials.
10—12 inches (Depends on Equipment Height)	As above.	Challenging: requires upper body strength of wheelchair users; ambulatory disabled may find walking difficult.	Provides useful "props" to support dramatic play. Children can manipulate the material itself. Provides some degree of playground accessibility for individuals with disabilities.	$12—25/ cubic yard
10—12 inches (Depends on Equipment Height)	As above.	Wheelchair accessible once matted down; challenging for ambulatory disabled who may experience balance prob-lems on uneven surfaces.	Provides useful "props" to support dramatic play. Children can manipulate the material itself. Provides some degree of playground accessibility for individuals with disabilities.	$80—95/ 10 cubic yards

SUMMARY OF SURFACING MATERIALS FOR USE UNDER PLAY EQUIPMENT

MATERIAL	FALL ABSORBING CHARACTERISTICS	ADVANTAGES	ISSUES TO CONSIDER
II. INORGANIC LOOSE MATERIAL (sand, gravel, stone dust, crushed stone, shells, rubber buffings, chopped tire, etc.)	Conforms to the shape of the falling child, spreading the area of impact while increasing its duration. The rubber products also trap air to provide cushioning.	Initial cost. Ease of installation. Does not pulverize. Not ideal for microbial growth. Generally nonflammable (except for rubber products).	Environmental conditions can reduce fall absorbancy (see page 115). Can be swallowed, blown or thrown. Spreads outside the containment area. Conceals animal excrement and sharp objects.
A. Sand	As above. Particles should be round and as uniform in size as possible. Select sand composed of hard round particles between 1/16 inch and 3/16 inch diameter.	Low cost (major cost is transportation). Preferable and more popular than pea gravel.	Small particles bind together when wet. Particles larger than 3/8 inch can cause serious eye injury when thrown. Species of original stone affects longevity. If used under play equipment, additional sand areas must be provided for play.
B. Chopped Tire	A shock absorbent material which also traps air between the particles to provide a cushioning effect.	Six inches has significant impact absorbing ability. The material retains most of its fall attenuating characteristics. Spreads outside its containment area.	Surface deteriorates with wear. Subject to vandalism. Is flammable.
III. SYNTHETIC COMPACT MATERIALS (rubber mats, synthetic turf on foam mats, rubber sheeting on foam mats, poured in place urethanes and rubber compositions)	Consists of a shock absorbing material such as rubber.	Low maintenance. Colors. Clean. Consistent shock absorbency. No displacement. Generally low life cycle costs. Good footing. Accessible. Harbors few foreign objects.	Initial cost, replacement after useful life. Vandalism. Seams, loss of color, water drainage, slip resistant surfacing. 200 G-force rating. Ease of maintenance. Attractive and complementary to the appearance of the playground. Warranty and estimated life of the material.

RECOMMENDED DEPTH	MAINTENANCE REQUIREMENTS	ACCESSIBILITY	PLAY VALUE	COST
10—12 inches. (Depends on Equipment Height)	Requires replacement and continuous maintenance to maintain approprate depth and remove foreign matter.	See specific materials.	Manipulative play value. Generally, they do not increase access to play areas for disabled, except chopped tire.	See specific materials.
Depends on equipment height; 10–12 inches minimume; 18-36 inches for sand play area.	As above.	Inaccessible to wheelchairs or ambulatory disabled; should not be eliminated from play areas because of its play value.	High value for manipulative play, especially when access to water (faucet or water element) is also provided.	$15-20/ton.
4–8 inches. (Depends on equipment Height)	As above.	Wheelchair accessible; inaccessible for ambulatory disabled who may experience balance problems when walking on this surface.	Provides for increased play area access for individuals with disabilities. Chopped tire may have some manipulative play value.	$2.50–3.00/ sq. foot.
Ranges from 1–6 inches thick; desired thickness depends on the equipment height and product resiliency.	Generally minimal.	Accessible.	Provides increased access for individuals with disabilities.	$5-$13/sq. foot depending on thickness and product resiliency.

12. LANDFORMS/TOPOGRAPHY

A variety of landforms and vertical elements should be provided to allow for a variety of experience in three-dimensional space, varied circulation within and between spaces and varied interaction of the body in space (rolling, crawling, sliding, balancing, jumping). They can also provide design opportunities for integrating fixed equipment into the landscape (NPFA, 1978a). Landform is often underutilized as a play opportunity in site design.

Planning Criteria

Play Value. Landforms and topography provide for large muscle activities, spatial experience and spaces for "refuge". Stimulation of orientation skills, hide-and-go-seek games, viewing, rolling, climbing, sliding, opportunities for fantasy play and imagination can be supported by landforms.

Programming. Good potential for places to support building activity, points of suspension and cantilevers.

Play Leadership. Landforms have good potential for supporting hiding/chasing and trailing games and present opportunities for building sites.

Safety. Steep slopes and sudden drop-offs must be avoided. Guardrails may be needed on paths and ramps.

Risk Management. Plan for regular maintenance. Changes in level, steps and ramps must be highly visible with no hidden surprises.

Accessibility. Ramps should be provided. "Summit" points need to accommodate wheelchairs and and provide support for other disabling conditions.

Integration. There is good potential for interaction when children help each other negotiate the challenge of varied topography.

Management/Maintenance. Height, slope, ground cover and protective barrier criteria need to be specified to avoid erosion on earthformed mounds.

179 *Landforms can be used to define gathering places.*

180 *Mounds support hide-and-go-seek and chasing games.*

181 *Grassy hills are excellent for rolling games.*

12.1 Range of Design Choices

Slopes, varied topography and landforms satisfy many play needs. They should be retained when they exist on a new site. Earth moving and related site improvements (e.g., drainage) can be an expensive aspect of site development. Opportunities will therefore vary depending on existing site conditions and budget.

The design approach can range from the importation of material to create a "mound" on a flat site, to complete "regrading" of the site to create a continuously varied ground surface with topographic features.

12.2 Topographic Features

Topographic features can be designed into the topographic form to add interest and a variety of play opportunities, as illustrated below.

a. **The Hill and Hill Circle** (Bunin, et al., 1980; Gordon, 1972)

A grassy hill, surrounding a tree, is graded gently for crawlers as well as for climbers to ascend to a plateaued summit, roll down on the grass or slide down on a protected enclosed fiberglass slide. The hill circle, surrounding the base of the tree, provides a quiet nook for children. It has a circular bench to sit on in a shaded area for individual play, for group interaction and socializing.

12.3 Minimum Provision (Seattle, 1986)

a. Provide a grassy hill, natural or constructed, as part of each play area (NPFA, 1986).

b. Provide a minimum of one or two earth berms, 4 feet to 5 feet high (200 to 400 sq. ft.) with varying slopes of 1:3, 1:4 and 1:5 for each play area.

c. Typical earth form slopes shall not exceed:

- 3:1 for mowable grass areas;
- 2:1 for cut or fill slopes with erosion control matting and special non-mowable ground covers.

d. During the construction of a play area, remove all rocks and debris larger than an adult fist to a depth of 12 inches.

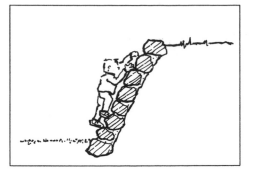

182   Rock face climbing wall stimulates large muscle coordination and sense of achievement.

183   The bridge stimulates social interaction, spatial orientation and sense of discovery.

184   Jumping "cliffs" can be provided, with proper attention to ground surface treatment for safety.

12.4   Drainage of Play Areas (Seattle, 1986)

All open areas should slope to drain, with the exception of loose surface areas under children's play equipment. Positive drainage can be reinforced by:

a.   Percolation layer.

b.   Tightline to storm system.

c.   Perforated line.

12.5   Surface Slopes (Seattle, 1986)

a.   Slope resilient surfacing 0—2%, provided with underdrainage.

b.   Provide a 2% minimum slope and cross-slope for asphalt surfaces.

c.   Provide a 1% minimum slope for concrete surfaces.

d.   Provide a 2% minimum slope for open lawn areas.

e.   Avoid crossing play areas with drainage swales which might cause children to fall.

12.6   Drainage Collection Systems (Seattle, 1986)

Subsurface drainage is required for all surfacing beneath children's play equipment.

A play area drainage system has to be considered in conjunction with the entire park drainage system in order to determine specific methods. A combination of surface and subsurface drainage must be considered for all sizes.

185 *Stepping stones and logs stimulate large muscle coordination and balancing skills.*

186 *To attain a sense of challenge and achievement, a height of 4'—5' for toddlers and 9'—13' for older kids is recommended.*

187 *A slide can be incorporated into a slope so the child cannot fall. The slide becomes more accessible. Sand at the bottom cushions the landing.*

188 *Hill and hill circle.*

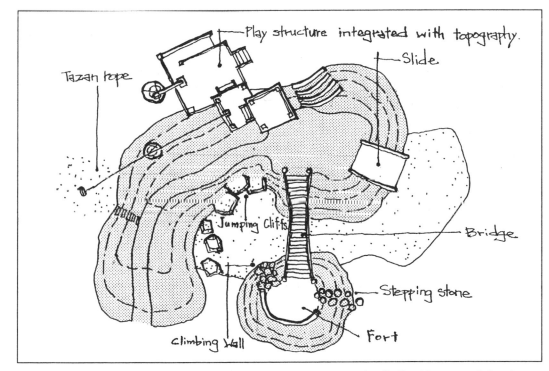

189 *Topographic form used as a design element to connect and unify fixed features of the site.*

13. TREES/VEGETATION

Trees and vegetation should be established to satisfy the need for shade, wildlife habitat, sensory variety, loose parts, softly edged spaces, space separation, hideaways and a friendly atmosphere.

Planning Criteria

Play Value. Vegetation is an intrinsically interesting setting that stimulates exploratory and discovery behavior, fantasy and imagination. It provides subtle visual complexity and is ideal for hide-and-seek games. Tree-climbing is a universally favorite activity. Trees add a highly significant positive ambience to play settings through their variable mix of sun/shade, color, texture, fragrance and softness of enclosure. Vegetation offers enormous play potential. There is no substitute for vegetation as a major source of play props: leaves, flowers, fruit, nuts, seeds and sticks.

Programming. Vegetation can be used to support many different program activities requiring spatial diversity and a stimulating atmosphere. Trees are good for building in, for hanging things on, for swinging on. Vegetation supplies a variety of play resources that children can harvest for themselves (Allison, 1975; Moore, 1986b; Moore & Wong, in press; Schools Council, 1974).

Play Leadership. Play leaders need to be knowledgeable about play opportunities that can be supported by vegetation and trees.

Safety. Choose appropriate tree species and place them so that problems of dropping limbs and "kitten-up-a-tree" (child climbs up, can't come back down and gets stuck) are avoided. Do not place trees so near structures that children can climb from one to the other, unless the structure is deliberately designed around the tree.

Risk Management. Appropriate species and locations should be chosen, avoiding toxic and allergy-related species. Regular inspections of health are required. Annual pruning regime needs to be established.

Accessibility. For children with physical disabilities, the experience of being in trees needs to be replicated by choosing appropriate low branching and weeping types, by not pruning off low growing vegetation, and by integrating vegetation into accessible settings. A conflict can occur with low hanging branches over pathways. Trees that a wheelchair can roll into or under should be placed away from pathways. Otherwise, they may present hazards for the visually impaired.

Integration. Trees provide opportunities for child-to-child play and for shared experience, especially with regard to play props. Vegetation is one of the single-most important elements for integration because it can be enjoyed and shared equally by all.

Management/Maintenance. A program of regular maintenance is needed. Public policy needs to recognize the value of vegetation and trees as a community and childhood resource. Local listings should be developed that identify the most appropriate regional species for different purposes such as play, wildlife habitat and visual enhancement. Species that support all three purposes clearly have high priority for installation. Listings of unsuitable toxic species should also be highlighted.

190   Plants and children grow together.

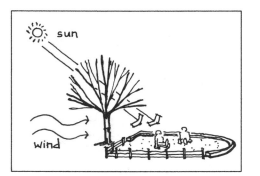

191   Trees are an excellent modifier of microclimate.

192   Vegetation marks the passing of the seasons.

13.1   How Trees and Vegetation Improve Play Settings

Trees and vegetation have no substitute as play setting elements. Children are especially attracted by a mix of natural and people-made elements (Mason, 1982). Emphasis should be on the integration of plantings into play settings, rather than creating segregated "nature areas."

a.   **Variety of Play Opportunities.** Vegetation settings greatly extend the range of play activity: collecting plant parts, climbing and playing in trees, hide-and-seek games and exploration.

b.   **Climatic Modification.** Vegetation is an effective modifier of climate because it is so varied and therefore provides a greater range of climatic choice than people-made structures. Trees are the best way to provide shade. Spreading, deciduous species that shed their leaves to let winter sunlight through are especially good (but have maintenance implications).

c.   **Seasonal Variation.** Vegetation marks the passing of the seasons and introduces children to a sense of time and natural processes.

d.   **Improved Surface Runoff and Erosion Control.** Broad-leaved deciduous trees can reduce the direct impact of heavy rain and extend the runoff period. Surface root systems bind the soil and help resist erosion.

e.   **Variety of Enclosure.** Size, shape and enclosure of play settings are greatly enhanced by being wholly or partly achieved with vegetation. A more varied spatial and textural setting is achieved with a complexity and subtlety beyond that possible through people-made elements alone.

Vegetated enclosures give a "boundary-depth" with more character than a rectilinear fence. Vegetated space divisions produce a great variety of shapes and forms, thereby increasing territorial ambiguity and extending the possible range of games and social interaction.

f.   **Sensory Variety.** Quality of the movement experience is greatly improved by vegetation (in conjunction with topography). Planting can be used along paths to create a sequence of texture, smell, light, shade and color. "Specimen" plants are important orienting elements.

193 *Planting adds soft, ambiguous enclosures and "boundary" depth to play areas.*

194 *Raised planting improves the quality of movement experience, especially for children in wheelchairs.*

Plants can teach about texture, fragrance and color (Seattle, 1986):

1) Vary texture of leaves: evergreen with deciduous; shiny with rough; serrated with smooth edges; thin with thick.

2) Vary form, size and shape of plants used near children's areas.

3) Select plants for seasonal changes: evergreen vs. deciduous; color through the seasons; early leaves, late flowers; flowers and fruit.

4) Consider opportunities for color in trees, ground covers, vines, annuals and perennials.

5) Select plants for fragrance.

6) Select plants for craft and culinary potential.

7) Select for auditory stimulation. Some plants, especially in the fall, produce interesting sounds when the wind blows through their dry leaves. Plants like bamboo and pine trees produce sounds year round.

g. **Indoor—Outdoor Transitions** can be softened with vegetation—especially for people whose eyes adjust slowly to changing light levels and glare.

h. **Manipulative Play Material (Play Props)** (Moore, 1986b). Plants are a valuable source of play material. Small horizontal surfaces (tables, benches, ledges, logs, rocks) should be provided to support this activity.

195 *Specimen trees can be landmarks for orientation.*

196 *Vegetation provides a great diversity of texture in play settings.*

197 *The fragrance of flowers is especially important to blind children.*

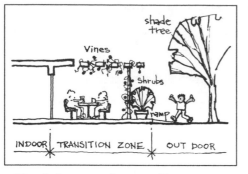

198 *Indoor—outdoor transitions.*

199 *Vegetation is a manipulative play material.*

Leave woods and natural areas in a rough state; avoid the tendency to "clean up," except for thorny material and dead branches and twigs which are at eye or neck height (Seattle, 1986).

i. **Craft and Culinary Activities.** A range of annuals and perennials can support specific activities such as cooking, dying and doll making (PLAE, 1981—87).

j. **Comfortable Social Setting.** Many children find natural environments more comfortable for social activity. Objects having a clear identity, such as trees, large rocks and ponds function as landmarks and produce a strong visual impact on the user. Mature shrubs make excellent hideouts and refuges (Kirby, 1987).

k. **Wildlife Habitat.** Vegetation provides, through establishment of plant communities, a range of habitat conditions for wildlife that cannot be matched by people-made settings.

It is important for children to observe wildlife (Leedy, 1982; Schicker, 1986). Select plants with fruits, cones, and seeds to attract birds, squirrels and other wildlife (Seattle, 1986).

Bird houses can be built so that children in wheelchairs can get a closer look.

l. **Open-endedness.** Vegetation of all types provides props and settings for imaginative play. Trees and large shrubs provide flexible open-ended situations that children can build onto.

200 *Shrubs provide excellent hideaway places.*

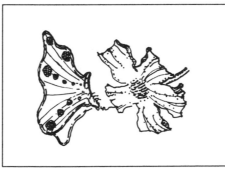

201 *Vegetation is a habitat for wildlife.*

202 *Trees become "woods" and "forests" to children.*

203   *Plants to play around.*

204   *Trees to play under.*

205   *Impact of vegetation on users.*

m.   **Play Area Identification.** Visually distinctive plantings or particular "specimen" plants can provide identity to a play area even though no manufactured equipment is present. Such identity plantings can signal "permission" to play.

n.   **Community Playground Aesthetic Value** (Los Angeles, 1987).

The overall design must be pleasing and attractive to the whole community. People of all ages respond to flowering shrubs, deciduous trees, rockeries, flower pots, herb gardens, etc.

13.2   Child—Plant Interaction

Opportunities should be provided for children to interact with plants using all their senses. These children and plant places extend in scale from a few blades of grass poking through a crack in the asphalt, to a large natural resource area. Whether small or large, simple or complex, the idea in supporting children—plant interaction is to maximize user impact while minimizing environmental impact.

13.2.1 Factors That Affect User Impact

The impact of plants on the users of a space is influenced by:

a.   **Age and Sex of Users.** Younger children appear to appreciate plants more readily than older children. Girls seem more appreciative than boys (Moore, 1986a).

b.   **Environmental Values of Users.** The degree to which children appreciate and understand plants depends on their cultural situation, family circumstances and their degree of participation in environmental education activities.

Ensure that local schools are involved in play area development and that environmental education is included in the curriculum.

c.   **Season and Climate.** Inclement weather reduces the amount of contact between children and plants. Regions with heavy winters have this disadvantage. Seasonal change, on the other hand, is an important dimension in the plant world, which children need to experience.

d.   **Type of Plant.** Some plants are more attractive to children than others because of their sensory qualities and play potential. Bamboo, for instance, is universally liked. All manner of flowering plants are attractive.

Injurious and toxic species must be avoided.

206 *Vegetation and trees can be incorporated into programmed activities.*

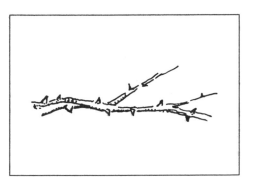

207 *Injurious and toxic species must be avoided.*

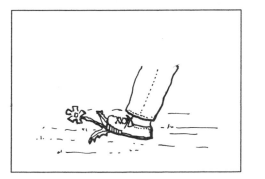

208 *Environmental impact of users on vegetation should be minimized.*

e.   **Density/Diversity of Plants.** Volume and variety of plants are important factors. An increase in either will increase the complexity and number of possible interactions.

f.   **Habitat Conditions.** Effective user impact will be increased if protective structures (fences, etc.) are designed to also provide maximum contact.

13.2.2 Factors That Affect Environmental Impact

The impact of children on designed vegetated settings is conditioned by several factors, including:

a.   **Age and Sex of Users.** Older kids, especially boys, are more aggressive.

b.   **Environmental Values of Users.** Attitudes towards vegetation reflect the cultural values of the community.

c.   **Season and Climate.** Inclement weather reduces the amount of human activity.

d.   **Maturity of Plants.** Larger, older plants are able to withstand impact better than smaller, younger plants.

e.   **Type of Plant.** Plants vary tremendously in their attractiveness to children, the amount of abuse they can withstand and their recovery time. Some plants, such as willow, have an attractive play potential and are naturally hardy (Moore, 1986b).

f.   **Habitat Conditions.** Plants are adapted to specific conditions. Some are more broadly adapted than others. Habitats can be more or less suitable for a given plant, depending on soil conditions, drainage, irrigation, exposure and associations with other plants.

g.   **Habitat Perception.** New, unconventional or bizarre planting will attract undesirable attention. A freshly planted tree, standing on its own, surrounded by asphalt, looks out of place. Kids will perceive it that way and probably rip it out. A group of trees, growing together with associated plants, looks very different and more natural, and will stimulate different behavior.

h.   **Habitat Protection.** The degree to which plants are physically protected by permanent barriers from direct impact is crucial. Staking, tying up and other management efforts to help the plants assume their natural position are important (see Hierarchy of Protection, below).

209 *A rock surrounded by a small amount of dirt provides a minimal niche for plant growth.*

210 *Raised planters and staking provide a hierarchy of protection for plants, children's play and wheelchair access.*

211 *Edges of buildings provide naturally protective interfaces for plantings.*

Each plant must be surrounded by several "lines of protection." For example, a small shrub may be tied to a stake; it may also grow in a planter and thereby be protected from traffic flow; the planter itself may be sheltered by being placed against a building or in a fenced-off area. There are many ways of implementing this principle.

i. **Density/Diversity of Plants.** The ability to withstand impact is a function of both density and diversity.

j. **Differentiation.** Any object projecting from, resting on, or close to the ground will create a small, protected niche within which plants and associated life forms are able to flourish.

13.3 Design of Child—Plant Interactions

a. **Protective Interface.** A design objective of any open space occupied by both children and plants is to achieve high user impact with low environmental impact.

Protective elements should divert children's kinetic energy sufficiently to avoid irreversible plant damage. They therefore need to:

1) Allow children to move in three-dimensional space;

2) Allow plants to grow in three-dimensional space;

3) Allow children to have intimate contact with plants (high user-impact);

4) Protect plants from excessive damage (low environmental impact).

Protective elements should be designed as multipurpose supporters of both plants and play by combining the principles of **separation** and **interpenetration:**

1) **Separation.** Separation of people zones from plant zones, vertically and/or horizontally is the main way of reducing environmental impact.

2) **Interpenetration.** Interpenetration of people and plant zones is the main way of increasing user impact. This can be done more easily on the horizontal plane, although vertical interpenetration is also possible (e.g., a climbing structure designed around a tree).

c. **Climbable trees.** Climbable trees are an example of vertical interpenetration. Platforms can be constructed to assist this function, more safely, with less environmental impact.

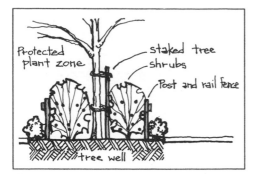

212 *Simple post-and-rail fences provide effective separation between people and plants.*

213 *Beanpole teepee (carpeted with sand), a simple form of child-plant interaction.*

214 *Tree climbing gives children a sense of achievement.*

13.4   Natives and Exotics

A mix of both native or naturalized and exotic plants should be used in play settings. Native plants provide hardy background planting. They are usually more resilient. Exotics add variety and interest.

13.5   Maintenance (Seattle, 1986).

It is important that plantings are maintained to avoid potentially hazardous branches and twigs at children's eye levels.

a.   For protection of both child and plant:

1)   Plant 2 inches minimum caliper trees or larger.

2)   Use heavy tree guards or stakes around plants until established.

3)   Avoid small lawn areas where they will provide access to roof tops.

4)   Avoid plants known to be poisonous in or near children's play areas.

b.   For barrier plants:

1)   Discourage foot traffic with denser branching or a thornless shrub substructure.

2)   Use soft branching plant material where children may fall into it or run through.

3)   Use low maintenance plant material.

4)   Use plants tolerant to foot traffic.

5)   Use multitrunked and multibranching plants.

6)   Use quick growing and "self perpetuating" plants which heal after breaking.

7)   Use hedge-like, thicket plants for small defensible areas.

215 Low-slung, ramped platforms can provide an accessible treehouse setting.

c.   **Because all trees can be climbed:**

1)   Select trees which develop strong trunks and horizontal branches, and are fast growing, thornless and low maintenance for children's areas.

2)   Provide resilient surfacing under trees and trim or prune existing trees for safety.

3)   Use trees and shrubs with fruit, cones or pods to provide props, but do so judiciously. Do not use such species in locations where "shedding" could be hazardous (e.g., on main pathways) or a severe maintenance issue.

14. GARDEN SETTINGS

Gardens are one of the best ways of enabling children to interact with nature, to learn about the ecological cycle and to cooperate with peers.

Planning Criteria

Play Value. Gardens provide for social interaction, fine motor skills development and sensory stimulation.

Programming Potential. There is excellent potential, with spin-offs into nutrition, food chain, nonfood uses of plants, economics of food, cross-cultural awareness and third world food problems (Moore & Wong, in press).

Play Leadership. Leaders need training in how to use gardens.

Safety. Tools need to be locked up. Gardens need to be enclosed.

Risk Management. There must be supervision, signs, checkout for tools, and a fenced enclosure.

Accessibility. Provide raised beds, U-shaped to allow easy reach to center, with easy access to water (for example, levers) and recoilable hoses. Compost boxes must be low to the ground to allow for wheelchair access. "Rolling" bins should be available for fertilizer.

Integration. Gardening is a good group activity, good for child-to-child assistance.

Management/Maintenance. Policy is needed to support the importance of gardening; extra training for staff and maintenance people should be provided.

Further Information

For further information on children's gardens:

a. Refer to *A Child's Garden* (1978), published by Ortho, 575 Market Street, San Francisco, CA 94105.

b. Contact the National Federation of City Farms, publishers of *City Farmer*, The Old Vicarage, 66 Fraser Street, Windmill Hill, Bedminster, Bristol BS3 4LY, England. Tel. 0272.660663.

216 Gardening stimulates cooperative work between children.

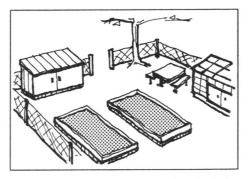

217 A basic enclosed garden includes raised beds, compost boxes, storage, etc.

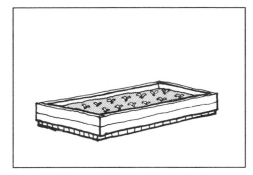

218 Raised beds provide order and a practical working arrangement.

219 Children's gardens must be enclosed.

220 Height and width of planting beds should allow wheelchair access.

221 Low-rise beds can be accessible to children out of wheelchairs.

222 Straw makes a comfortable, tidy ground cover in gardening areas.

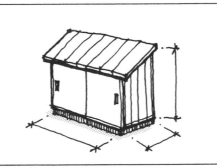

223 Lockable, secure storage is essential in a garden setting.

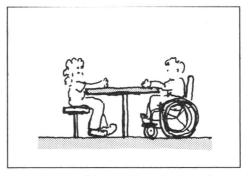

224 Accessible tables are essential for working and social interaction.

225   *Gardens provide a good vehicle for special events.*

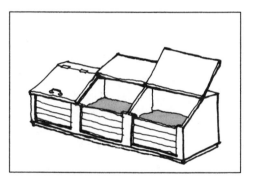

226   *Tri-compartment compost box with lids and removable boards provides the most practical means of composting. Compartments must be low to the ground to allow for wheelchair access.*

15. ANIMAL SETTINGS

Animals stimulate a caring and responsible attitude towards other living things. They provide therapeutic effects and offer opportunities for learning about biology.

Planning Criteria

Play Value. Animals can have a particularly powerful therapeutic effect on children. A source of wonder and fascination, they are living things that children can interact with, talk to and invest in emotionally.

Animals provide companionship in nonthreatening ways and almost always come back for more contact. This can be critical for a child with limited self-esteem who has little contact with other living things (Schneekloth, 1985).

Caring for animals can produce a sense of responsibility and pride in children. Having animals around provides an opportunity to learn to care for other living things. But it is important that these lessons be learned under the guidance and direction of caring adults (Schneekloth, 1985).

The strong motivation to care for animals makes them a powerful socializing medium for children. Documented childhood memories of animal care are very strong (Moore, 1986c). Animal care stimulates a sense of personal competence, self-esteem and autonomy (*Children's Environments Quarterly*, Vol. 1, No. 3, 1984).

Programming. Animals may relate to many program themes and can be a theme in themselves. They provide an excellent tie to children's literature (Moore & Wong, in press) and a connection to conservation education.

Play Leadership. Leaders need good knowledge of animals appropriate for using in play programs (HAPA, 1978; PLAE, 1981—87).

Safety. There are risks of bites, scratches, disease and insect pests.

Risk Management. Animals need proper housing and care. Parents and children must be made aware of animal needs and informed of the risks of interaction.

Accessibility. Some species have substantial potential for close contact and interaction with children, e.g., rabbits, hamsters, guinea pigs, gerbils and tortoises. Fish in their natural habitat and in aquaria have good potential, too. Ponies have a powerful potential for children with disabilities.

Integration. Excellent potential for shared experience between children of different ages and abilities and between adults and children.

Management/Maintenance. Policies are needed that protect both animals and users, including a rotation plan for larger animals. Different animals need housing in different ways. Requirements for adequate care vary. Sheep and goats are a potential agent of maintenance by being allowed to graze grass areas.

In one adventure playground in England, a young mentally retarded man became the animal caretaker which was a great source of pride for him. He eliminated the need for teachers to be always present while still allowing the children the chance to interact with living things.

227 Caring for animals instills responsibility . . .

228 . . . and promotes respect for other living things.

229 Bird song provides a positive acoustic ambience.

15.1 Appropriate Types of Animals

a. **Nonharmful insects and insect-like organisms** should be considered an important aspect of the play setting. The vast majority of insects are beneficial to the human race, do not bite, do not eat valuable materials or spread disease. They are an inevitable part of any vegetated setting. Caterpillars, butterflies, moths, ladybugs, beetles, pillbugs, spiders, millipedes and snails are some that are particularly attractive to children (Moore & Wong, in press).

b. **Birdlife.** There are specific habitat requirements: high places for nesting, sources of nesting materials and food producing plants. It is difficult for children to make close contact with birds (except if caged); nonetheless, birds add a positive ambience to play settings (movement, color, song). Birds in large, naturalistic caged settings are a possibility.

c. **Small animals, amphibians and reptiles.** Typical species include salamanders, squirrels, toads, mice, moles, snakes, lizards, etc., that are adapted to specific habitat conditions. Gerbils are a popular caged animal. Tortoises are fascinating, and easy to care for.

d. **Fish, frogs and pond life.** These are very attractive to children and have minimum habitat requirements (see Chapter 16, Water Settings).

e. **Domesticated and farmyard animals.** Rabbits, guinea pigs and hamsters are the most popular and easiest to care for. Several others are appropriate (chickens, goats, sheep, pigs, ponies and donkeys) and have become a traditional aspect of the playground scene in some countries (Broadway, 1979; *Childhood City Newsletter*, 1981).

15.2 Habitat Requirements for Attracting Wildlife to Play Settings

Two habitat requirements are essential: shelter and sustenance (food and drink). In many cases, vegetation fulfills both requirements (Schools Council, 1974). The presence of vegetation will support a dramatic increase of the population level and diversity of organisms, particularly insects—herbivorous ones first, then their carnivorous predators (Moore & Wong, in press).

Pioneer vegetation provides basic habitats for populations of small organisms (insects, arachnids, millipedes, sow bugs, etc.) that in turn provide a food source for larger animals (amphibians and birds) that walk, crawl or fly to the site from surrounding areas. In order to encourage this colonization process and the building up of a biotic pyramid, a

230 Aquatic habitats support many animals that fascinate children.

231 Rabbits and other domesticated animals are particularly appropriate for integrated play settings.

232 All animals are adapted to particular habitat conditions; some have more specific requirements than others.

census of wildlife living around the site, in neighbors' gardens and on vacant lots is useful. Staff from the local university, high school or parks department can help give advice, carry out the census and/or work directly with the children.

Three complementary strategies are possible in encouraging wildlife to a play setting:

a.   Create basic habitat conditions and see what happens;

b.   Once a census has been made of what's around, create habitats attractive to specific organisms;

c.   Introduce organisms directly and see what happens.

Specific ideas for making the site more attractive to wildlife include (Moore & Wong, in press):

1)   **Diversity of vegetation**—the primary habitat. Include volunteer wild plants, ground covers, wall covers, shrubs, trees, etc. Pay attention to specific food producing plants.

2)   **Dark undersides** and cavities are necessary for all kinds of "crawlers" and insects. Place logs, rocks and other heavy objects on the ground, with cavities beneath.

3)   **Chip pile.** An excellent habitat for "burrowers." A load of chippings from the parks department or city street tree crew dumped in a quiet corner of the playground with reasonable drainage will support a rich community of organisms. Children will spend hours hunting through the surface of the pile to see what they can discover.

4)   **Compost Heap.** Set aside a corner where prunings and weeds can be piled to decompose. Within a short time it will become a hive of activity and a resource for anyone who wants to lift off the top layer and take a look. Eventually, compost will be useful for mulching garden areas.

5)   **Wood Pile.** Wood piles provide a great habitat for insects and other organisms. Logs must be tied together so that they don't get scattered around.

233 *Undersides of rocks and logs provide ideal wildlife niches.*

234 *Large, decomposing logs provide an excellent habitat for small organisms.*

6) **Large Logs.** Large, heavy, decomposing logs provide useful self-contained ecosystems. Full or partial shade is important to keep logs moist.

7) **Water Places.** Ponds provide self-contained ecosystems (see Chapter 16, Water Settings). Wildlife can be encouraged by carefully designing the bottom and edge conditions and by creating landings, islands and marshes.

Birdbaths are also worth considering.

15.3 Birdscaping

Local species of birds can be attracted by creating environmental conditions which support avian life. The most important are food, cover and nesting sites.

Basic bird needs are not a complicated enterprise. Remember that a diversity of vegetation ranging from large tree canopies and small trees to a shrubby understory jungle punctuated by weedy, seedy wild annuals and perennials can create a bird oasis even if it is relatively close to busy city traffic and heavy child impact.

15.4 Guidebooks

The School Outdoor Resource Area. Schools Council (1974), London: Longman.

16. WATER SETTINGS

Water features and aquatic environments are highly valued by children (Moore, 1986a), they support a variety of terrestrial and aquatic wildlife and add a substantial aesthetic dimension to any recreation setting.

Planning Criteria

Play Value. The play value of water is tremendous because of its multisensory character: sounds, textures, changes of state and feelings of wetness. Water is a primal element and holds endless fascination for young children. It excites and relaxes. Children seldom miss opportunities for water play be they in the bathtub, in puddles, in swimming pools, especially after rain (Schneekloth, 1985). Water is often combined with sand and other play props.

Programming. Aquatic settings support a vast range of play and learning opportunities: exploring, fishing and wildlife activities, dam building and engineering works, "panning for gold," flotation and boat building (Moore & Wong, in press).

Play Leadership. Leaders need knowledge of how to use water as a program resource. Sensitivity to parental reactions to children getting wet is important.

Safety. Setting standards for water features is difficult. It is said that children can drown in 1 inch of water, but facts about actual water related mishaps are hard to find. Sharp drop-offs must be avoided. Careful edge treatment is essential. Edges must be physically defined. Bottoms must be gently shelved. Maximum water depth must not exceed 14 inches. Bottom covering must be slip-proof. Water must circulate or recirculate and must be sufficiently oxygenated to maintain adequate water quality.

Risk Management. Regular water quality tests are needed. Watch for empty bottles/broken glass. Stress parental awareness of risk management and procedures to reduce parental anxiety.

Accessibility. Edge treatments are critical to accommodate vision-impaired users. Wheelchair transfer places are needed to enable children with mobility impairments to get close to the water or to make contact with it: lean-over spots, decks, stacksacks full of sand, etc. Develop inflatables to allow children to float on water.

Integration. Water provides good potential for shared activity and interaction.

Management/Maintenance. Policies are needed to address the use and value of water to children, about maintenance of aquatic features and the different options available.

235 *Still water feels calm, reflects the sky and surrounding elements, and is contemplative.*

236 *Running water feels animated, and stimulates interaction and experimentation from children.*

16.1   Water on Handicapped Adventure Playgrounds (HAPA, 1978, slightly edited)

All HAPA playgrounds have artificial streams, some with waterfalls, running beneath wooden bridges into shallow ponds, not more than 14 inches deep. The water is supplied with a pump system causing it to circulate continuously once the pond is full enough. The movement of the water helps to keep the pond and stream clean and clear. Good filter systems keep the drains free from leaves, mud and sand. Emptying and sweeping out the bed of the stream and pond gives as much pleasure to the children as playing in the water when they are full. A bridge is fun as a place to cross over or as a place from which to simply sit and watch. It is also interesting to paddle through underneath, or to sail under on a raft or boat. A bridge should be built high enough over the water for these purposes, but it must also be accessible for everyone.

16.2   Purposes of Water in Play Settings

Water settings range in scale from a dew covered leaf, to a fully developed pond system, to an elaborate fountain structure. They embody three related functions:

a.   Life support oriented towards program purposes, wildlife habitats and aesthetic appreciation.

b.   Play support emphasizing physical contact with water as a play material (sand, water and plant part combinations are particularly powerful).

c.   Cooling-off for hot weather (possibilities range from hoses to spray pools).

16.3   Physical Properties of Water Relevant to Design

a.   Water is essential to all biological life.

b.   Water is an incredibly attractive play material, which is a child's way of experiencing all life's dependency on water.

c.   Water can be combined with earth or sand in a spectrum of aquatic conditions from clear water, to mud, to damp earth, to intermittently wet sand.

d.   Water flows downhill on the line of least resistance until it reaches the lowest level.

e.   Water can be sprayed upward—vertically or at an angle—under normal faucet pressure.

f.   Water is subject to change in state from liquid to solid to gas.

237   Water cascade.

238   Hose-filled ponds and streams are a simple means of providing temporary water-play features.

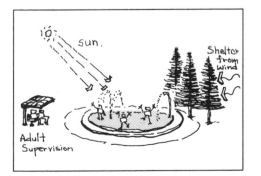

239   Basic water-play and cooling-off settings need sun, shelter from the wind and adult supervision.

g.   In order to evaporate, water takes its latent heat from its surroundings.

h.   Some materials float, some sink.

16.4   Types of Aquatic Features

Wherever possible, preserve existing natural water features. Natural streams, creeks, ponds and puddles enhance play. Consider them within the context of overall park design.

The most common aquatic features are:

a.   Marshes

b.   Ponds

c.   Pools

d.   Streams and creeks

e.   Channels

f.   Fountains

g.   Hose-filled ponds or streams

16.4.1 Water Play Areas (Seattle, 1986)

Water play areas are powerful playground attractors. Water can be used by the child in many ways: to splash, pour, mix with sand and dirt, float boats, etc. Acoustic qualities are attractive and valued.

Wherever feasible, provide water as a play element.

Water play areas can be wading pools, spray pools, play pools, streams, bubblers, sprinklers, troughs or even a running hose bib in a sand box; the possibilities are endless.

Safety is a primary concern. Contexts vary from water in body-contact, water-play features to natural resource features. Water depth must be carefully considered, on physical and programmatic circumstances. Far more research is needed concerning specific design

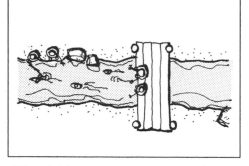

240 *Bridges are very attractive to children and provide a simple means of getting close to water.*

241 *Stepping stones allow close contact with water.*

242 *Child operated water pump.*

standards for water features. As drowning is a risk, caution must be exercised. The following are critical aspects:

- Areas around water features must be nonskid and well drained.
- Water areas must be sunny and protected from the wind.
- Simplify plumbing and pump systems for water features.
- Simplify forms and construction methods for water features.
- Provide for adult supervision in water play areas.

16.4.2 Hose-filled Temporary Ponds (CMHC, 1979)

A simple play stream or an elaborate recirculating and filtering system can be devised, depending on use, funds and climate.

a. A stream may be of any size and shape providing it drains to the lowest point.

b. The depth of water should be 6 inches maximum. Careful judgement should be exercised according to the age and abilities of the children.

c. The stream bottom should be either reinforced concrete or asphalt.

d. The edge of the stream should be lined with flat smooth stones laid in mortar.

e. A footbridge may take any shape.

f. The drain should be located at the lowest point. It should be connected to a dry well or sewer depending on local conditions and requirements. A screw-in plug attached to the bottom with a chain is a standard plumbing house fixture; a screen mesh at the top of the drain should be provided.

g. Islands of wild grass or sand can be added design features.

16.5 Design Criteria for Water Settings

a. **Varied Movement.** Both horizontal and vertical movement exemplify the innately liquid character of water.

b. **Continuity.** Water works as a continuous system at many scales, in both natural and people-made systems. Elements, functions and forms should be juxtaposed and integrated into a total system, albeit at a small scale.

c. **Channel Character.** Streams can be wide or narrow, shallow or deep, fast or slow, rough or smooth, straight or curved.

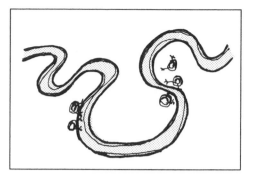

243   Wandering   channels   allow   more water access.

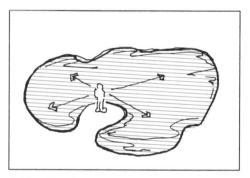

244   Headlands give an overview and island sense.

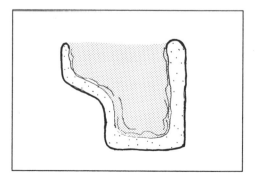

245   "Vernal" puddles fill with rainfall.

d.   **Edge Character.** Both streams and ponds can have a wide variety of edges from hard to soft, deep to shallow, fenced to unfenced, etc..

e.   **Balanced Impact.** Design strategies should maximize user-impact and minimize environmental impact:

1)   Protection of the Land—Water Interface can be achieved by fences, barriers and rocks. Rocky shorelines, stepping stones or projecting platforms are all good impact reducers because they help keep feet clear of the fragile meeting of land and water.

2)   Marshes are particularly impact-resistant, provided they retain a couple of inches of water—most kids really don't like getting muddy.

3)   Water-play elements located away from life-support elements will help draw high energy play activity away from fragile resources.

f.   **Interpenetration.** Forms can be designed that support close contact between users and water. They include wandering channels, deltas, headlands, stepping stones, inlets and bridges.

g.   **Multiuse.** Water features should be designed for use when empty (roller skating, wheeled toy play) or for winter use (skating, sliding) in cold climates.

16.6   Hard Surface Settings

Play areas often contain large areas of asphalt that in effect are giant catchment basins.

a.   **Hoses** can be used to explore the subtle variations in surface and slope in an apparently uniform asphalt terrain. Rates of flow can be measured in different places to assess relative gradients. Natural lines of drainage can be plotted for future reference.

b.   **"Vernal" Pools or Puddles** can be small, permanent modifications to the flow of water, if located away from main foot traffic. They provide a modest water play setting. Over time, silt and debris will collect against the "dam," providing a microhabitat for small plants and organisms. Studies can be made of the changing situation.

Paved areas can be designed to create puddles but should be limited to a specific area. The maximum depth of puddles should not exceed 1 inch nor 1 square yard per event (Seattle, 1986).

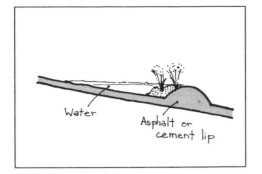

246   *Small plants grow out of accumulated silt.*

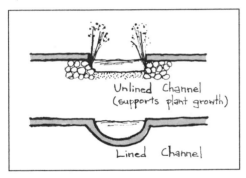

247   *Potholes and channels provide water access too.*

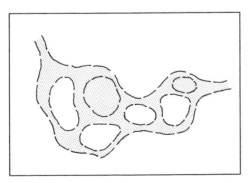

248   *Deltas are a simple means of providing a "hard" water system.*

c.   **Potholes and Channels** can be designed into asphalt areas in various shapes and sizes, coincident with natural drainage lines (which may be discovered in hose experiments). Channels can be straight or curved. In a short period of time plants will invade and create a modest aquatic habitat.

d.   **Deltas and Pools.** By making excavations bigger, deeper and/or more complex a more varied system can be created.

16.7   Diversified Hard and Soft Settings

A complex of elements cut out or built into asphalt surfaces can go together to make a diverse setting, including willow thickets, minimarshes, pools and channels.

16.8   Soft Settings

Soft settings can be developed in nonasphalted areas. They can be more subtle, complex and extensive. The system illustrated here contains two ponds, a marsh, an island, a stream and a bridge (the Environmental Yard, Berkeley, California).

A scaled down version of this kind of setting would be feasible, if adequately protected. The choice of features and their juxtaposition are highly dependent on the disposition of the site, topography and drainage pattern. Many alternatives are possible.

16.8.1 Water Circulation/Recirculation Ponds

A pond is fascinating for children.

It should have gently sloping sides and be a maximum of 14 inches deep, so that vehicles can be driven through it and children can play in the shallow water at the edge without tripping. It should be kept clean and the water changed regularly; an efficient drainage and filter system is essential. By installing an electric pump, the water can be made to circulate and flow along a stream into the pond. This stream of running water provides marvelous opportunities for play, such as making dams and water falls. Rafts and boats can be floated on the pond. St. Francis Park in Portland, Oregon, has an outstanding example of a recirculating water-play setting.

If natural rainfall is insufficient to keep ponds topped up, they will need to be connected to the public water supply. The water supply can be via a float valve installation. Recirculation systems are required for larger installations.

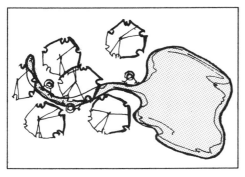

249 *Inlets provide additional shoreline and an intimate water-play setting away from the large pond.*

16.9 Pools, Fountains, Cascades and Sprays

These features provide play oriented water activity and also promote diversity. Fountains and spray ideas are infinite.

a. **Pools** (Seattle, 1986)

1) Locate in sunny, highly visible areas.

2) Pools must have a shelter house nearby for:

- safe storage of chlorine and chemicals;
- supervision visibility and safety;
- storage of water play equipment and props.

3) Pools must have adult supervision when water is being used.

4) Provide benches at pools in both sun and shade locations.

5) Spray areas and areas of shallow running water are preferable to standing water.

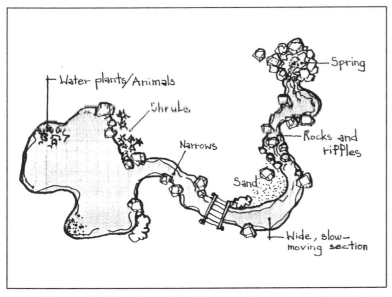

250 *Prototypical "hard," recirculating aquatic system with full water treatment.*

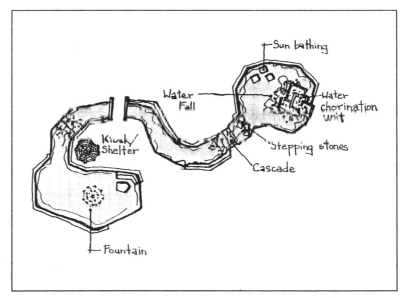

251 *Prototypical "soft," recirculating aquatic setting.*

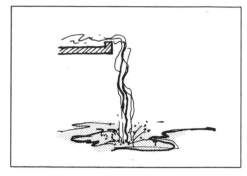

252 *Waterfalls are a stimulating feature for people of all ages; sheer drops, however, can be hazardous.*

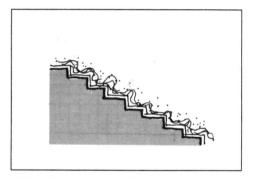

253 *Cascades avoid the sheer drops of waterfalls but achieve a similar effect of falling water.*

254 *Rocks and ripples provide added interest to running water.*

6)   Use fine spray mist which is most comfortable in all-weather situations.

7)   Spray areas and water collecting areas must have nonslip surfaces.

8)   Provide several depth areas in all pools: shallow part for tots and parents; deeper parts for older children. Undulating bottom surfaces provide an exciting variety of water spaces. The slope toward the center of the pool should be less than 1:12.

9)   Provide several drains and water sources for any kind of pool. This lessens the time needed to fill and drain the pool and provides play opportunities for more children.

10) Locate fill and drain valves above grade in locked boxes or in shelter if immediately adjacent to pool.

11) Provide a hillside, on-grade water slide wherever possible with a convenient hose bib or water source for continuous running water when in use.

12) Provide many different sources of spray which can be easily installed by a play supervisor:

   •   quick coupling stand-pipe hose attachments;
   •   surface spouts;
   •   hose bibs, hoses, nozzles, fire hydrants.

b.   **Fountains** (Seattle, 1986)

Consideration should be given for other types of water spray such as fountains and waterfalls.

c.   **Water Tables** (Gordon, 1972)

Water is a most intriguing material to young children, yet it often lies beyond the restricted reach of children in wheelchairs or of hands that control crutches and are not free to touch—to feel—to make contact. How can this basic material be made accessible? At graded heights and allowing for insertion underneath of standardized wheelchairs of three different sizes (fitted to children on individualized measurements), water tables are fed by an artificial waterfall—a water sluice—that serves as a diagonal overhead bridge under which both wheelchair-bound and ambulatory children can pass.

Water tables should meet sanitation standards and be at heights accessible to a variety of user groups (Seattle, 1986).

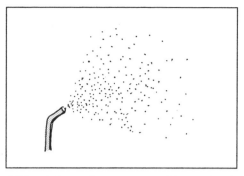

255 A fine "mist" spray provides a simple cooling-off function.

256 Fountains provide an important aesthetic dimension to playgrounds.

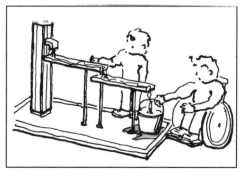

257 Water tables provide access to water for wheelchair children. There are many design alternatives.

16.9.1 Water Entrapment (Seattle, 1986)

In programmed play settings where feasible allow water to be manipulated with stoppers and other moveable water entrapment devices along water courses.

16.9.2 Aeration and Stagnation (Seattle, 1986)

All water in public contact must meet all applicable health and safety standards and be aerated, chemically treated or replaced regularly as necessary to prevent stagnation.

17. SAND SETTINGS

Sand, along with water, is the most popular play material because of its softness and malleability. It has even more potential when combined with water.

Planning Criteria

Play Value. Sand is an excellent medium for creative play and social interaction. It is easy to move and mold. It can be dug, sifted, sculpted, poured, thrown and drawn upon. It is the ultimate loose part.

Programming Potential. In some ways, very structured activities are unnecessary because of sand's inherent play characteristics. Combined with water sand has good potential for constructional play.

Play Leadership. Leaders need to appreciate potential.

Safety. Sand is commonly used as a safety surface. Broken glass, cat and dog toilet can be a problem. It is also easy to slip on when spilt onto concrete or asphalt.

Risk Management. Adequate containment is important. Regular inspection and maintenance is needed. Do not locate it next to residential backyards where domestic animals might be attracted. It will go rancid if covered from light.

Accessibility. This is a difficult problem which can be solved to some degree by rolling out plastic carpet over sand surface to support wheelchairs. Ramps are usually necessary, too. Sand in bearings of wheelchairs can be a problem. Multi-level sand areas at wheelchair height can be attractive to all children and provide opportunities for high accessibility.

Integration. Sand offers good potential for parallel play. Cooperative play and social interaction can result from children playing in close proximity in sand areas.

Management/Maintenance. Pro-sand policies are required. In many instances it is preferable to use tan bark or wood chips as a surfacing material. Separate sand play areas should be provided even when sand is used as a surface under play equipment.

17.1 Sand on Playgrounds

Sand can serve both as a play material and as a safety surface. *Sand play* areas should be explicitly designated.

A playground sand area should be like a beach—deep, wide and near to water. It should be near a path and have a ramped approach so that children on wheels can get in easily and not fall in by mistake. Playing with hoses and buckets of water in the sand is fun and easily managed if there is a supply of water nearby. If the sand area is at least four feet deep with good drainage below and no covering over it, it will be perfectly hygienic. Rain, air and sunshine keep it so. If it is exposed to falling leaves in autumn or to cats and dogs at night time, a fine meshed cover can be put over it when necessary (HAPA, 1978).

13.2 Sand Playability Criteria

a. **A small grain size** will allow the material to be molded and to "stick together."

b. **Low dust content** will minimize the "dirty" aspects of material sticking to clothes and limbs, and reduce the risk of dust being blown into children's eyes.

c. **Moldability** makes sand easy to "smooth out" and incorporate fine detail when sculpted.

d. **Cakiness** allows material to remain stuck together after molding.

e. **Digability** makes digging with hands or small implements easy.

f. **Specification** for sand areas or boxes shall (Seattle, 1986):

   1) Be a balanced mix of particle sizes ranging from coarse sand (not more than 1.5 mm) to very fine;

   2) Pack well when moist;

   3) Be well washed, clean, free of dirt, clay, silt oxides or iron or other contaminants.

g. **Depth of sand** in larger sand-play areas shall be between 18 and 24 inches (Seattle, 1986). The sand pit shall be deep enough (about four feet) for children and leaders to dig using proper garden spades (HAPA, 1978).

258 *Sand should be 4 feet deep (HAPA)/ 18—24 inches (Seattle).*

259 *Sand play areas need shade in summer and sun in winter. They should be sheltered from cold wind.*

17.3   Design Principles

Sand play areas are one of the most commonly misdesigned elements in playgrounds and parks. Sound design principles include:

a.   **Ambient microclimate.** This is essential for extensive sand play. Shade in hot weather and sun in cool weather should be provided with shelter from prevailing winds. All sand play areas should be sited to receive sun for part of the day for natural cleansing (Seattle, 1986).

1)   Shelter from prevailing winds.

b.   **Enclosure.** Sand material must be kept in place to thwart children from disturbing or running through the creative sand play of others. Enclosures provide a psychologically calm atmosphere. Shelf-like play surfaces can be designed in, along with places to sit or "perch" with peers. Enclosures must be made wide enough to support such activities.

1)   If using concrete, provide an apron with a minimum of 18 inches around the sand pit on all sides flush with grade for sweeping sand back into pit (Seattle, 1986).

2)   Provide lids for sand areas when practical. Lids, preferably screen material, must allow light and air circulation for natural cleansing (Seattle, 1986).

3)   Sandpits should be designed with a minimum 3-foot wide sand walk-off apron sloping 2% to 3% into the sandpit to permit sand to flow back into the pit (Los Angeles, 1987).

4)   The perimeter enclosure of sandpits should be level. Sandpits should have positive drainage systems, preferably a storm drain and daylight. Level sandpits are required because sand flows and tends to seek its own level (Los Angeles, 1987).

c.   **Accessibility.** Sand pits should be designed to facilitate transfer of children from wheelchairs to the playing surface. Alternatively, sheets of rubber or beach rings can be laid across sand surfaces to provide wheelchair access.

Provide handrails along the perimeter to help youngsters maintain balance as they go into and out of the area independently. (Gordon, 1972)

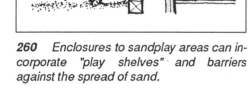

260   *Enclosures to sandplay areas can incorporate "play shelves" and barriers against the spread of sand.*

261   *Sand areas must be accessible to children and adults.*

262   Shelves provide sitting places and...

263   ...a support for sand play with loose parts.

264   Natural elements such as rocks and vegetation add interest and additional play opportunities.

d.   **Size.** Sand areas must be large enough for many children to play without getting in each others way.

e.   **Play Surfaces.** Sand tables, rock or stone worktops and shelves provide necessary support.

f.   **Toy Play.** Children like to play in sand with small toys—especially pocket-sized trucks, animals and vehicles, or they find other props including on-site vegetation. This activity is supported by providing a variety of work and play surfaces.

g.   **Adequate Drainage.** This is necessary to avoid waterlogging. The best methods will depend on site conditions.

Provide controllable drainage to allow for programmed moisturizing of sand for compaction (Seattle, 1986).

h.   **Vegetation.** Growing within or immediately adjacent to sand areas, vegetation greatly enhances the range of fantasy play by supplying plant parts (Moore, 1986b). Many types of plants are feasible, from grass and wild plants to mature trees.

i.   **Water Supply.** This is essential for good sand play. A spring-loaded or dripping, tamper-proof faucet works best. Hoses may also be used.

Provide a limited-flow water source next to sand areas, such as hand water pumps or trickling water troughs, to allow for sand and water play. Locate drinking fountains away from sand play areas (Seattle, 1986).

j.   **Boundary Enclosure.** A variety of places for individual and small group activities should be provided. Sand areas should be sized and shaped to encourage smaller groups of 1—4 children to play together; these sub-areas can be linked to create a larger sand area, accommodating more children overall (Seattle, 1986).

k.   **Separation.** Sand play areas must be separated from active play equipment (Seattle, 1986).

Keep sandpits far enough away from any building, to prevent tracking sand onto floors (Los Angeles, 1987).

265   *A water supply should be located adjacent to sandplay areas.*

266   *Separation of sand play areas from zones of high activity is necessary.*

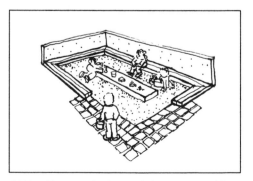

267   *Prototypical sandplay area with a table in the center.*

1.   **Age Groups.**   A variety of sand play opportunities should be provided.   Sand for toddlers should be at a shallow sand bench or table to allow stand-up play (Seattle, 1986).

Sand play for 4 year olds and older can be at ground level.   Several smaller areas are better than a giant one.   Children play in groups of one to four, making tunnels, canals, castles and mountains.

17.4   Sand Pit   (CMHC, 1979)

Control of sand overspill is helped by the center "table."   Another deterrent is to round the outside edge of the pit with a half log, curved side up, attached to the wood timber sides; if bricks or concrete are used, this curved edge is easily accomplished.   Cobblestones or flat paving stones around the sand pit help take sand off the feet and improve the appearance (but can be difficult for wheelchairs to traverse).   The depth of sand below the edge also prevents blowing; however, it may need a step down for little children and a ramp for wheelchairs.

Hedging or another type of wind screen may be necessary for some sites.

If cats are a problem, nylon netting that allows rain and purifying sun through can be stretched over the sand when not in use (never cover completely as sand will go rancid). A handy rake or scooper permanently stored nearby is a simpler solution.   Sand must have water available and be kept damp.   Storage close at hand for sand toys is necessary.

17.5   Elevated Sand Table

An elevated area containing sand or water provides access for those in wheelchairs.   Flat areas are also useful for toy cars, crafts, etc.

They should be located on platforms of varying heights with the table positioned at the joining of two platforms.   This position allows one table to accommodate wheelchairs of different heights.

268 *Multilevel sand tables provide the greatest range of accessibility.*

269 *Sand tables can accommodate wheelchairs and...*

270 *...the corners allow children to play together.*

17.6   Raised Sand Area

Sandboxes should be provided both at ground level and above ground for wheelchair users without transfer skills.

A raised sand area can be built into a berm. The raised end should provide 27 inches vertical clearance and 18 to 24 inches between the edge of the box and the base.

271 *Elevated sand surfaces let children in wheelchairs interact with peers.*

18. PLAY PROPS AND MANIPULATIVE SETTINGS

Props should be recognized as an essential part of any play environment. They help children manipulate their environment to stimulate imaginary and dramatic play. There are two major categories: 1) a wide variety of small natural and synthetic "found objects" such as insects and small mammals, sticks and stones, bottle tops and popsicle sticks, logs and rocks, plant parts, sand and dirt; and 2) larger manufactured items such as modular systems, wheeled toys and dress-up clothes. Play props provide an immediate low-cost method of enhancing existing play settings, as long as it is not thought of as a panacea to integration.

Manipulative settings range from found objects in fixed settings to adventure playgrounds.

Planning Criteria

Play Value. Play props and manipulative settings provide critical support for social, imaginative and creative play and promote: (PLAE, 1981—87)

a.   Fine motor skill development, which is as important as gross motor skill development.

b.   Social-emotional development stimulated by intimate social interaction, different in style to the larger scale interaction of traditional games.

c.   Cognitive skills inherent in manipulating the physical environment to solve child-initiated problems.

d.   Independent living and self management skills by giving children a sense of control over their environment.

e.   Social-organizational skills, providing children an opportunity to work together to implement their own projects.

f.   Self-concept development which is supported by children's increased opportunities to differentiate themselves from their surroundings by using props.

g.   Language skills providing experiential richness and social interaction thus stimulating a greater diversity of verbal expression.

Programming Potential. They are essential to creative programming.

Play Leadership. All play leaders should be skilled in the creation and use of play props and manipulative play settings.

Safety. Very small loose parts present a danger from sucking and swallowing. They may also be thrown.

Risk Management. Adequate storage facilities are needed. Disbursment must be monitored. Hazardous items should be discarded.

Accessibility. Many props are more or less accessible, depending on disability.

Integration. They offer tremendous scope and opportunities for integration. Excellent potential for children working together.

Management/Maintenance. Policies are needed to support the importance of play props. Checkout systems needed. Low cost sources need to be identified and assessed.

Areas where play props are used must be designed carefully and screened to avoid unsightly appearance to passersby.

Most props require supervision and effective play leadership.

272   *Manipulative settings offer more play value.*

273   *Play settings with loose materials stimulate interactions between children of different abilities.*

274   *Fixed-but-moving parts such as gates must be recognized as play objects.*

18.1   The Value of Manipulative Settings

An effective play environment should allow for combinations of fixed features and loose props. Fixed, open ended features provide a beckoning "stage," stimulating the child to build onto them. Children use an undulating wall, fence or ground surface to run toy cars along; they build a shelter between two shrubs or use pieces of vegetation to make a "mixture" on a park bench.

Play props are especially important in unsupervised settings. When the stimulus of play leadership is missing, children must rely on their own inventiveness to manipulate and shape their personal environment. Play props can be used in any number of interchangeable ways, at many scales, ranging from an individual child playing with a few twigs, a softdrink can or dirt, to large scale group construction of "forts" and "clubhouses," to dramatic play using dress-up clothes or races using wheeled toys.

Children must be able to manipulate and interchange parts of their environment. It is a fundamental part of normal development, and essential for children with disabilities who depend on touch for much of their environmental information. Play settings should contain a continuum of fixed and movable parts including:

a.   Small "found objects" (plant parts, sand, cartons)

b.   Larger manufactured parts (large blocks, tires, boards, etc.) with adequate leadership and storage.

c   Fixed-but-moving parts such as: (small scale) latches, door knobs, hooks, gears and handles; and (large scale) gates, turnstiles, windows and doors.

d.   Fixed parts such as structures and bounded areas which provide for permanence and stability (adapted from Schneekloth, 1985).

18.2   Empowerment: Children Making a Place of Their Own (adapted from AEC, 1980)

Responsive elements allow a child to learn properties of the physical environment and develop skills in manipulating it.

A physical environment that responds to a child's manipulations encourages exploration and discovery. Amorphous materials, like sand, water and mud invite activity and interaction. Play props can be manipulated, put together and torn apart. They are the ingredients that children use to make their own environments.

Play props might be wood and tools, large pieces of lightweight styrofoam, fabric, old tires or modular blocks. Children might make their own forts, cities or teepees, and then tear them down for the next project. Play props allow children to test out their relationship to the physical environment and learn relationships between cause and effect in a safe, free-play situation.

Place-making is empowering for everyone, but especially for children, as they are rarely given the opportunity to build with anything larger than blocks. The opportunity for children with special needs is even rarer, because there is often an exaggerated concern for their safety and protection. The confidence and ability to adapt one's physical environment is an important step toward independent living.

When children identify an area as their own they will take better care of it than if it were a public space (Moore & Wong, in press).

18.3 Types of Manipulative Settings

There are six main types of manipulable settings (as described in a—f below), providing varied play potentials, and a continuum of control by the child: **found objects** or ad hoc props in existing settings; **purpose-made props** such as those created by children or leaders during structured activity programs; **modular systems** designed for user applications; **large wheeled vehicles** that users can manipulate at will; **adventure playgrounds** created from scratch, where all parts and their dispositions are decided by the users; and **natural settings** that can be integrated into all five of the preceding types.

a.   **Found Objects in Fixed Settings.** Play settings usually contain microscopic play props. These include:

1)   Small objects and materials. All manner of sticks, stones, dirt and dead leaves can be used in two ways.

- As "tools" they enable the child to interact more fully with another material, e.g., to scratch dirt with a stick, throw a rock in a pond or bang a piece of play equipment to make a noise.
- As "props" in dramatic fantasy play, e.g., stones as "money," dead leaves as "soup," or a piece of wood as a "microphone."

Often such materials are swept away and the setting becomes too tidy. In adult eyes, they are so microscopic that their play value is overlooked easily. But for young children they represent valuable play materials.

275   Pebbles, stones, shells, sticks and small toys are essential loose parts.

276   Sand and dirt—the most common loose play items.

277   The use of most manufactured objects must be carefully monitored.

A major problem of having play props in an asphalt or structured area is that they look out of place, and so small-scale that they appear to be litter. Vegetated areas help disguise play props so they look less obtrusive and part of the setting.

2) **Small Manufactured Toys.** Children bring or have supplied on-site their own small toys (cars, trucks, soldiers, dolls, etc.) to use as props. Small wheeled toys of all sizes are particularly important.

3) **Sand, Dirt and Water.** These materials may be used individually or in combination with each other, and with small objects.

4) **Ephemeral Objects.** These include manufactured items such as cardboard boxes, plastic cartons, softdrink cans—"bits and pieces" which find their way onto the site by accident (or by design). Part of their attraction is the surprise factor. But such materials quickly deteriorate, needing careful management and disposal.

Natural materials are also valuable such as scrap lumber, logs and truckloads of clean leaves for making leaf piles in the fall (often available from the local parks and recreation department).

Recycled material can sometimes be sanded, painted or varnished to prolong its life. Large storage cupboards may be necessary to protect the more attractive items from being taken away. Replacing, repairing and constantly adding new loose material is worth the effort in terms of child development and sustained play value.

5) **Heavy loose parts.** Some items are too heavy to be moved off the ground, although they could be moved around with difficulty by a group of children working together. Large blocks of lumber are the most appropriate example. Because of their weight, they are not likely to be scattered all over the site, so they can be easier and less time consuming to maintain.

The heaviest loose parts should only be moveable by adults and can serve such purposes as space definition.

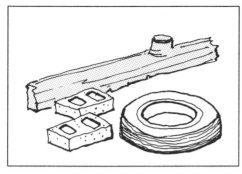

278 *"Stuff" includes all manner of larger, longer-life props.*

279 *Dress-up clothes of all types are essential for dramatic play.*

280 *Swedish Blocks and Playchest.*

b.   **Purpose-made Props.**

These include objects with a fixed form (puzzle types) and manufactured parts with a flexible or modular form (lightweight panels or blocks). Adequate storage and supervision is essential (Seattle, 1986).

1)   **Dress-up Clothes.** A large chest of dress-up clothes (collected together and replenished from time-to-time) is an essential resource for dramatic play programming.

2)   **Foam Mattress** (Gordon, 1972). For children with restricted movement who are unable to walk or to sit alone without support, a foam mattress can be extremely valuable. Using the mattress, a child can be prone but still experience the sensation of open space, can see the sky instead of a ceiling, can become aware of clouds and of a tree responding to winds and can observe the play of other children.

3)   **Inflatables.** Inflatables have a great potential for use by children with and without disabilities. This area of equipment use requires further research. Inflatables are forms which contain air. They can be easily blown up or deflated for easy storage. This type of equipment requires supervision.

c.   **Modular Systems**

Manufactured play props like giant tinker toys or outdoor modular blocks can be provided under supervision.

Adult-size ladders can be sawn in half. Adult-size sawhorses can be used by older children, but some smaller sizes are suggested. Barrels, sturdy boxes in any size, and large, hospital-type detergent containers can also be added (CMHC, 1979).

Play settings can be designed to be added to when the play leader arrives with a kit-of-parts. Moveable walls can be suspended from permanent structures. Other props can be added by children.

1)   **Swedish Blocks and Storage Playchest** (CMHC, 1979). These blocks are similar to kindergarten blocks but are designed for outside use. The addition of boards and other loose material extend their play value. The playchest is sturdy and houses the 145 blocks; it also serves as a playhouse, store, space ship or other play object. The double-hinged top lies flat against the back to discourage use except for locking up. The blocks are expensive initially, but

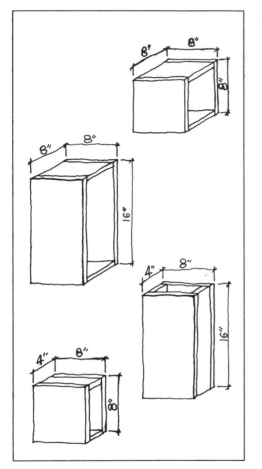

281   *Hollow blocks are an excellent play props system.*

they fascinate children of all ages and are indestructible. Quantity is very important—you can never have too many. Specifications are listed below.

- The chest
    - 1500 mm (5 ft.) long, 900 mm (3 ft.) deep, 900 mm (3 ft.) wide.
    - Must be treated with exterior finish and could have a padlock.
    - Double hinged lid flat against back when not in use.
    - Drain holes in the bottom.
    - Raisers approximately 38 x 90 mm. (1 1/2 x 3 1/2 in.)
    - Drop down front for clambering in and playing "store." Support with chains and heavy duty hinges.
- The blocks
    - Cut lengths of 65 x 140 mm (3 x 6 – nominal) hardwood:
      12 @ 1200 mm (4 ft.) long
      24 @ 600 mm (2 ft.) long
      169 @ 300 mm (1 ft.) long.
- Round all edges. Finish blocks with mixture of good, heavy duty, hardwood floor sealer plus colored oil stain.

2)   **Hollow Blocks** (CMHC, 1977). These are specially recommended for preschool play groups where the size of the group is controlled. Sizes are units of one another and form modular systems. The sizes, shapes and weights were designed by Caroline Pratt, U.S. educator, to fill specific developmental needs. With the addition of boards ladders and other miscellaneous props, a play group may need no other equipment. Shallow storage means easy access and clean-up. Where vandalism is not a problem, they can be stacked against a wall by size and left out all year. They are great fun in the winter.

The final dimensions of these blocks are crucial to their success. Therefore it is important to pay careful attention to the dressed dimensions of the wood (wood of a nominal 20 x 190 mm (1 x 8) and 20 x 90 mm (1 x 4) should be used).

Ten blocks of each size make a good set for a group of 25 children.

3)   **Moveable Adventure Village.** Developed by PLAE, Incorporated, this building system was manufactured from standard 3/4-inch thick-walled PVC pipe and fittings. Cardboard and cloth infill panels complete the package. It is ideally suited to use with a traveling playbus program. Within a few

282   Wooden boards and boxes are favorite play props.

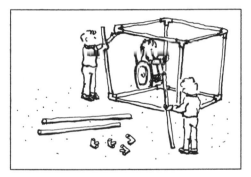

283   Plastic pipes and fittings are a type of modular system.

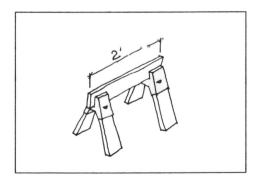

284   Sawhorses can be made with standard brackets.

minutes, in a local park or shopping center, a group of children and play leaders can erect a "village" environment that can then become a setting for a thematic workshop such as "Wild West," "Living on the Frontier" or "Adventure Village." The kit of parts and activity program guides are available from PLAE, Inc.

d.   Large Wheeled Vehicles. (HAPA, 1978)

It is very important for children who are physically disabled to have the means for independent mobility.

New methods for allowing independent exploration are being invented. Various commercially produced vehicles including large bicycles, hand-propelled tricycles and garden trucks can be useful. HAPA has specially-designed wheeled toys.

When buying wheeled toys, make sure they are robust enough to withstand intense use. Note that something designed for a particular child may not be suitable for others. Solid tires are preferable to inflatable and industrial wheels are stronger than toy ones.

Special electrically operated vehicles can be bought or made for children with severe physical disabilities. These are naturally very popular with many children so it is best that such vehicles are kept locked away until needed.

Battery-driven, hand-propelled and push vehicles should be considered, including old prams, baby walkers, supermarket trolleys, bicycles and garden trucks. A bean bag or a specially designed wooden corner seat placed in a trolley or truck, for example, can help many children be more mobile.

e.   Adventure Playgrounds (Allen, 1968; Bengtsson, 1970; Shier, 1984). A concept imported from Europe, adventure playgrounds are similar to other manipulable settings, but with one critical difference — they are staffed by trained play leaders.

Play leadership describes the multirole relationship between children, **adults and the community, requiring special training and experience. In some European countries it exists as a separate profession (animateur, social pedagogy) alongside allied education and recreation professions.

A skilled playleader increases the scope of adventure play by:

1)   Providing of tools (hammers, saws, nails).

2)   Managing construction materials.

285   Special wheeled vehicles adapted to children with disabilities offer valuable play experiences.

286   Plant parts make excellent play props.

287   Adventure Playgrounds with trained play leaders are the most developed form of manipulable play settings.

3)   Disposing of materials that have lost their usefulness.

4)   Inspecting children's constructions and play sites for safety.

5)   Involving children nondirectively in constructive activity.

6)   Being a role-model, friend and confidant to children.

7)   Maintaining liaison with community groups and individuals to facilitate communication and interaction—specifically through voluntary participation and contribution to the playground in time, money or materials.

An adventure playground may also contain an enclosed building for storage, shelter, meetings and social events.

Adventure Playgrounds are the most developed example of responsive play settings, but because of the difficulty of managing and maintaining them, they are rare. Ways should be found to incorporate adventure play elements into designated play settings.

f.   **Natural Settings.** Natural materials provide many opportunities for children to manipulate their environment. Rocks, pebbles, leaves, sticks, twigs, branches can be built into boats, forts, castles and costumes. They can be stacked, linked, piled, poured. Children's imaginative use of these objects is boundless (Seattle, 1986). Children have such a strong affiliation with vegetation as a play resource that it is vitally important to ensure a good supply (see Chapter 13, Trees/Vegetation for further details).

Natural settings provide good support for manipulative activity. Low maintenance vegetation areas should be set aside in playgrounds and parks for this purpose.

Settings of any size containing dirt, water, trees and flowering plants can provide a setting for manipulative play, if designed and managed appropriately. In park landscapes, such play functions may not be recognized. This inevitably results in conflict between management and children, when plants get broken and/or dirt is dug up and scattered around.

Suitable materials include plants such as bamboo and willow. "Prunings" from streets and parks may be available from the city parks department. If this is not done, children may deliberately harvest other plants and run the risk of being

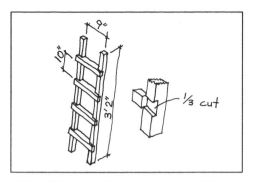

288 *Short ladders make useful play props, but need careful supervision.*

labeled "vandals." Larger pieces of vegetation are suitable for constructing self-designed shelters, forts, huts and clubhouses.

1) Select plant materials near play areas which recover quickly from being pulled and broken (Seattle, 1986).

2) Organize maintenance crews to provide piles of natural play props in some play areas on a seasonal basis: piles of autumn leaves, a yard of extra dirt, a half-load of tree clippings. Expect to do a "sweep-up" later (Seattle, 1986).

In areas of 1500 sq. ft. or larger, a considerable variety of manipulable play can be provided. The area should be dirt-surfaced and enclosed with a strong, high fence. An accessible gate (42 inches wide) and a "squeeze-through" 9—12 inches wide entrance should be provided, plus a larger 8 foot gate for vehicle access.

Suitable building materials for use by children include scrap lumber, prunings from the city parks department, cardboard boxes and packing crates. Corners, edges and other areas which are small enough to be spanned with available materials are ideal sites for shelter building.

Props which find their way onto the rest of the playground can be periodically returned to the compound. Every so often materials should be replenished and unusable materials discarded.

18.4   Setting Management

Manipulative settings and play props must be carefully designed and managed by adults who understand the importance and function of manipulative play. Parent education must be stressed. One of the best ways to promote the concept of props and loose parts is through programs that use them to demonstrate their potential for integration. Community artists have a critical role to play here.

Play props always present management problems—real and imagined. Specific settings must be created to provide for loose-parts, so they can be both available and manageable. Adequate storage must be provided, especially for manufactured props. (In West Germany, storage sheds are provided in parks and managed by paid, retired people.)

Playground and park settings must be viewed as dynamic, ever changing environments that respond to user needs.

19. STAGE SETTINGS

To support group productions, performance and a sense of community, children and adults need a well-defined, slightly elevated accessible stage space and adjacent audience space.

Planning Criteria

Play Value. A stage supports dramatic and fantasy play, performance activities, presentation of self and teamwork.

Programming Potential. It is a place for informal gathering, community events, festivals and performances.

Play Leadership. Leaders should understand the role of performance and be trained to use the full potential of staging facilities.

Safety. Drop-offs at the edge of the stage must be avoided.

Risk Management. Signage is required to indicate proper use.

Accessibility. Ramps and warning strips are required.

Integration. Stages provide good potential for children to feel "on stage" together, audience and performers.

Management. Policies and schedules of use should be established. Stage facilities also offer excellent opportunity for community participation in the parks and play settings.

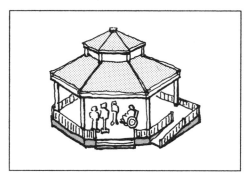

289 *Traditional spaces such as gazebos make excellent staging places.*

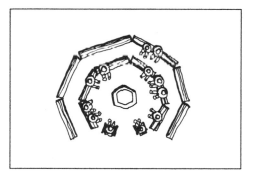

290 *Accessible campfire circles or mini arenas provide a basic staging area for average-sized groups.*

291 *In this accessible stage for up to 15 children, wooden posts are nailable and support all manner of "scenery" and shade props.*

19.1 Types of Staging Areas

a. **Verandas, Gazebos, Terraces and Decks.** These traditional indoor-outdoor elements serve an important social purpose. Many variations can be designed. In fact, in most climates, partially enclosed, covered spaces must be provided in order to make effective use of the outdoors.

Such structures have great potential as staging areas and can provide a major support for program activity. Picnic tables inside such structures can provide convenient work surfaces. Storage should be incorporated.

b. **Campfire Circles/Mini-Arenas.** Depending on the number of concentric rings provided, large groups can be accommodated. A fireplace is not essential but should be given serious consideration.

There are several ways of constructing campfire circle forms to accommodate groups of up to 25.

If there are more than two or three rings, they should be "raked" to assist visual and acoustic contact. Circles can be made of utility poles, railroad ties, lengths of regular or irregular tree trunks. Accessibility for wheelchair users should be taken into account.

c. **Group Program Spaces.** The primary purpose is to provide comfortable places where groups of children and leaders can meet for program activities. The maximum feasible group is about 15 (a "seminar" size).

Design possibilities are many to serve such functions as eating and hanging out for older kids and teenagers. They can be places where neighbors and parents can meet informally, especially if adjacent to preschool facilities.

d. **Stages and Arenas.** Groups larger than 15 or so need special consideration. Spaces are needed to cater to groups ranging in size from 25 to a couple hundred or more, to accommodate dramatic art, mime, music activities and large community gatherings.

Spaces of this size must be located away from traffic noise and visual distractions. Large arenas or stages consume space and have a high cost relative to their social utility, yet the availability of such a facility can have a substantial effect on interaction and development of children and the community at large.

e. **Amphitheaters.** (Bunin, et al., 1980) Steps and narrow aisles in amphitheaters can be troublesome barriers for wheelchair users. Designing an accessible am-

292 *Stages can be altered to fit program needs.*

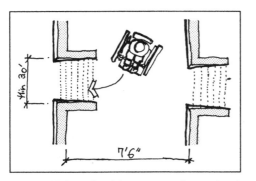

293 *Aisles should accommodate wheelchair access.*

phitheater will benefit all patrons by allowing them to choose their seats with minimum effort and maximum safety. The amphitheater illustrated below is raked steeply enough to require steps, but is also graded and ramped to provide wheelchair access to four of the five seating levels and the stage. The design can be adapted easily to fit site conditions and programming needs.

1) Provide firm, wide paths leading to amphitheater and support facilities (restrooms, parking, concessions).

2) Pathway surfaces should be slip-resistant under wet and dry conditions.

3) Whenever possible, grade site to provide access at several different seating levels without the use of steps or ramps. Otherwise, provide ramps (in addition to stairs) at least 4 feet wide with a slope of 1:15 or less.

4) Provide wheelchair seating in as many different viewing areas as possible.

5) Cross aisles may be used to seat wheelchairs if 4 feet of clear aisle space is provided behind the chair.

f. **Groups of Picnic Tables.** Half-a-dozen or so picnic tables can be assembled into a group program area. Placing them under lightly shaded, sun-filtered trees is ideal, ensuring microclimatic comfort.

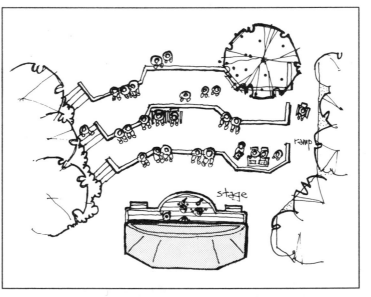

294 *Prototypical amphitheater accessible to wheelchairs.*

20. GATHERING, MEETING AND WORKING PLACES

To support social development and cooperative working relationships, children need small, comfortable gathering places where they can meet and work together in small (2—7), medium (7—15) and large (15+) groups (Moore & Wong, in press).

Planning Criteria

Play Value. Gathering, meeting and working places are critical for social interaction.

Programming Potential. They provide support for programming activities.

Play Leadership. They support leadership functions.

Safety. Table surfaces must not be located under a climbable element. Surfaces must also be nonflammable.

Risk Management. Table surfaces should be placed in partial shade at appropriate heights for wheelchair use and should be washable for hygiene.

Accessibility. Table surfaces must be open.

Integration. Gathering, meeting and working places support social interaction.

Management. Different types and sizes are required for different sized groups and different purposes. It should be possible to reserve these spaces in public parks. Work tables should be wider than standard picnic tables and have a continuous, smooth surface. Corners should be rounded, heights varied and benches flexible to accommodate varied group configurations.

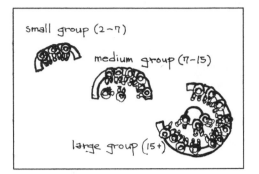

295 *Spaces should be provided for groups of different sizes.*

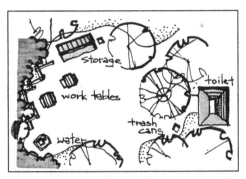

296 *Prototypical, multipurpose meeting and working place with work tables, water, trash cans, storage and toilets nearby.*

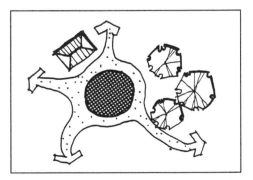

297 *Some meeting places may be located at points of high access and visibility.*

20.1   Importance of Places for Meeting and Working

Social interaction is basic to playing and learning. If appropriate meeting places are provided, social relationships can be extended to greater breadth and depth. Gathering, meeting and working places range in scale from a couple of children sitting on a log to an entire working group.

Many playgrounds are uncomfortable for children and adults alike, and harbor boredom and aggression rather than positive social development. Children need privacy at times. Quiet, secluded places should be provided where children can gather, where imaginations can have free rein.

The distinction between "work" and "play" is not made by young children in their informal activity. Although play often has a work-like character, "work" to a child usually means activities which are organized and directed by adults.

For adults and children to work successfully outdoors, comfortable, practical places are essential. They must be designed as "gathering spots," having a multipurpose quality to accommodate meeting, working and playing at different times for different people.

When playing, children often need a place to sit and relax alone, with a friend or an adult. Adults need places to sit and watch over their children or to talk to each other. Some children have limited stamina and need places to rest.

20.2   Design Principles

a.   **Location.** Some meeting and working settings should be located at points of high accessibility, at main path crossings or entrances. Other places should be located in the reverse circumstances, so that small groups can meet and work in private.

A prime area for meeting and working activity is at the point of transition from inside to outside. It is usually important to locate work places adjacent to storage facilities, so that tools and materials are close at hand. Proximity to a sink and water supply is often necessary.

For programming convenience, working places can be located adjacent to staging areas.

b.   **Microclimatic Comfort.** Protection from exposure and wind is always necessary. Summer shade and winter sunshine are necessary in most temperate and Mediterranean climatic zones. In wet climates protection from rain must be provided. This means that a choice of "open," "covered" and "enclosed" places is necessary.

298   Other places may be in quiet, private retreat-like surroundings.

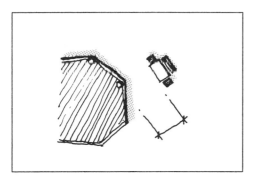

299   Work table adjacent to staging areas adds convenience.

300   Ambient microclimate is an important consideration in designing meeting and working places.

c.   **Social Support.** There are many ways of making places that facilitate and support social interaction (Moore & Wong, in press).

d.   **Diversity of Body Support.** Anthropomorphically correct, properly dimensioned and proportioned elements must be designed to support the human body. However, in outdoor settings, over-design should be avoided. People in general, and children in particular, use outdoor furniture in many "undesignated" ways, reflecting subtleties of social interaction. The anthropometric requirements of children with disabilities add further to the need for diversity.

e.   **Multilevel Structures.** Different levels designed into meeting and working places will support different body positions and a broader range of social interaction. Many fixed structures such as fences, play structures and stairways can be designed as places for people to sit and interact.

There should be many different places to sit, rest and lie down in each play setting. Conventional benches with backs and arms are needed at entrances and along paths. In addition, there should be platforms and edges that are easy to sit on, dry places on the ground to sit and lie down and soft areas for sitting and lying.

Some sitting places should have special benchrests and grab bars. Benches that can be straddled for children who need to prop themselves on their elbows should be provided.

f.   **Sense of Enclosure.** Physical enclosure should provide a feeling of privacy but not so strongly that children feel claustrophobic. The pleasure of privacy is often increased by retaining visual contact with the external surroundings. A range of settings should be provided, having a varied sense of enclosure from very private to open.

g.   **Identity.** Areas which are identifiable visually can foster a feeling of affiliation and recognition, and contribute to a "sense of place." Clear, strong identities make choosing a rendezvous point easy. Being able to say, "see you on the round bench" or "on the rocks" or "by the cherry tree," avoids frustrating confusion.

A well differentiated environment containing a hierarchy of "named" places is essential for effective behavior management and for clarity of communication between inside and outside. Playleaders must be able to give clear geographic instructions in changing from one activity to another.

301 Intimate enclosures stimulate close social contact.

302 Multilevel structures support different body positions and a variety of social interaction.

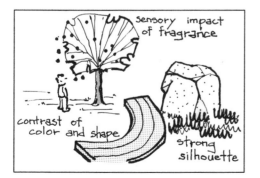

303 Meeting and gathering places need a sense of identity.

Identity can be designed through the use of:

1) **Contrast:** between place and background, of color, texture and form.

2) **Strong, clear shape:** a geometrical or semigeometrical form.

3) **Sharp silhouette:** strong, vertical planes, especially "skylines."

4) **Sensory impact:** "accent", or "identity," plants having a strong smell, texture, movement in the wind, fall color and fruit.

20.3   Types of Meeting, Working and Gathering Places

a.   **Built-in, ancillary places.** Places serving other main functions (such as stairways, rails, low walls and structures) can be designed to accommodate social interaction, "hanging out" and private daydreaming.

The most action oriented play structure can become a quiet social sanctuary at off-peak times. Fences can be made comfortable to sit on; people-plant settings—almost by definition—must include comfortable seats and "perches."

b.   **Small group settings.** Places are needed whose primary functions are social and work related, where small groups can meet ("solos," "duets," "trios" and "quartets").

The most simple work settings are off-the-ground surfaces: benches, tables, seats with places to lodge small instruments, materials, clipboards, etc.

c.   **Logs, Rocks and Found Objects.** Simple sitting and working spots can be created using heavy objects in the 100—300 pound range, like logs or rocks, that can be moved by a group of adults but not by children. Found objects can be used individually or grouped according to the social purpose in mind.

d.   **Self-made Places.** Children can make temporary social settings for themselves, if given:

1)   An adequate supply of building materials/loose parts.

2)   Suitable "building sites."

3)   Understanding leadership (see Adventure Playgrounds, Section 14.3e).

e.   **Designed Gathering Places.** Meeting and working settings of many types can be made from a variety of materials.

304 *Meeting spaces can be built into play structures.*

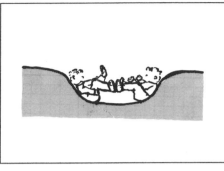

305 *Small group (duet, trio and quartet) meeting spots are important.*

306 *Worktables—a basic meeting and working facility.*

307 *Logs, rocks and other readymades.*

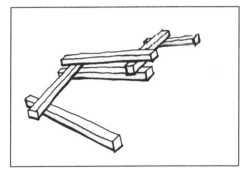

308 *A simple gathering place made from large timbers . . .*

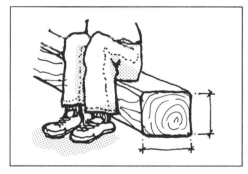

309 *. . . provides seating at a comfortable height.*

310 *A temporary "clubhouse."*

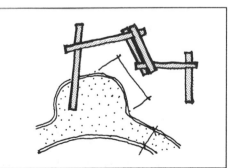

311 *Places should be accessible to wheelchair users from main path.*

312 *Physical layout can be introduced to a blind child with a 3D model.*

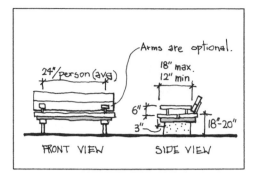

313 *Standard park bench with arms and back.*

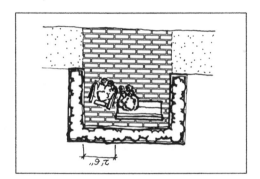

314 *Spaces beside benches for wheelchairs*

315 *Small platform for sitting and working on.*

20.4   Seating (Seattle, 1986)

a.   Provide seating at every playground, sand and water locations.

b.   All benches for adults should have arms and backs. Provisions for arm and back rests increase comfort. Arm rests are also helpful for getting into and out of seats and benches.

c.   Group benches in various configurations for sitting alone or in groups.

d.   Choose materials which do not retain heat or cold. Avoid rough materials or those that may splinter (Robinette, 1985).

e.   Sitting heights of 18—20 inches are preferable.

f.   Sitting surfaces below 12 inches width are uncomfortable for many adults. Likewise, widths beyond 18 inches become awkward for normal leg lengths.

g.   Provision for heel space of 3 inches makes rising from seated positions easier.

h.   Seat surfaces should be pitched to shed water.

i.   Include a space beside bench for wheelchair or stroller (about 30 inches wide for average wheelchair, Bunin, et al., 1980).

j.   Seating areas should be located adjacent to (but not obstructing) pathways and developed trails, particularly along inclines.

k.   Texture change in walkways adjacent to seating areas will cue the blind to location of benches.

l.   Benches that contrast in color from surroundings are more easily distinguished by visually impaired people.

20.5   Work Tables

a.   Provide tables with seating at every play area for eating, games and crafts. A covered table extends the life of the play area for misty or rainy weather (Seattle, 1986).

b.   Allow table widths of 18 inches and table lengths of 24 inches per person.

Table heights should average 29—33 inches.

c.   Round off or chamfer all exposed corners or sharp edges.

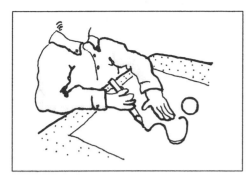

316 Smooth tabletops with rounded corners and no recesses should be provided.

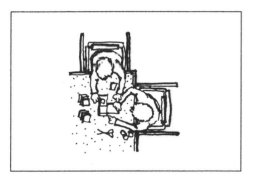

317 Table corners are good for pairs of children to work.

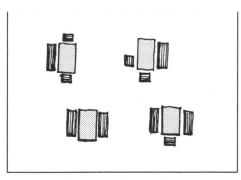

318 A mix of worktable configurations.

d. Keep table tops smooth with no recesses that might hold water or food particles.

e. Provide a clear lateral space, at least 30 inches wide, beneath the table to accommodate average width of a wheelchair. Provide 18 inches clear leg space under tables measured from outside of table top to nearest support of table leg.

f. The tops of accessible tables should extend past the legs by 19—25 inches at both ends with 29 inches minimum clearance between the underside of the table and the ground (Bunin, et al., 1980; Nordhaus, et al., 1984).

g. Provide a 4 ft. minimum clearance around the table at the accessible ends (5 ft. is preferred). Provide a 3 ft. minimum clearance at the sides (4 ft. preferred).

h. Bench and table materials should be comfortable to touch in hot and cold weather.

i. Tables and seating should be placed on level, hard surface pads.

j. Accessible tables should be located on level sites adjacent to a firm, stable-surfaced path (Bunin, et al., 1980)

20.6 Fireplaces and Grills

Fire is needed for a variety of program activities: candle making, leather branding, pottery work, etc.

Children are fascinated by fire, as most adults are. However, they have very few opportunities to learn how to handle it safely. They need to learn about it, its uses for heat and cooking, its dangers and ways to control it. Fire is also very soothing, much like water, in its ability to draw out our thoughts and create opportunities for quiet reflection (Schneekloth, 1985).

Make a special place for fire. Make sure children know the rules and how and when fire is permitted. Let the children cook, burn trash and leftover materials, sit around and tell stories and enjoy its warmth.

Obviously any fire on a playground must be under the constant supervision of an adult, but for many children who may rarely have the chance to see an open fire, the experience of gathering sticks, building, managing and extinguishing bonfires is both interesting and instructive. Cooking on campfires and barbecues is always popular and it is easy to make

319 *Vary table heights for different sized children.*

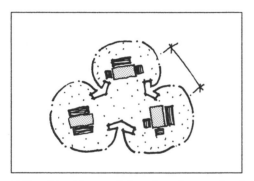

320 *Provide spatial variety for a mix of social distances.*

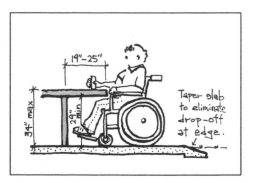

321 *Minimum table dimensions for adults and children in wheelchairs.*

a raised fireplace using bricks and a metal grill, so that chairbound children can join in frying sausages, hamburgers and pancakes (HAPA, 1978)

a. Grills are preferable to fireplaces. Cook surfaces should be 30—36 inches high and within the comfortable horizontal reach from a wheelchair (15 inches). If fireplaces are used, the grates should be raised 18—24 inches (Nordhaus, et al., 1984).

b. Use rotating grills; place them downwind from camping and seating areas. Handles should not conduct heat and must be easy to grasp.

c. Use a distinctive paving texture around grills and fireplaces as a warning to children and people with visual impairments.

d. Cooking surface height should accommodate both seated and standing people (Bunin, et al., 1980).

e. Some grills and fireplaces should be accessible by a firm, level path.

f. Front of grill should be flush with front of fireplace.

20.7   Water Faucets (Nordhaus, et al., 1984)

Water sources should be accessible to meeting and working areas and must be placed within reach of a person in a wheelchair or small child:

a. The height of faucet should be between 36 and 40 inches.

b. Faucets should be located on a hard surface pad adjacent to an accessible pathway. Use materials that will not become soft or slippery when wet. Do not use gravel!

c. Pads should be a minimum of 3 ft. wide by 4 ft. long.

d. Openings in drain gratings must be less than 1/2 inch.

e. Use lever type controls.

20.8   Drinking Fountains (Bunin, et al., 1980; Nordhaus, et al., 1984; Robinette, 1985)

Drinking fountains must be usable by a person in a wheelchair. Keep in mind that many people with disabilities require water frequently.

a. Place controls and spout at the front. Lever controls are preferred but large push buttons are also good.

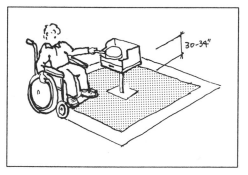

322 *Use a distinctive paving texture around grills as a warning to people with visual impairments and children.*

323 *Comfortable reach dimensions for children in wheelchairs.*

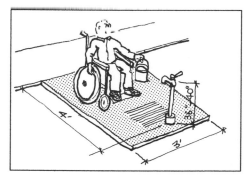

324 *Provide 3 feet by 4 feet hard surface pad at water hydrants. Use drain grates with openings of less than 1/2 inch.*

b.　　In order to accommodate reach of average wheelchair user, faucets should be 3 feet to 3 feet 4 inches high; for children 18—24 inches. Spouts no more than 36 inches above floor, 34 inches preferred.

c.　　Knee space 27 inches high should be provided.

d.　　Allow 30 inches by 48 inches of clear floor space.

e.　　Alcoves should be a minimum of 30 inches wide.

f.　　Fountains and faucets should be accessible by firm level paths and should not protrude into pathways.

g.　　Openings in drain should not exceed 1/2 inch.

h.　　Dual fountains accommodate children and people in wheelchairs as well as standing adults.

i.　　Lower fountain should be cantilevered 17—19 inches from upright or wall.

j.　　Provide a minimum 29 inches vertical clearance below fountain nozzle to give legroom for wheelchair users.

k.　　A minimum 18 inches wide paved area around outdoor fountains avoids both mud and puddles.

20.9　Trash Receptacles (Bunin, et al., 1980; Nordhaus, et al., 1984)

a.　　Trash receptacles should be located adjacent to meeting and working areas on a hard surface pad adjacent to an accessible pathway.

b.　　The opening mechanism must be within comfortable horizontal reach from a wheelchair with the opening 3 ft. or less above the ground. The opening mechanism should be operable with one hand.

c.　　Use trash receptacles which have rounded corners and are free from sharp edges.

d.　　Provide receptacles which can be used with a single arm motion.

e.　　Locate cans adjacent to, but not obstructing, trails and pathways to avoid hazards for the visually impaired.

f.　　In areas where scavenging animals pose a problem, use a cover mechanism that will allow trash to be thrown away with a single arm motion.

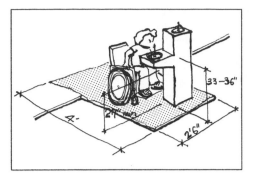

325 *Wall hung drinking fountains are preferred.*

326 *Trash receptacles should be adjacent to an accessible hard surface pathway.*

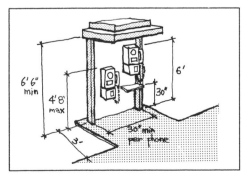

327 *Centrally located outdoor telephones are a critical play setting asset, especially as a safety device.*

g.   Locate litter receptacles at the points children are likely to enter or leave a play area, whether a marked formal entry or not (Seattle, 1986).

20.10   Outdoor Telephones (Robinette, 1984)

All groups of telephones should have at least one lower height telephone for use by wheelchair users.

Phones for the disabled should be no higher than 4 feet to the coin slots. Provisions for braille instructions, volume controls on headsets and push button dials are helpful for many individuals.

Provide adequate lighting on the underside of overhangs for nighttime use.

Package shelves are a helpful convenience to all people.

20.11   Toilets (Bunin, et al., 1980)

a.   Approaches to toilets should be graded or ramped with a slope no greater than 1:12.

b.   A 5 x 6 foot stall is accessible to most people and will permit a side transfer from wheelchair to toilet.

c.   Grab bars at least 3 feet 6 inches long to the side of the toilet and 3 feet long in back of the toilet will allow most people to transfer from wheelchair to toilet.

d.   Grab bars should be 1-1/2 inches diameter and no more than 1-1/2 inches from the wall (otherwise, arms can slip and be trapped between bar and wall).

   Note: There are enormous amounts of information on access and restroom facilities. Clear standards have been set and adopted. Therefore, the subject is not discussed here in detail (Cary, 1978; Harkness & Groom, 1976; Peoples Housing, 1983).

20.12   Electrical (Seattle, 1986)

All electrical conduit and wiring should be underground in and around a children's play area.

Provisions for utility metering, weatherproof electrical enclosures, transformers and the like should be located away from children's play areas and in locked vaults or utility rooms.

328 *Nighttime lighting is an important consideration in site planning.*

20.13 Lighting (Seattle, 1986)

The decision to include lighting in the play area must be made carefully. A lighted play area may give the illusion of safety and security after dark and invite children to play in an unsafe area.

Lighting is most appropriate at drop-off and pick-up points and restroom buildings.

20.14 Bike Racks (Seattle, 1986)

Provide bike racks at every play area. Evaluate play areas for their attraction for 6 to 12 year olds as an indicator of how many will be needed.

Locate bike racks in several places throughout each play area to minimize the chances of their falling into the path of play.

21. STORAGE SETTINGS

Facilities are needed to store play equipment and materials, loose parts and maintenance materials and equipment.

Planning Criteria

Play Value. Although not expressly intended, storage places are often settings for social interaction.

Programming Potential. Storage areas provide essential program support.

Play Leadership. Leaders must be able to manage storage facilities effectively.

Safety. They must be lockable and not climbable.

Risk Management. Careful checks must be made for toxic and inflammable materials.

Accessibility. It is critical that users have easy access to storage facilities including employees, play leaders, supervisors and children.

Integration. Not applicable.

Management. Policies which recognize the importance of secure storage facilities are needed. For example, the provision of "rentable" facilities for groups who deliver programs.

329 *Playstore: an attractive place serving many needs for security and storage.*

21.1 Function of Storage Facilities

Storage space should be designed as an integral part of an environment to facilitate all activities that go on within the space. Unfortunately, some manufacturers do not see a sufficient profit margin in the supply of storage. But this can be overcome by making it a multipurpose, integral play setting component.

Proper storage space helps to reduce clutter that can limit activities. Accessible storage areas that are clearly defined, labeled and properly placed will encourage children to initiate, carry out and clean up after their own activities (AEC, 1980).

Some children with disabilities use special equipment such as canes, walkers, wheelchairs or crutches. Storage for these items should be accessible to a child who might be crawling, standing or sitting. It should also be unobtrusive, so that it does not make the space look as if it is only for children with disabilities and unnecessarily increase the stigma attached to special equipment.

21.2 Outdoor Storage Cupboard

Size and arrangement will depend on the number of objects to be stored and the number of users. Storage cupboards can be incorporated into the design of playhouses or climbing structures for maximum accessibility. The outside of a storage unit can be made playable. It can be designed so that when it is empty, it can be used for play, but should not have play as its primary use.

Storage units should not be too deep; this encourages junking and makes it difficult to see what is inside. The aim is to make play materials as accessible as possible. If the store opens wide during play time, children will be able to select toys and put them back when done, making it easier to maintain and supervise. Air holes should be provided in case a child gets locked in.

Walk-in storage can be designed, but shelves must not be too deep and the passage must be kept uncluttered. Good storage can make all the difference to the "playability" of a playground.

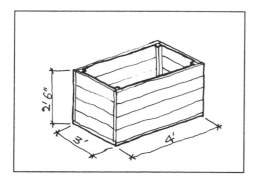

330 *Storage box.*

a. Overall dimensions will vary, depending on storage needs. Storage needs are almost universally underestimated. A minimal unit might measure 3 feet 6 inches deep by 6 feet wide.

b. Doors should be lockable. Pull-down or roll-down garage doors should be considered. Indeed, a garage type space is a good model to meet storage needs.

c. Shelves need sturdy support for heavy play equipment.

21.3   Storage Box (CMHC, 1978)

This box, combined with loose material and blocks, appeals to children's imaginations. Open side to the sky, it becomes a cave or hold of a ship; covered by boards, it is a secret place; with a trap door, a second story can be added; turned on its side with the addition of blocks, it may be a quick playhouse; open side down with short ladders or block steps, it is a lookout platform and on its end, an even higher lookout.

Exact dimensions are not important although the size should allow the box to be tipped and managed by three-year-olds. If it is too big, requiring adult help, the imaginative possibilities are limited; if it cannot be moved at all the play value is lost. A group of 20 children should have at least two such boxes. The aim should be to provide as many as space and budget permit.

21.4   Field Houses

Auxiliary spaces are needed outdoors as resource centers and program bases. Storage is an integral aspect. On most recreation sites, some kind of field house is necessary for the effective use of the outdoors. Several alternatives are possible. Buildings may be provided by the conversion of existing buildings or the construction of new ones. A third alternative is to import a prefabricated portable building. Some manufacturers include them as catalog items.

In most cases the building should be located near the geographical or activity center of the site.

Once constructed, a field house can be used as a protected garden space; or it can be lined with polyethylene to make a greenhouse; or roofed over to make a covered workshop or storage area; or lined with plywood to make a place for animals or a tool shed. It should be convertible from one use to another.

21.5   Storage Compounds

To store large items of equipment and bulky materials such as sawn lumber, a chainlink fenced enclosure can be used. An advantage of chainlink fencing is that it is almost indestructible—a property that can be used to great advantage in building high-security, indoor-outdoor places.

PART C:

PFA Guidelines in Action

22. PFA GUIDELINES IN ACTION: REBUILDING A PUBLIC PLAYGROUND AT FLOOD PARK , SAN MATEO COUNTY, CALIFORNIA

22.1 Overview

Flood Park was constructed in the 1930's as a WPA project for the citizens of San Mateo County. For fifty years it served the recreational needs of its constituents, operated by the San Mateo County Parks and Recreation Division of the Department of Environmental Management. In 1982, a new Master Plan for the park's future development was approved. When some of the community groups using the park raised concerns over the scope and direction of the plan, the County Board of Supervisors commissioned a study to address the needs of park users with respect to "whole access," that is, the accessibility of the park's facilities to all users. Project planners and designers were Moore Iacofano Goltsman and Lawrence Wight & Associates.

The goal of the Flood Park Barrier Free Access Design Project was to improve accessibility to the park's facilities and amenities for all people, with attention to the specific needs of three user groups:

a. Children with and without disabilities.

b. Adults with disabilities.

c. The elderly.

22.2 Community Needs Assessment

a. **Community Workshop.** In October 1985, a community workshop was held to bring together the park's various constituent groups. Flyers were distributed and telephone contact was made with recreation and community service organizations to publicize the workshop.

Participants defined the term "people with special needs" as those whose needs were not presently being met. They included:

1) Developmentally disabled.

2) Emotionally disabled.

3) Physically disabled (both temporarily and permanently).

4) Those with stamina limitations: the very young, the active elderly and the frail or institutionalized elderly.

5) Economically and culturally disadvantaged.

6) New residents (such as immigrants).

7) Hearing impaired (both from birth and adventitiously acquired).

8) Visually impaired.

In a further workshop segment, participants defined a "whole access" environment as one which:

1) Allowed physical and programmatical access to all user groups.

2) Provided safety, security and support.

3) Offered all users maximum independence.

4) Facilitated access to all of the park's "natural" experiences.

b. **Walking Tour.** The group was given maps and instructions for a specially prepared walking tour of the Flood Park site. Eleven stations, including the play areas, were set up to serve as observation points for an environmental assessment. At each station, participants were asked to jot down constraints and possibilities for whole access and general comments about the park's facilities and amenities.

c. **Community Workshop Results.** Participants' observations identified the following issues to be addressed:

1) Physical accessibility: surface materials, slope, pathway width, proximity of activity areas to vehicle loading areas, use of restroom facilities.

2) Program accessibility: use of activity areas by people with a wide range of disabilities; promotion of activities that permit participation by people with and without disabilities; maximization of experience of the natural settings for all park users.

3) Communication accessibility: development of a map and signage program to provide information about the historical aspects and locations of the park's facilities; provision of telecommunication devices for the hearing impaired.

d. **Children's Design Workshop.** A second workshop, for children of the Flood Park community, was held a week later, sponsored by PLAE, Inc.

The goals of the workshop were to demonstrate how park facilities might be utilized and to gather information directly from children about what types of elements they would like to see in the play areas.

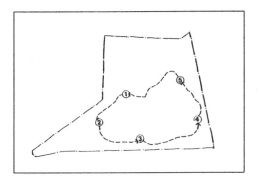

331   *Walking Tour Map*

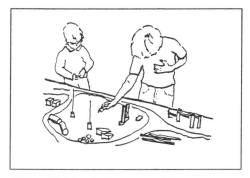

332   Children's design model.

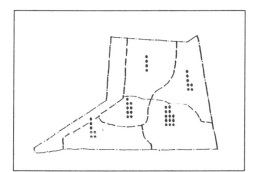

333   Behavior Map

A 4x8 foot model of the playground with basic outlines of pathways, buildings and existing play structures was set up. Two tables loaded with model-making parts (corks, straws, marshmallows, packing material, spagnum moss, rocks, toothpicks, netting, sticks, modeling clay and yarn) were set up, and children were encouraged to create models of their own play settings. Twenty children, including a minibus of children with disabilities, participated.

e.   **Children's Workshop Results.** The children proposed many imaginative play setting designs, ranging from practical to whimsical. Flags, pennants and banners were planted atop various structures, adding a circus feeling to the playground. Water features were prominent, with a stream flowing into a small pond where boats sailed. Another pond was for jumping in. Elevated structures with ramps were popular. The most complex play structure design was a net hidden by trees, shrubs and flowering bushes.

Adding a festive atmosphere to the event, multicolored, helium-filled balloons surrounded the model. Toward the end of the workshop, children attached notes to the balloons about their designs and asked other children who found the balloons to send in more ideas.

f.   **Use Analysis.** A complete analysis of the site was made, incorporating observations about current uses, vegetation, facilities, equipment and behavioral mapping data.

g.   **Accessibility Survey.** An accessibility survey was conducted to identify physical barriers in each use area. This information was compiled into a series of maps and analyzed for future park development.

h.   **Preliminary Design Alternatives.** Design alternatives were prepared based on the community workshop findings, analytical data and the accessibility survey, and presented for review by staff, parks commissioners and the Board of Supervisors.

i.   **Master Plan.** A play area master plan incorporating PFA guidelines was produced and a phasing plan developed. The site and a selection of setting designs are presented on the following pages.

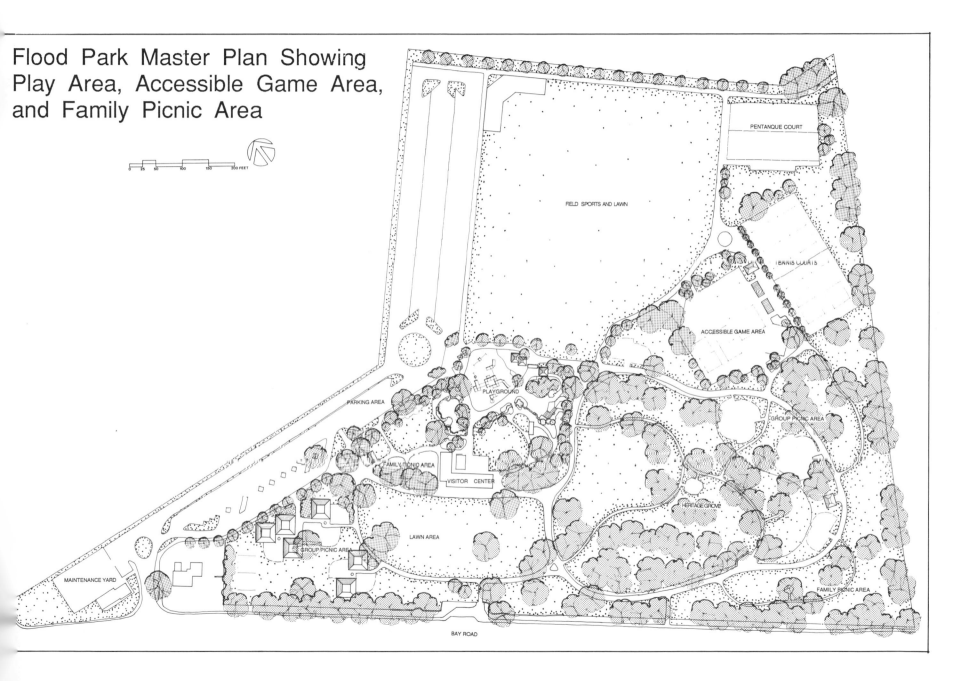

Flood Park Master Plan Showing
Play Area, Accessible Game Area,
and Family Picnic Area

0   25 50   100   150   200 FEET

MAINTENANCE YARD

PARKING AREA

FIELD SPORTS AND LAWN

PENTANQUE COURT

TENNIS COURTS

ACCESSIBLE GAME AREA

PLAYGROUND

FAMILY PICNIC AREA

VISITOR CENTER

GROUP PICNIC AREA

LAWN AREA

HERITAGE GROVE

GROUP PICNIC AREA

FAMILY PICNIC AREA

BAY ROAD

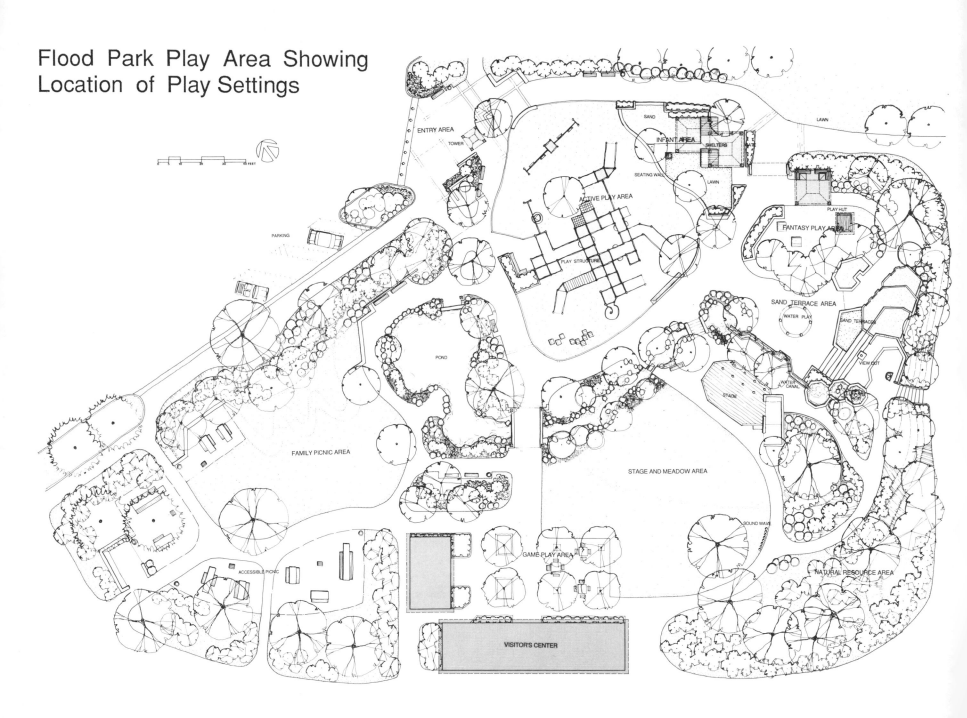

Flood Park Play Area Showing Location of Play Settings

ENTRY AREA

TOWER

SAND

INFANT AREA

SHELTERS

LAWN

SEATING WALL

LAWN

ACTIVE PLAY AREA

PLAY HUT

FANTASY PLAY AREA

PARKING

PLAY STRUCTURE

SAND TERRACE AREA

WATER PLAY

SAND TERRACE

POND

VIEW OUT

WATER CANAL

STAGE

FAMILY PICNIC AREA

STAGE AND MEADOW AREA

SOUND WAVE

ACCESSIBLE PICNIC

GAME PLAY AREA

NATURAL RESOURCE AREA

VISITOR'S CENTER

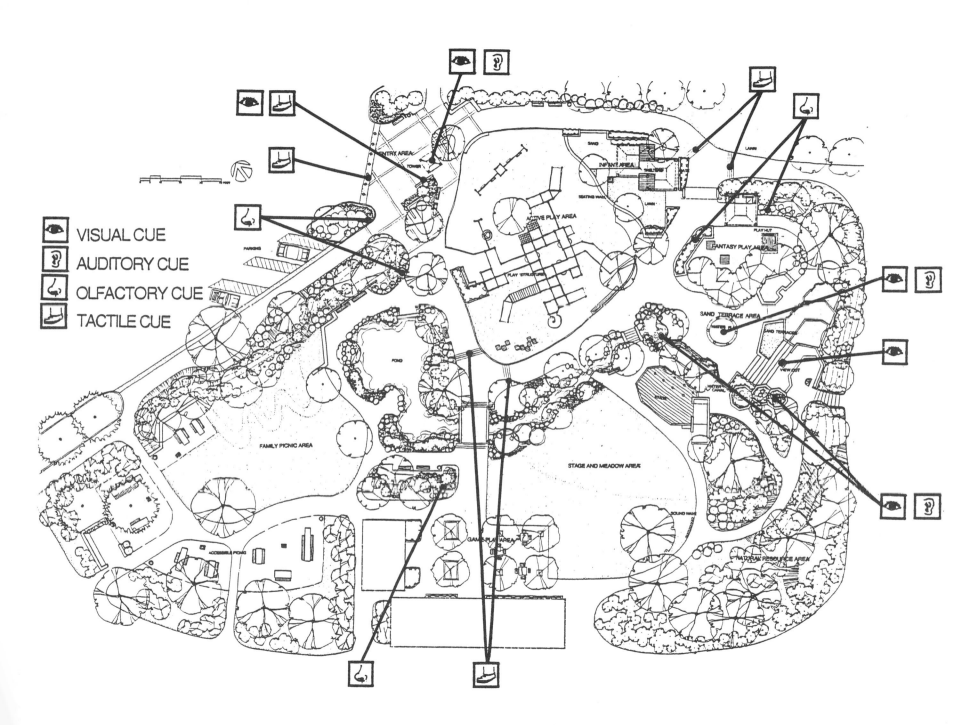

VISUAL CUE

AUDITORY CUE

OLFACTORY CUE

TACTILE CUE

Flood Park Play Area Entry Setting

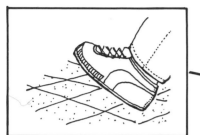

Textured pavement to indicate transition between sidewalk and park

Drop off zone in entry setting and close to picnic area

Parking for handicapped persons

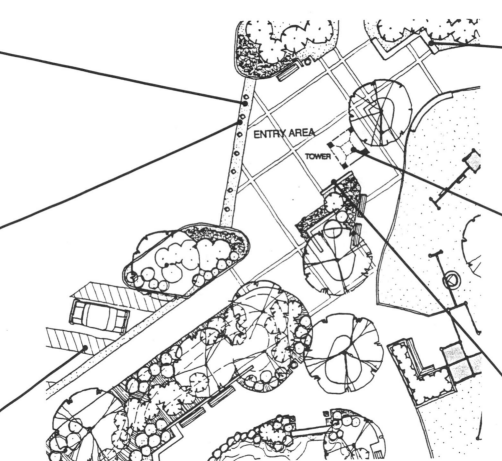

ENTRY AREA

TOWER

Seating wall provided as a gathering place

Landmark to enhance sense of arrival

Park information and user orientation displayed in entry setting

Entry Setting in Elevation

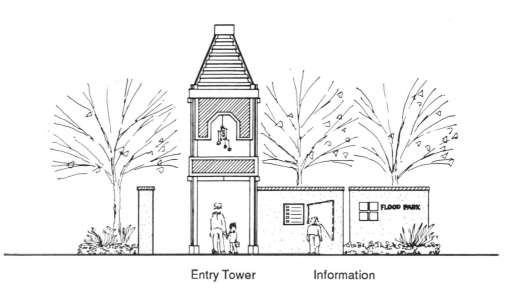

Entry Tower   Information

Section through Infant Play Setting

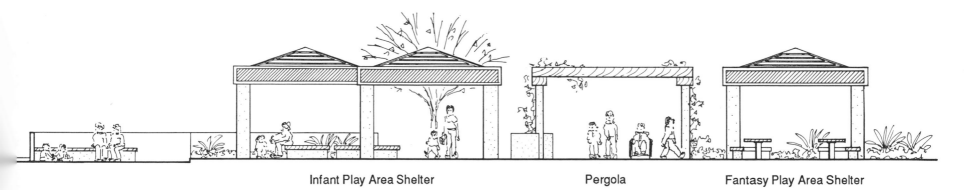

Infant Play Area Shelter   Pergola   Fantasy Play Area Shelter

Manufactured Equipment and Sand Settings

Resilient surface under swings

Play structure with spaces for socializing

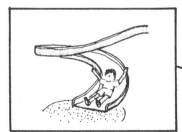

Spiral slides provide challenging play

Series of small platforms to sit, jump and play on

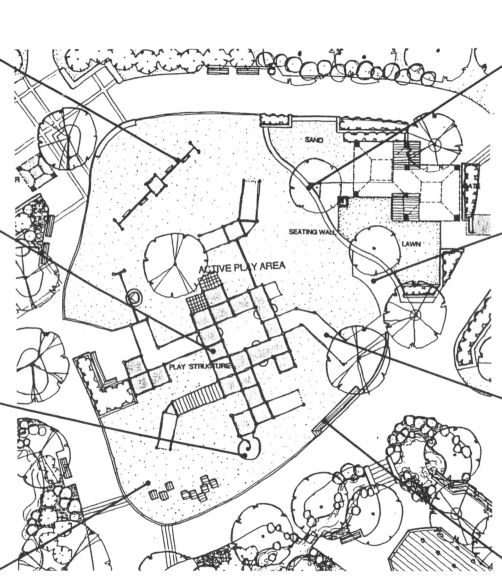

Seating wall at the boundary of infant play setting and manufactured equipment setting

Wheelchair access in close proximity to play action

Accessible setting with resilient surface

Gathering/meeting/working setting with small fence and counter

Infant Play Setting

Edge of sand area designed as a multipurpose space

Small water source provided to allow manipulation of sand

Small play structures as attraction to children

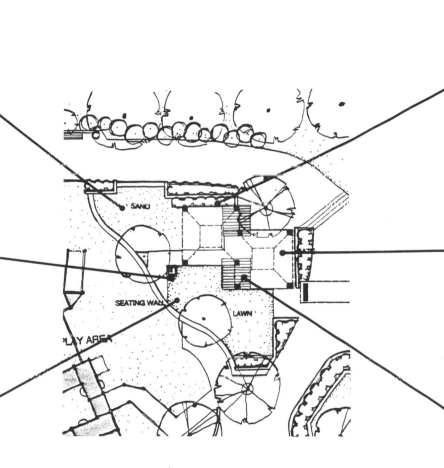

Landscaping treatment at edges

Sheltered sitting areas for parent supervision

Platform for sitting, resting and supporting objects

Fantasy Play Setting

Accessible worktables

Trees provide natural play materials in manipulative settings

Play hut gathering/meeting/ working setting

Vegetation as a play prop

Entry setting to play area

Diversity of play props encourages imaginative play

Small platform for sitting and working on

Existing trees for climbing

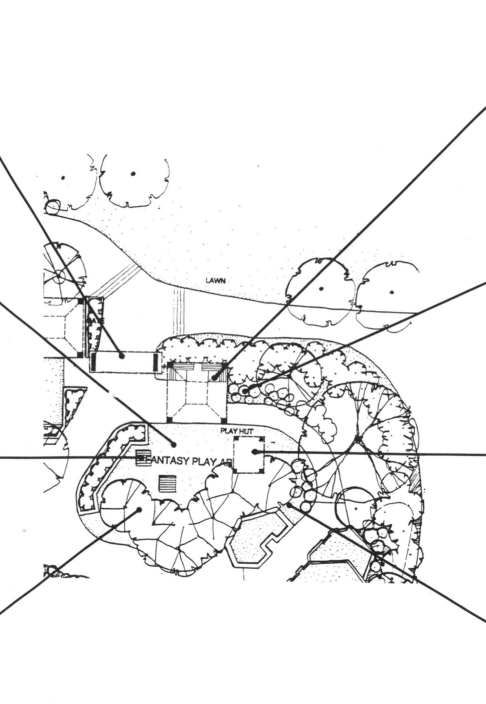

LAWN

PLAY HUT

FANTASY PLAY AR

Sand Setting

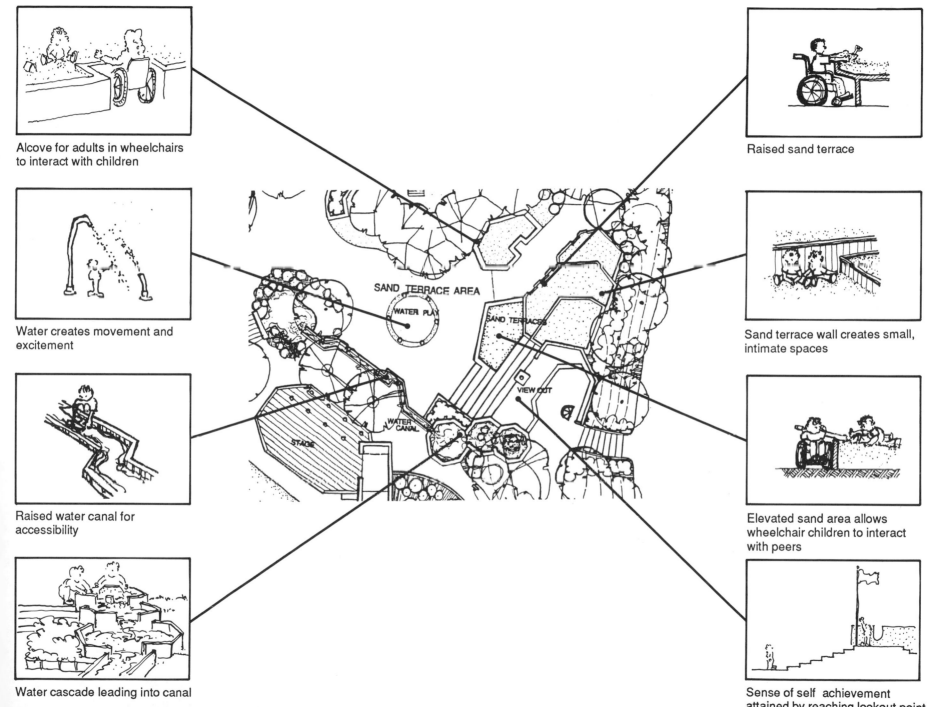

Alcove for adults in wheelchairs to interact with children

Water creates movement and excitement

Raised water canal for accessibility

Water cascade leading into canal

Raised sand terrace

Sand terrace wall creates small, intimate spaces

Elevated sand area allows wheelchair children to interact with peers

Sense of self achievement attained by reaching lookout point

SAND TERRACE AREA

WATER PLAY

SAND TERRACES

VIEW CUT

STAGE

WATER CANAL

Section through Sand Play and Water Settings

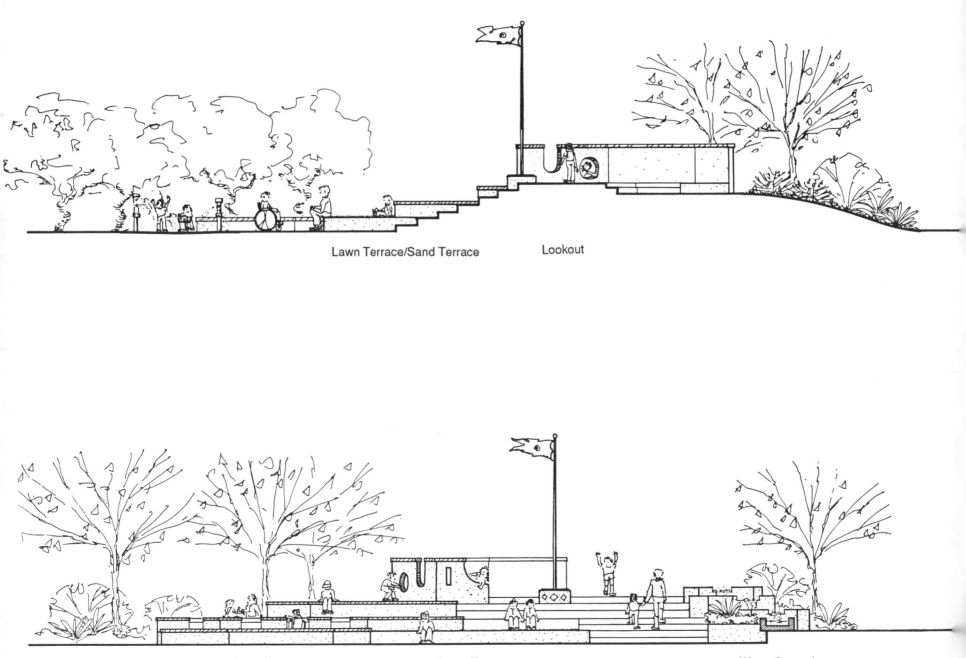

Lawn Terrace/Sand Terrace   Lookout

Sand Terrace   Lawn Terrace   Water Cascade

Staging and Multipurpose Meadow Settings

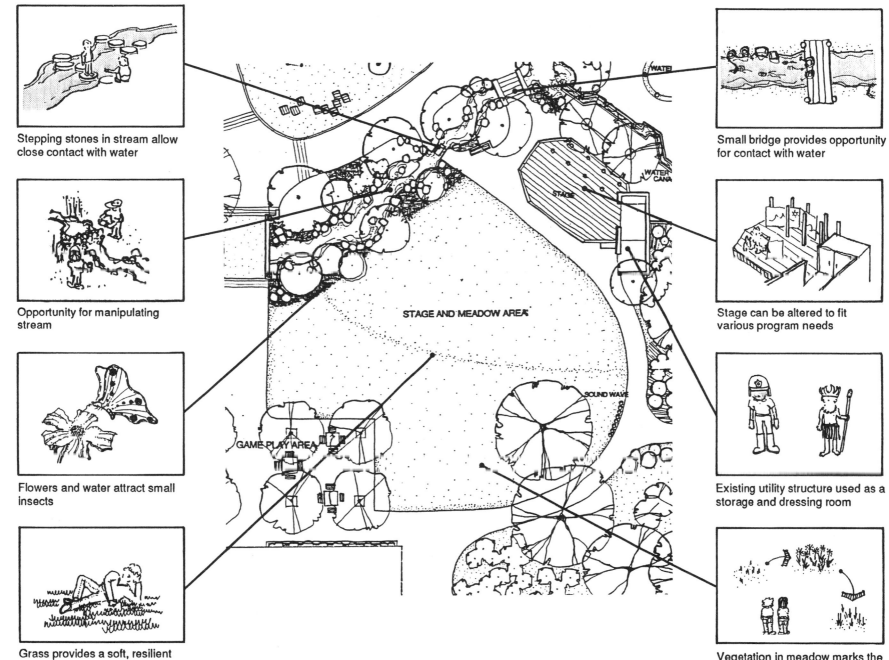

Stepping stones in stream allow close contact with water

Opportunity for manipulating stream

Flowers and water attract small insects

Grass provides a soft, resilient play surface

Small bridge provides opportunity for contact with water

Stage can be altered to fit various program needs

Existing utility structure used as a storage and dressing room

Vegetation in meadow marks the passing of the seasons

STAGE AND MEADOW AREA

GAME PLAY AREA

SOUND WAVE

STAGE

WATER CAN

Gathering/Meeting/Working Setting at Visitor's Center

Storage space for items used for play programs and events

Information about programs and community events

Use of visitor's center as a hub facility for an event

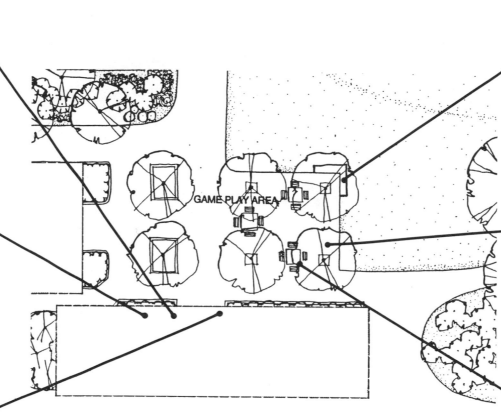

GAME PLAY AREA

Seating wall at the edge of the meadow and pavement

Tree canopy creates an intimate space

Small table used for games and socializing

Multiuse Family Picnic Setting

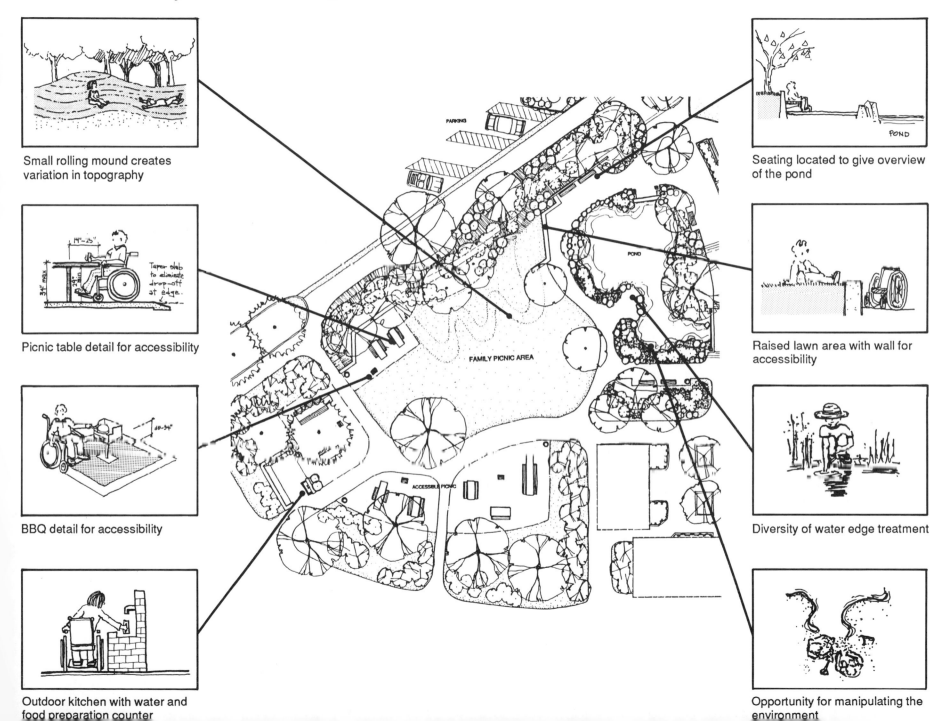

Small rolling mound creates variation in topography

Picnic table detail for accessibility

BBQ detail for accessibility

Outdoor kitchen with water and food preparation counter

Seating located to give overview of the pond

Raised lawn area with wall for accessibility

Diversity of water edge treatment

Opportunity for manipulating the environment

Multipurpose Accessible Games Setting

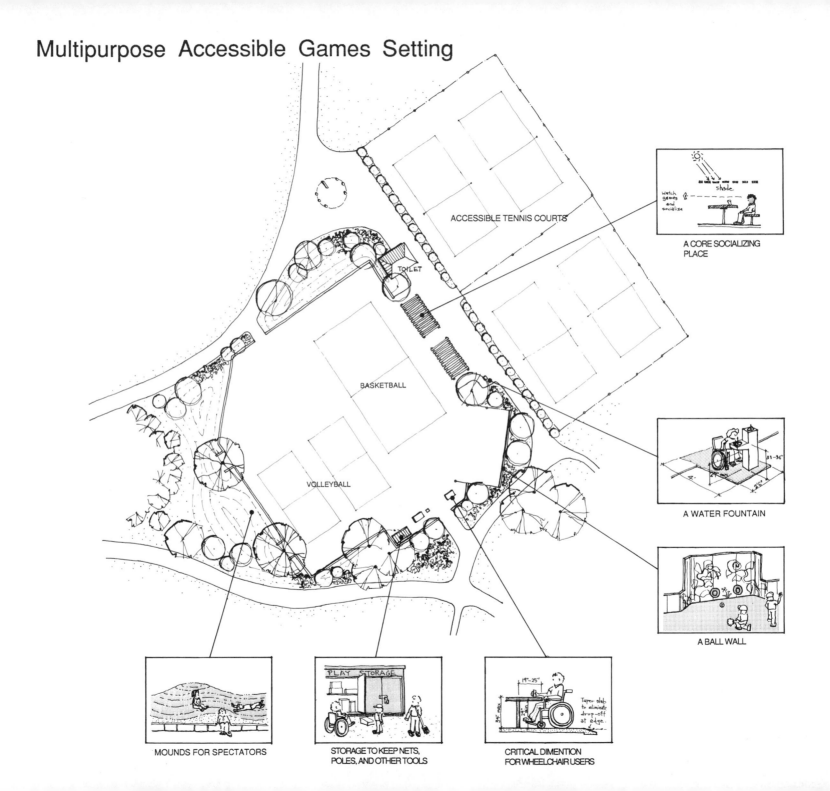

ACCESSIBLE TENNIS COURTS

TOILET

BASKETBALL

VOLLEYBALL

A CORE SOCIALIZING PLACE

A WATER FOUNTAIN

A BALL WALL

MOUNDS FOR SPECTATORS

STORAGE TO KEEP NETS, POLES, AND OTHER TOOLS

CRITICAL DIMENTION FOR WHEELCHAIR USERS

Play Station Locations

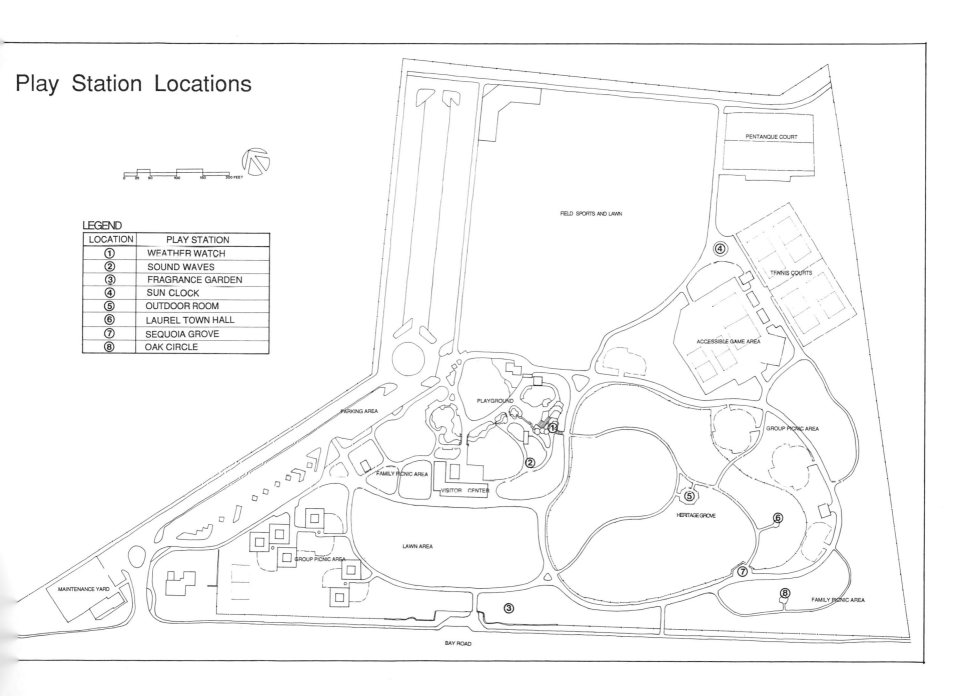

LEGEND

LOCATION	PLAY STATION
①	WEATHER WATCH
②	SOUND WAVES
③	FRAGRANCE GARDEN
④	SUN CLOCK
⑤	OUTDOOR ROOM
⑥	LAUREL TOWN HALL
⑦	SEQUOIA GROVE
⑧	OAK CIRCLE

PENTANQUE COURT

FIELD SPORTS AND LAWN

TENNIS COURTS

ACCESSIBLE GAME AREA

PARKING AREA

PLAYGROUND

GROUP PICNIC AREA

FAMILY PICNIC AREA

VISITOR CENTER

HERITAGE GROVE

LAWN AREA

GROUP PICNIC AREA

MAINTENANCE YARD

FAMILY PICNIC AREA

BAY ROAD

0 25 50 100 150 200 FEET

Play Station

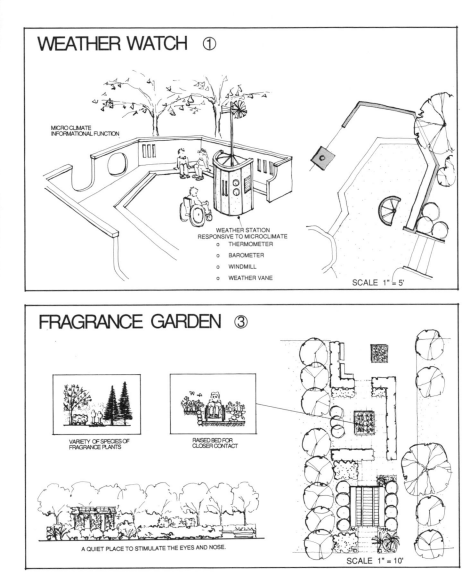

WEATHER WATCH ①

MICRO CLIMATE
INFORMATIONAL FUNCTION

WEATHER STATION
RESPONSIVE TO MICROCLIMATE
- o THERMOMETER
- o BAROMETER
- o WINDMILL
- o WEATHER VANE

SCALE 1" = 5'

FRAGRANCE GARDEN ③

VARIETY OF SPECIES OF
FRAGRANCE PLANTS

RAISED BED FOR
CLOSER CONTACT

A QUIET PLACE TO STIMULATE THE EYES AND NOSE.

SCALE 1" = 10'

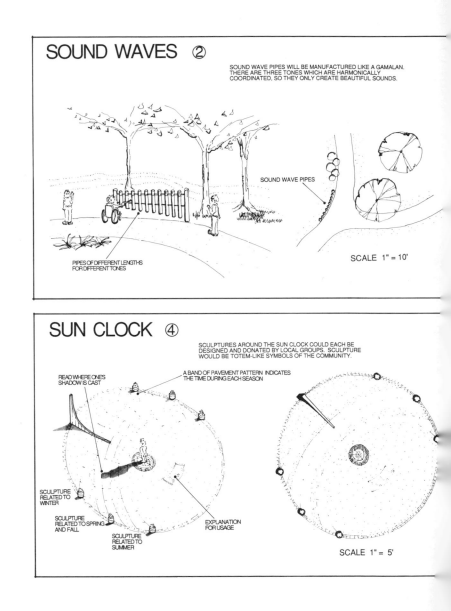

SOUND WAVES ②

SOUND WAVE PIPES WILL BE MANUFACTURED LIKE A GAMALAN.
THERE ARE THREE TONES WHICH ARE HARMONICALLY
COORDINATED, SO THEY ONLY CREATE BEAUTIFUL SOUNDS.

SOUND WAVE PIPES

PIPES OF DIFFERENT LENGTHS
FOR DIFFERENT TONES

SCALE 1" = 10'

SUN CLOCK ④

SCULPTURES AROUND THE SUN CLOCK COULD EACH BE
DESIGNED AND DONATED BY LOCAL GROUPS. SCULPTURE
WOULD BE TOTEM-LIKE SYMBOLS OF THE COMMUNITY.

READ WHERE ONE'S
SHADOW IS CAST

A BAND OF PAVEMENT PATTERN INDICATES
THE TIME DURING EACH SEASON

SCULPTURE
RELATED TO
WINTER

SCULPTURE
RELATED TO SPRING
AND FALL

SCULPTURE
RELATED TO
SUMMER

EXPLANATION
FOR USAGE

SCALE 1" = 5'

OUTDOOR ROOM ⑤

PLACE FOR GATHERING IN THE MIDDLE OF HERITAGE GROVE.

INFORMATION ABOUT NATURAL SYSTEM.

PLACE FOR LECTURE OF NATURE STUDY PROGRAM

DIRECTIONAL SIGN

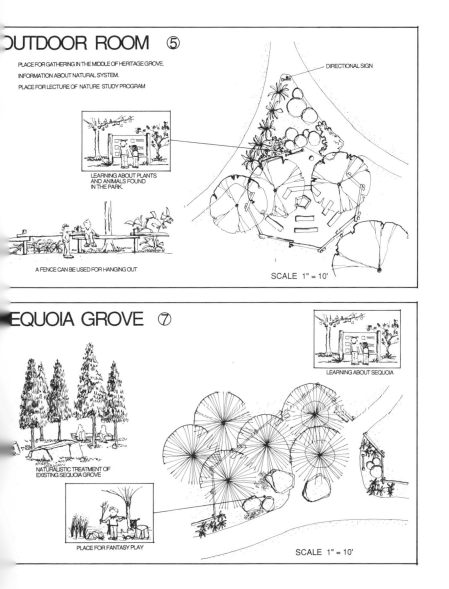

LEARNING ABOUT PLANTS
AND ANIMALS FOUND
IN THE PARK.

A FENCE CAN BE USED FOR HANGING OUT

SCALE 1" = 10'

LAUREL TOWN HALL ⑥

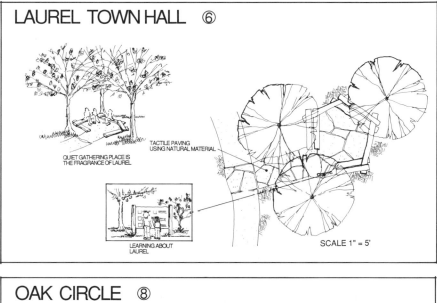

TACTILE PAVING
USING NATURAL MATERIAL

QUIET GATHERING PLACE IS
THE FRAGRANCE OF LAUREL

LEARNING ABOUT
LAUREL

SCALE 1" = 5'

SEQUOIA GROVE ⑦

LEARNING ABOUT SEQUOIA

NATURALISTIC TREATMENT OF
EXISTING SEQUOIA GROVE

PLACE FOR FANTASY PLAY

SCALE 1" = 10'

OAK CIRCLE ⑧

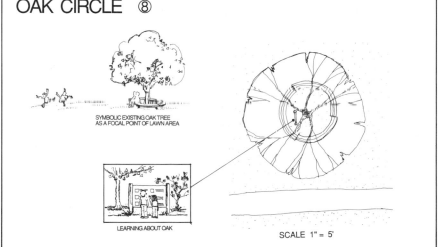

SYMBOLIC EXISTING OAK TREE
AS A FOCAL POINT OF LAWN AREA

LEARNING ABOUT OAK

SCALE 1" = 5'

Accessibility Levels, Pathway Materials and Slope

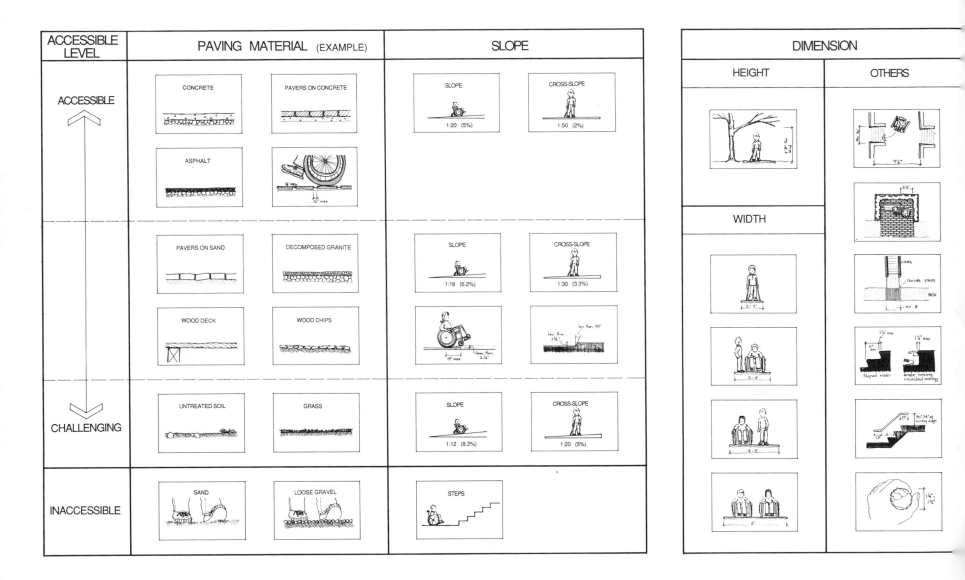

ACCESSIBLE LEVEL	PAVING MATERIAL (EXAMPLE)		SLOPE	
ACCESSIBLE	CONCRETE	PAVERS ON CONCRETE	SLOPE — 1:20 (5%)	CROSS-SLOPE — 1:50 (2%)
	ASPHALT			
	PAVERS ON SAND	DECOMPOSED GRANITE	SLOPE — 1:16 (6.2%)	CROSS-SLOPE — 1:30 (3.3%)
	WOOD DECK	WOOD CHIPS		
CHALLENGING	UNTREATED SOIL	GRASS	SLOPE — 1:12 (8.3%)	CROSS-SLOPE — 1:20 (5%)
INACCESSIBLE	SAND	LOOSE GRAVEL	STEPS	

DIMENSION	
HEIGHT	OTHERS
WIDTH	

Pathway Improvement Plan

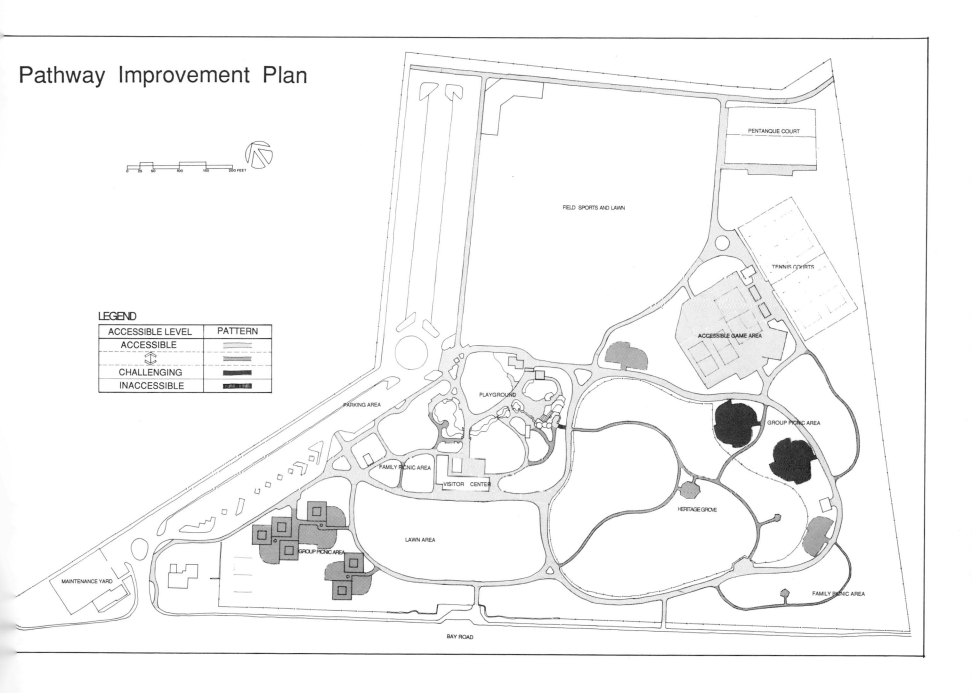

0 25 50 100 150 200 FEET

LEGEND

ACCESSIBLE LEVEL	PATTERN
ACCESSIBLE	
CHALLENGING	
INACCESSIBLE	

PENTANQUE COURT

FIELD SPORTS AND LAWN

TENNIS COURTS

ACCESSIBLE GAME AREA

PLAYGROUND

PARKING AREA

GROUP PICNIC AREA

FAMILY PICNIC AREA

VISITOR CENTER

HERITAGE GROVE

GROUP PICNIC AREA

LAWN AREA

MAINTENANCE YARD

FAMILY PICNIC AREA

BAY ROAD

22.3   Play Setting Evaluation and Design Criteria

Based on the results of the Flood Park community workshops and a design program of play settings, reflecting the opportunities and constraints of the site, a plan checklist (with the additional criteria of maintenance and cost) was developed. This checklist then became a decision-making tool to weigh the trade-offs required for each setting before moving into the design development phase. The checklist is presented on the following pages and *can* be adapted as a design programming tool for other play settings.

FLOOD PARK PLAY AREA PLAN CHECKLIST

SETTING TYPE	PLANNING CRITERIA					
	Play Value	Program Potential	Safety	Mgt/Maint.	Access/Integration	Issues
Pedestrian Entrance. • Tower. • Map. • Signage. • Seating. • Vegetation.	Orientation. Historical. Tactile map of park. Understand aqua-duct connection to Hetch Hetchy Resevoir.	History Play Station.	Bollards to separate pedestrians from cars. Map protected with shade.	Vegetation. Signage upkeep.	Tactile map, signage with raised letters, tower as landmark with wind chimes as audio cue. Full wheelchair access.	Tower right-of-way. Art work commission.
Pathways • Major. • Minor. • Trails.	Wide enough for circulation & wheeled toy play.	Self programmed.	Fire truck ac-cess. 5' narrow paths. Edge detailing, signs/seating off pathway.	Clear pathways, good repair. Vehicle policy.	Level pathways. Change in ground texture at cross roads and at signage & seating. Seating max. every 100'.	Bicycles, skateboards, cars on paths. Cart checkout?
Climbing Area • Manf. Equip. • Slides. • Swings. • Linked structures.	Active play, large muscle, graduated chal-lenge for ages 3—12, easier smaller events on one side.	Preprogrammed play events.	Protected fall zones within & around equip. Seating for adults to supervise. Sand under large equip. 12" deep.	Sand off paths. Clean sand daily. Safety checks, monthly detailed inspection of equipment.	Grab bars and rails, textured platforms at height changes, all after a corner or with defined texture accessible, tire swing with resilient surfaces, including entrance of structure.	Relocation of existing equipment.

FLOOD PARK PLAY AREA PLAN CHECKLIST

SETTING TYPE	PLANNING CRITERIA					
	Play Value	Program Potential	Safety	Mgt/Maint.	Access/Integration	Issues
Infant/Toddler Area • Sand Play. • Water Play. • Sensory Path. • Equipment. • Signage. • Seating. • Vegetation.	Exploratory, environmental awareness, manipulation, motor skills, social skills.	Parental guidance.	Soft surfaces, no glass or other harmful items. Gates on entrance/exit. Appropriate vegetation. Nontoxic materials.	Sand contained. Animal droppings cleaned daily. Check for harmful substances.	Adjacent to large play area so parents can view children .Older and younger children can see each other. Multisensory cues.	
Fantasy Play Area • Picnic/worktable. • Clubhouse. • Small stages. • Vegetation.	Dramatic skills, social skills, role play, quiet play.	High potential. Child programmed.	Careful selection of grasses & natural ground covers. Observable from a distance.	Wild grass, rough cut, no large power mower.	Dirt pathway, clubhouse with wind chimes in roof for audio cue. Accessible club house.	
Sand Play Area • Raised sand amphitheater. • Sand shelves.	Fine motor & social skills. Dramatic, creative manipulative play.	Self programmed.	Edge detailing. Sitting steps 24" wide, hard sur–face. Shelf visible 6" above sand.	Keeping sand in boxes. Sand swept off steps.	Seat access at different heights in center of activity area. Edge detailing provides cues. Wheelchair access. Universal play activity.	

FLOOD PARK PLAY AREA PLAN CHECKLIST

SETTING TYPE	PLANNING CRITERIA					
	Play Value	Program Potential	Safety	Mgt/Maint.	Access/Integration	Issues
Play Mound • Seating. • Topography. • Vegetation.	Overview. Quiet play.	Child programmed. Flood Park Flag contest.	Retaining wall. Edge details.	Erosion potential. Ground cover carefully. maintained	Multiple means of access. Landmark helps to orient, gives overview of area. Good from infant to senior, across disabilities. Slope 1:20.	
Water Play • Spray	Sensory stimulation Social skills.	Child programmed.	Potable water. Nonslip surfaces.	Clear drains.	Fully accessible, lever handles.	
Water • Spring. • Waterfall. • Raised chute. • Stream. • Pond.	Exploratory. Sensory stimulation. Social skills. Environmental education.	Child-programmed, self-programmed, high programming potential.	Water depth. Edge details. Pond surface, observable from a distance.	Glass in water. Water quality. Filtration system. Daily check. Wild life mgt. for pond.	Access at various points and at various heights. variety of water experiences at varying levels of accessibility. Quiet to active play across ages.	Chlorination. Natural system most important design element for play.
Stage Area • Platform. • Adobe Bldg. • Lawn. • Storage.	Dramatic, social skills. Community place.	High programming potential.		Lawn mowing.	Stage access with ramp 1:10 over 15'. Access over lawn difficult.	Electrical wiring in adobe building.

FLOOD PARK PLAY AREA PLAN CHECKLIST

SETTING TYPE	PLANNING CRITERIA					
	Play Value	**Program Potential**	**Safety**	**Mgt/Maint.**	**Access/Integration**	**Issues**
Table Games • Seating. • Vegetation. • Surfacing.	Intergenerational. Problem solving. Social skills.	Self programmed.	Loose parts. Hard nonslip surface.	Loose parts.	Loose seats for wheel-chair access, pedestal base on tables.	Check out games in ranger area.
Outdoor Kitchen • Sinks. • Counter.	Support area for barbecue.			Keeping it clean.	Sink and counter height.	
Family Picnic • Tables. • Grills.	Support area. Social skills.	Family programmed.	Grill area.	Keeping it clean.	Loose benches for wheelchair access at any point. Grills with place to hold platters.	Loose benches.
Restrooms • Men. • Women.	Support area.		Observable.	Keeping them clean.	Fully accessible.	Prebuilt modular systems.
Planting • Trees. • Shrubs. • Flowers.	Environmental education. Play props. Fantasy play.	Child programmed. High programming potential.	Observable. Nontoxic, nonallergenic.	Pruning, leaf pick up, protection for new vegetation.	Branch overhang height. Ability to get into and near vegetation.	

PART D:

Programming and Management

23. PLAY PROGRAMMING

This chapter provides an overview of play programming for integration of all children. At a future date, the subject will be presented in detail as a separate Play For All publication.

Play opportunities should provide challenging experiences for all children in safe, healthy, stimulating and accessible environments. Creating a fully integrated community recreation program is difficult but not impossible to achieve if the public agency makes a commitment to implement such a program.

23.1 Case Study Program

Over the past seven years, PLAE, Inc., of Berkeley, California, has developed a prototype program as an action-research effort to discover how to integrate children with disabilities in a program serving over 1200 children, one third with developmental, physical, emotional or learning disabilities. The ages of the children range from six to sixteen. Several conclusions have been reached as a result of this experience (Iacofano, et al., 1985):

a. The greater the range of outdoor settings the wider the assortment of programmed activities that can be supported.

b. A broad range of activities allows more children of different ages and ability levels to participate at the same time.

c. A programmatic base in the community arts, instead of sports, offers many opportunities for participation by all children.

d. A thematic approach to workshop activities, in combination with skilled play leadership, provides a structure which allows children to work together through dramatic and fantasy play. It also helps adults relate positively to the program and to better understand its value.

e. The "play value" of play settings is highly dependent on how they are programmed and managed, especially for the integration of children with disabilities.

23.2   Play Programming Criteria for All Children

Based on the above findings, PLAE has developed a management model for providing direct community recreation services to all children. The model takes into consideration the range of settings, the program of activities, play leadership and the physical setting.

a.   **Environmental Diversity.** A variety of physical settings must be provided to support varied programming and to accommodate different leader abilities and skills.

b.   **Environmental Control.** Both children and staff must have control over their environment. Lockable storage, use of restroom facilities, large trash receptacles, electricity and water are necessary.

c.   **Defensible Space.** For leaders to feel free enough to take risks and be adventurous in programming, the environment must be easily supervised. Play leaders need to see who is entering or leaving the activity area and be able to locate children easily. However, this does not mean that the environment must be totally open or without walls, buffers and other subdivisions.

d.   **Adaptability/Flexibility.** Programs must remain open to changing situations and the individual needs of participants within a structural framework.

e.   **Arts-based Programming** provides a context for innovation, creativity and the discovery of one's relationship to the world.

f.   **Choice of activities.** A variety of activities are required to engage and capture children's imaginations:

1)   Activities that make everyone a star.

2)   Trust-building activities.

3)   Risk-taking activities.

4)   Activities that promote sharing and cooperation.

5)   Activities that allow for creative expression.

6)   Activities that are fun!

7)   Group problem solving.

8)   Construction activities.

9)   Activities that are "larger than life."

g. **Fantasy.** As children's natural springboard into play, fantasy stimulates imagination and creativity. The conscious incorporation of fantasy into a program supports and nourishes children's natural ability.

h. **Spontaneity.** Providing play props, loose parts and a variety of scrap materials that can be transformed into something else allows children to take an activity initiated by the play leader and expand on it. For example, with simple building materials, children can create structures around which elaborate fantasy dramas may unfold.

i. **Product.** Products are an important part of the play experience They show accomplishment. Products can be ends in themselves or they can become parts of a larger group project such as a circus performance.

j. **Cooperation.** A team approach to projects helps children work together. By assigning individual responsibility for parts of a project, children have an individual accomplishment which leads to a group product. A balance is struck between encouraging the development of self-potential and fostering community awareness and positive social interaction.

k. **A Creative Atmosphere.** The play environment is a place to experiment, take risks and make mistakes.

l. **Play Leadership.** Play leaders and animators are the backbone of any play program. They are highly skilled professionals trained in the use of creative arts and physical settings to create play events that are stimulating and challenging for a wide variety of children. Animators create a context for fantasy and dramatic play by introducing activity scores, scripts, props and loose parts that help involve children and facilitate use of the environment to their fullest potential.

Animators can provide a positive role model for all children, modeling qualities such as autonomy, practical skills, cooperation, flexibility, willingness to listen and the desire to change and grow.

m. **Openness.** Integration of all children is promoted as disabled children and non-disabled children are involved in the same program. Accommodations for children with a variety of disabilities are present and are readily made when leaders are able to adapt a tool or an activity on the spot.

n.   **Empowerment.** Play programs can empower children to utilize their full capabilities and to learn how to participate in the making of decisions that affect them.

o.   **Behavior Management.** An organized program structure is important to children's safe play experiences. Positive limits can be set and children can participate in solving problems and taking responsibility for their own behavior.

p.   **Communication.** Staff that works well together and communicates openly contributes to making an environment where children feel safe. Children benefit from seeing positive interactions between staff.

q.   **Parent/Staff Interaction.** A healthy relationship between parents and staff is essential for supporting child development.

r.   **Setting, Program and Leadership.** Physical environment, program and leadership must be managed as a system: the environment sets the stage and context for program activities for execution by creative play leaders. This interaction of physical setting, program and leadership is the heart of the management model.

24. RISK MANAGEMENT STRATEGIES

This chapter is a revised and updated version of a paper that originally appeared in Children's Environments Quarterly (Moreland, et al., 1985).

Safety, security and liability have become major factors in determining the quality of children's environments and play programs. Swings and suspended nets are being eliminated from some playgrounds. Thickly planted areas, typically used by children for hide-and-seek games, for exploration of nature and other creative activities, are being omitted from the design of new play spaces to permit higher visibility for adult supervisors. Installed playground equipment has come under intense scrutiny and design standards have been called for by consumer agencies and federal, state and local governments.

Rising insurance rates have forced many play and recreational programs out of business while others have been curtailed. Recent concerns about potential child abuse in child care programs have focused attention on the qualifications and experience of program staff. When children with special needs are enrolled in a program, special safety concerns create even more anxiety for those responsible.

24.1 Who is Responsible?

Given this growing plethora of pressures on organized play, one may seriously ask whether professionally run programs are going to be possible at all in the future. The outcome lies clearly in the hands of those directly involved: public and private programming agencies, play equipment manufacturers, designers, equipment specifiers and the insurance industry.

In the forefront are the public agencies responsible for both programs and settings. Their ability to engage in successful risk management will largely determine whether quality play programming has a future; or whether it will be overcome by the growing number and size of liability suits; or whether it will simply fade away, by default, as creative staff become disenchanted with the many bureaucratic rules, regulations and conservative attitudes endemic of risky situations.

24.2 What is Risk Management?

Where does the risk management concept come from? It is a relatively new subject, even on the broader frontiers of management practice. It is an excellent example of contemporary philosophy of management as both science and art. The key assumption is that any life worth living is a risky business. One cannot learn except by taking risks: "Nothing ventured, nothing gained," the saying goes. However, the other critical assumption is that risk is not the same as danger or hazard.

The objective of proper risk management is to ensure that hurt, injury or accident is **prevented**; not to eliminate risk, but to reduce the potential for negative consequences to acceptable levels. Accidents cannot be eliminated entirely. Tragedies do occur. The natural environment, human relations, life itself, are to some degree, by their very nature, unpredictable. Chance (conception and birth is the obvious example) and truly "unforeseen circumstances" will always be present. Risk management is a strategy of "reasonable means" to prevent tragedy while allowing risk.

24.3   The Criterion of Reasonableness

What constitutes reasonableness is the crucial judgement: getting hit by a car is a common cause of serious injury and death among children, yet even the most modest suggestions for control (low speed limits, diverters, necked crossings, cul-de-sacs, speed bumps, etc.) are usually met with howls of protest by adult drivers who evidently feel them to be quite unreasonable suggestions in relation to saving a few children's lives (Appleyard, 1981). Like other social issues, they do not strike home except at a personal level. A highly visible campaign in the Netherlands to control residential traffic was started by a journalist whose own child had been killed by a car. The campaign was successful because, in this case, people were eventually **persuaded** that the traffic control proposals were reasonable.

24.4   Risk Management is both Art and Science

This is where the **art** of risk management comes in: the preparation of convincing arguments, the use of telling examples, the implementation of effective community/public relations. These strategies must stimulate all concerned to be involved in helping to define "reasonableness," Once defined, they must be made operational as management objectives and properly communicated back to the community.

The **science** of risk management also enters the picture, providing descriptive facts and figures of accidents and incidents, where they occur and under what circumstances (information that is still pitifully sparse).

24.5   Risk Management in Practice

Successful programs for children with and without disabilities depend on a complex environment which offers diverse opportunities for stimulating and challenging play

(Goltsman, Moore & Iacofano, 1982). Paradoxically, the elements of a complex environment carry greater inherent risks, both real and perceived. A manipulative environment gives children and program leaders objects which can be used for creative play activities but which may be especially difficult to control safely (Beckwith, 1985), particularly when such items are introduced spontaneously. Desirable environmental and programmatic elements from a child development perspective appear to be in direct opposition to safety and liability concerns. The purpose of risk management is to mitigate this apparent conflict. A proactive approach depends primarily on the **prevention** of incidents which jeopardize the safety and security of the child. Key strategies are as follows:

a.   **Reporting Incidents.** For incident reporting and management purposes, four types of situations in which safety and security problems (incidents) may arise have been defined:

   1)   **Child-to-Self:** Situations in which the individual child experiences an accident through interaction with the environment. Examples include falling down while running, and falling from a tree or wall.

   2)   **Child-to-Child:** Situations in which two of more children provoke harm or injury to one another. Examples include fighting, accidents during games, and the pressuring of children by peers into risky behaviors.

   3)   **Adult-to-Child:** Situations in which the health and safety of a child are jeopardized by actions taken or not taken by an adult in charge. Examples include physical or sexual child abuse and accidents due to negligence.

   4)   **Outside Influences to Child:** Situations in which factors enter from outside the play environment to affect the safety and security of the child. Examples include unauthorized persons entering the environment, litter and pollution and roaming animals.

b.   **Incident Data Analysis.** An evaluation process should be developed to determine where accidents occur and if they are environmentally related. Questions should be asked about where the accident occured, who was involved, the time of day, the nature of the injury and what actions were taken after the accident.

c.   **Shared Environmental Control.** Control over the physical environment is essential to the safety and security of children. Because program settings are often on public park or school property, use of the site must be negotiated and relationships with other programmed activities must be maintained. By inviting the involvement of others, potentially difficult or dangerous interactions are minimized and the situation is used to build up community support.

d.   **"Defensible" Program Space.** To provide further for the safety of children during program events, a more decentralized use of the site is required. "Play stations" can be established with individual play leaders at each station to supervise smaller groups of children. In this sense, the territory occupied by the program can be defined and monitored more naturally (Newman, 1972).

e.   **Shared Site Maintenance.** Maintaining the program site to eliminate potential hazards to children should be the joint responsibility of the programming organization and the community. In complex settings, a finer, more subtle approach to routine maintenance is often required than that normally provided for conventional equipment settings. Willing play leaders who understand how the environment functions as program space can support a nonjanitorial approach to maintenance and even engage users in the process.

Children can participate in occasional "Trash Pickup Contests"—essentially games where children work cooperatively to gather bottles, cans, paper and other litter.

f.   **Supervision.** Effective supervision of children's outdoor play activities is the key to both safety and the maximization of play opportunities.

Supervision goes beyond the passive overseeing of activities to include provision of activities which stimulate the imagination, promote the integration of all children and extend the learning experiences inspired by children's play.

Play leaders must serve as positive role models. They should be recruited from a variety of cultures and abilities/disabilities to help children appreciate cultural diversity. The following are specific safety first considerations:

1)   Staff should be trained in Red Cross first aid and CPR techniques as well as site safety procedures.

2)   The site should be prepared to facilitate rapid emergency response. A telephone, emergency transportation procedures, and first aid supplies should be readily available.

3)   Staff should be trained in promoting positive play experiences. This will minimize the chance of children engaging in high risk activities due to boredom.

4) An adequate staff-to-child ratio is necessary. Staff-to-participant ratios vary in different programs. An ideal ratio is 1:5. A workshop of twenty-five children typically has three adult supervisors and at least two teenage aides. Additional aides may be hired, depending on the types of disabilities represented in the group. Higher ratios produce benefits that tend to outweigh the costs: parents feel more secure and satisfied and the staff feels more capable of providing adequate security.

g. **First Aid Preparedness.**

1) Children should receive adequate instruction regarding rules. These rules should be periodically reviewed.

2) Parents should receive a copy of rules. Leaders should meet with parents of participating children and explain common sports hazards and methods of preventing accidents. Parents should be instructed to review these accident prevention measures with their children at home.

3) Emergency procedures should be developed for dealing with both major and minor accidents during program participation. Important considerations include:

- Parent's release form for emergency treatment;
- First aid procedures;
- Location of first aid equipment;
- Cardiopulmonary resuscitation;
- Location of nearest telephone;
- Location of nearest hospital emergency room;
- Transportation to the emergency facility;
- Procedure for notification of parents; and
- Maintenance of a file of phone numbers where parents and other individuals (who parents may designate as alternative contacts), may be reached. These procedures should be reviewed and updated on an annual basis.

4) A copy of the emergency procedures manual should be maintained on the site at all times.

5) The site should be prepared in order to provide a rapid emergency response. Access to a nearby telephone should be maintained at all times. Emergency

numbers (ambulance, hospital emergency room and poison control center) should be posted in a visible place near the telephone.

6) First aid supplies should be readily available, including ice or "instant ice packs."

7) A procedure should be developed for periodically checking and replenishing first aid supplies. Maintaining a list of supplies which are included in the first aid kit can facilitate this process.

8) Adequate staffing should be maintained to ensure supervision of remaining children if one leader must accompany a child to an emergency treatment center or provide first aid on site.

9) Provide staff training. All staff should complete an American Red Cross certified first aid course.

10) At least one staff member who is certified by the American Red Cross in cardiopulmonary resuscitation should be present on the site at all times. Other staff should be aware of the names of staff members who are certified in CPR.

11) Under no circumstances should an untrained staff member attempt CPR; serious injury can result.

12) Inservice training on emergency procedures should be required of all staff on an annual basis.

13) All staff should receive a copy of the emergency procedures manual and be encouraged to review it periodically.

h. **Training.** Play leadership training for both staff and aides is essential for providing safe yet challenging play activities. Play leaders need to learn how to give appropriate directions and avoid the kind of pitfalls that can lead to accidents.

On-the-job training can take place in a setting where prospective play leaders work with trained staff as apprentices. Trainees can learn proper use of potentially hazardous materials such as fire, ropes, hammers and saws in situations involving children.

Play leadership seminars can teach staff about the programming organization, its policies and goals. Trainees become aware of potential site hazards, learn procedures for managing accidents, learn how to handle behavior problems and how to include children in cooperative play activities.

i.   **Built-in Risk Taking.** Built-in risk taking within program activities provides a safe yet challenging experience for children. Recognizing that children like to climb on things that are potentially dangerous, safe programs of activity can be designed. In the PLAE workshop "Treasure Island," for example (*Treasure Island PLAE Score*, 1986), children "escape from the shipwreck to the life raft (climbing net)." Workshop leaders and aides are on hand to assist. To add to the perceived challenge (but not to the risk), the sand pit under the net is flooded with a few inches of water. "Shark fins" (cutout cardboard props) stick out menacingly (but not dangerously) from the water beneath the net.

Children love to jump off walls, rope swings, rooftops and other challenging places. In Treasure Island, blindfolded "pirates" jump off a plank positioned over a sand pit made safe with layers of foam rubber. Thus, children are provided with a heightened experience of jumping and risk taking.

Insuring the safety and security of children is easier if they participate in programmed activities. Play leaders must provide direction as well as supervision. Children are more actively engaged in programmed activities if they are cooperatively structured. Working and playing with play partners, in teams and in small or large groups, keep children actively engaged and less exposed to unforeseen risks.

j.   **Programming for Spontaneous Play.** To maintain high quality play programs, spontaneous (potentially hazardous) play must be integrated into programmed activities. In this way, children can have fun and seek challenge, while play leaders direct and supervise their activities.

Recognizing that children like to wade into ponds, jettison pieces of wood across water surfaces and build bridges, similar activities are programmed in the "Treasure Island" PLAE workshop. Play leaders help children collect empty plastic milk cartons to increase flotation. Together they construct more substantial, safe "rafts" that serve the same purpose and allow all children to participate.

Children's behavior can be directed appropriately to reduce risks to acceptable levels while not defeating children's creative play. To achieve this requires sensitive, carefully trained play leaders. They must be flexible enough to allow spontaneous play activities to be safely incorporated into the program theme, thereby supporting the goal of child integration.

k.   **Community-Based Management.** Parents, children and community members should be involved in the planning, design and operation of settings and programs. Parents of program participants can serve on the Board of Directors. Routinely solicited evaluations from both children and parents can provide comments and suggestions for incorporation into future programming. Community needs assessments can be conducted before new programs or services are implemented.

l.   **Community Involvement.** As the population served by a newly integrated program expands, efforts to involve families in a participatory way must also grow. Parent-child workshops can be sponsored, free events can be held in parks for families and other opportunities for increased family participation in the program development can be proposed, such as picnics where parents, children and play leaders can meet.

Radio shows and community slide presentations can build a solid foundation of mutual respect and support. Over the years, an extended "program family" can evolve that includes all former participants. Hundreds of families can be touched so that parents and children approach the play leaders easily with suggestions and criticisms as well as praise. Whenever concerns arise, the personal relationships which have developed among the participants and staff provide a basis for working out difficulties.

m.   **Multilevel Communication Between Parents and Leaders.** The safety and security of children is strongly supported by community based management. Parent board members can help develop a rapport with parents of children in the program, seeking their input and feedback. This makes parents feel more secure about the risks their children may take.

Program descriptions can be made available to parents in advance so that problems their children might have can be anticipated. Parental feedback can also be solicited through post-program evaluations to help identify concerns.

Program registration forms should require parents to provide information on their child's special needs: the need for extra attention because of shyness, assistance in eating because of an orthopedic disability, medication requirements, etc. Such forms can provide play leaders with information about the adults authorized to pick up the child, whether the child will walk home, emergency and doctor phone numbers, parent's wishes when minor scrapes occur, and so on. In cases of unusual need, additional aides may be called in to supplement workshop staff.

Parents should also receive a complete description of the program setting and risk management policies. They should be apprised of accident policies which can be adjusted in individual cases. Parents should be informed about the staff's level of supervision, the staff's experience and qualifications, and the level of safety and security the program realistically can provide. The purpose of these efforts is to make sure parents are fully aware of the risks and allow them to make properly informed choices on behalf of their children. The aim should be to minimize the anxiety of parents so that they can go about their business without fretting about their children's welfare.

Communication is the crucial link in providing a children's program that parents feel comfortable with. Professional leadership training helps staff learn the language to use when describing the program to others, how to communicate effectively with parents and how to respond to parent requests and desires. The end result is that parents understand the risks and opportunities their children face. They appreciate the goal of providing a stimulating play environment and feel equipped to share in the responsibility for their children's well-being.

n.   **New Risk Management Models.** There is no such thing as a completely safe play environment. Children will naturally seek out potentially hazardous physical challenges. Instead of removing all hazards, thus creating sterile and unstimulating play spaces, careful programming can lead to safe activities that satisfy children's need for enjoyment and challenge. This suggests the need for new models of supervised programming that can be incorporated into public recreational environments so that risk can be more sensitively balanced with creative play.

Communication is the key to effective risk management. Everyone connected with the program—staff, parents, children, administrators, community members—must share ultimate responsibility for child safety and security. Opportunities for families and community members to participate in the management of programs must be provided. In this way, when incidents occur, they can be managed from a base of preparedness and mutual understanding.

The greatest challenge being faced by providers of children's play and learning environments is not just to avoid major lawsuits for broken bones or astronomical insurance premiums; it is the responsibility for raising a generation of young people who have the opportunity to play in healthy and stimulating surroundings.

24.6   Taking Action

The *Play For All Guidelines* were developed to meet the challenge of balancing safety with child development objectives. Since the *Play For All* Stanford conference, many inquiries have been received requesting assistance in applying the guidelines to local communities.

The following is a process which has been developed by *Play For All* staff to assist parks and recreation departments, schools and child care agencies in applying the guidelines:

a.   **Develop a Safety First Policy.** The development of a safety first policy is a proactive approach to providing healthy, safe and developmentally appropriate outdoor play environments. It involves a consciously applied set of strategies designed to:

1)   Mitigate the known and perceived safety hazards in an environment and in organized programs.

2)   Prevent harm and injury.

3)   Establish a process for handling and documenting incidents that occur.

4)   Share responsibility for safety and security of children with their families.

b.   **Create a Site Master Plan Based on the PFA Guidelines.** After initiating a safety first program, every site should be analyzed for its appropriateness as a children's play and learning environment. This is an important task in the construction of new playgrounds or the rehabilitation of existing ones. A thorough inventory of the characteristics of each site should include, but not be limited to: location; site function, natural features and utilities; human and cultural features; existing equipment; and social and geographical setting within the community.

A site master plan should be developed. The master planning process should involve administrators, staff, maintenance personnel, risk managers, parents and children in setting goals for the site and developing a program of activities to meet those goals. The master plan can then be designed to support selected activities. Consideration should also be given to ensure that all children's play environments are accessible to children with disabilities. A phased development plan can be created to prioritize improvements to allow strategic improvements to be made as funds become available.

The following steps might be taken in order to develop a positive response to the safety issue:

1) **Task Force.** Create a task force to oversee the project. Members of the task force should include business managers, site personnel, maintenance staff and community members.

2) **Budget.** Determine how much money is needed:

   - Assess the amount of money being spent on legal action related to play environment injuries.
   - If there are no accidents, find out the direct costs of managing the site.
   - As a starting point, take the above information to the local insurance pool or risk manager and ask for 5% of their exposure to begin the process of upgrading the play environment.

3) **Master Plan.** No matter how small, create a master plan for the site. This master plan should involve task force members in establishing goals and a list of priority site improvements.

4) **Site Evaluation.** Using the goals and activities identified in the master plan, evaluate the existing site.

   - How do the existing equipment settings and other settings support the goals and activities identified in the master plan?
   - Is the site and its equipment safe, accessible, and well maintained? Do they support the desired play behavior? (Use a safety checklist as a guide.)

5) **Current Equipment Usage.** Using the site evaluation information as documentation, decide what needs to be removed, replaced or adapted.

6) **Phased Improvement Plan.** In most situations, all the desired site improvements cannot be afforded at one time.

   - Create a phased improvement plan to guide purchase and maintenance decisions and to help community groups decide on projects they want to support through fund-raising, gift purchase or, when appropriate, building new settings.
   - Create a set of guidelines and procedures for the design, purchase, installation and maintenance of the site.

7) **Document the Process.** A clear record of the process and decisions made will help future users evaluate current needs in light of previous decisions.

c. **Share Responsibility and Risk.** Since no play environment is completely safe, parents must be involved in sharing the responsibility of operating a play environment or program which can promote healthy child development. Providing opportunities for parent involvement in policy development, maintenance of the environment and program planning and implementation creates a sense of parent ownership.

Everyone connected with a play environment—staff, parents, children, administrators, and community members—must ultimately share responsibility for child safety and security. Real opportunities for families and community members to participate in the management of programs and environments must be provided. In this way, when incidents occur, they can be managed from a base of mutual understanding.

Children will naturally seek out physical challenges that can be hazardous. Rather than creating sterile and inappropriate outdoor play spaces, careful design, programming, maintenance and supervision can lead to safe activities that children both enjoy and find challenging.

This responsibility can be best met through the development of local safety first policies, creating site master plans to guide future play area development and involving parents and community members in sharing the risk and responsibility for play programs and environments.

APPENDICES

A. ABOUT DISABILITY AND INTEGRATION

The editors wish to thank the Bay Area Outreach Program (BORP) for permission to include this edited selection from *We Can do It: A Training Manual for Integrating Disabled People into Recreation Programs.*

A.1 Mainstreaming/Integration (Fitzgerald, 1982)

Mainstreaming is sometimes used as another word for *integration.* Even though the two terms have been used interchangeably they mean different things. Mainstreaming connotes the placing of a few "different" people (a disabled, racial or sexual minority) into a regular program or activity, thereby implying that the other "regular" people have more power or authority. Integration implies that both groups have equal status and are moving toward a common point of reference. Even though mainstream is more commonly used in education and government circles, a word with more positive connotations can help affect more positive change.

Integration is a dynamic process with the individual progressing through a continuum of various stages from the segregated experience at one end to the totally integrated experience at the other. Not all disabled people are ready to be integrated; some need support services which can prepare them for the next stage on the continuum. Progression through these various stages permits disabled and able-bodied people to have increasingly greater opportunities for social interaction at a pace that is appropriate for the individual.

A.1.1 Integrated Recreation

Not many years ago, everyday activities such as school, employment and recreation were unavailable to disabled people. Disabled people had separate schools, sheltered workshops and segregated recreational facilities. In fact, many disabled people were institutionalized and kept out of sight from the able-bodied community. During the early 1970's, Wolf Wolfensberger introduced a concept called "normalization" —introducing disabled people to a more "normal" environment. This represented a change from the prevailing attitudes towards disabled people.

Although normalization applies to all aspects of one's life, when applied to recreation, it created a new strategy for disabled recreators. In addition, change was brought about by federal and state legislation mandating that a continuum of services be given in the "Least Restrictive Environment" to disabled children.

Budget cuts in community and social services played an important factor too. Many community agencies had to pool their resources in order to stay open. When organizations which had provided recreation to disabled consumers were cut back or closed, city and university recreation programs were asked to provide services. It was found that offering integrated recreation activities in existing programs was very cost effective. All of these factors led to the development of integrated recreation.

A.2   Legislative History

There have been a great number of Federal laws which have implications for recreational opportunities for disabled persons. The major laws are:

a.   **Vocational Rehabilitation Act of 1963.** Funds for training and research in recreation for the ill and handicapped were included in the 1963 revision of the original Vocational Rehabilitation Act of 1954. This was the first Federal action recognizing the importance of recreation services for disabled persons. Following this action, several colleges and universities received funds to implement training programs at the graduate level in "recreation for handicapped individuals." A foundation for growth and development of training in therapeutic recreation was formed.

b.   **The Architectural Barriers Act of 1968 (Public Law 90-480).** This law requires physical aaccessibility and simply states that:

"Any building or facility constructed in whole or in part by federal funds must be made accessible and useable by the physically handicapped."

Therefore, any construction, remodeling or site development must be accessible and useable independently by physically disabled.

c.   **Rehabilitation Act of 1973 (Public Law 93-112).** This document is a comprehensive revision of the 1963 Vocational Rehabilitation Act, removing emphasis from "vocational" rehabilitation and focusing on total rehabilitation of all disabled persons. Several features of this legislation that impact recreation include:

1)   **Title II - Research and Training.** This title continues authorization of funds for training of recreation professionals to work with disabled persons and research in this area.

2)   **Title III. Section 304 - Special Projects and Demonstrations.** This section authorized grants for "Operating programs (including renovation and con-

struction of facilities, where appropriate) to demonstrate methods of making recreational activities fully accessible to handicapped individuals."

3) **Title V. Section 504 - Rehabilitation Act of 1973 (Public Law 93-112 as amended by PL-516 and PL 95-602).** "No otherwise qualified handicapped individual in the United States . . . shall, solely by reason of handicap, be excluded from the participation in, be denied the benefits of, or be subjected to discrimination under any program or activity receiving Federal financial assistance."

While the Architectural Barriers Act demands *physical access* in programs and facilities, Section 504 requires barrier free *programming* for physically disabled persons. Barrier free programming includes making the program available in alternative locations when the site itself cannot be made accessible. It also addresses access to programs related to people with sensory impairments.

d. **Rehabilitation Act Amendment of 1974 (Public Law 93-516).** This legislation authorized the planning and implementation of the White House Conference on Handicapped Individuals which was held in May 1977. Recreation was one of sixteen major areas of concerns addressed. Recommendations for increased Federal funding, better accessibility in parks, monuments and recreation programs, more consumer involvement in planning, program implementation and employment evolved from conference sessions.

e. **Education of All Handicapped Children Act, 1975 (Public Law 94-142).** This law amends Public Law 90-380, greatly expanding educational opportunities for disabled children. PL 94-142 requires a free, appropriate education for all children. The major emphasis in the rule is the word "appropriate" and specific guidelines are given for what is considered appropriate education. An individualized education plan is required for each child, which includes evaluation of their present level of educational performance, establishing specific educational goals, a statement of services to be provided to reach these goals and a continuum of placements to be given in the least restrictive environment. Recreation as a related service is included in the law. The definition of recreation as it pertains to this rule includes assessment of leisure functioning, therapeutic recreation, recreation in schools and communities and leisure education. This law begins to promote leisure and recreation as a very significant aspect in the total education of disabled children.

A.3   Descriptions of Disabilities

A.3.1   Visual Impairments

People with visual impairments have a wide range of ability and limitations. Someone who is legally blind is defined as having measured vision of 20/200 in their better eye with correction. This means that they are able to see at 20 feet what a normally sighted person is able to see at 200 feet.

There are many kinds of visual impairments, each with a wide range of ability and limitation. Someone who is described as legally blind may be able to read large print and move about without mobility aids in many or all situations. They may also be able to perceive light and darkness and perhaps even some colors. However, someone else who may also be legally blind, may not have any of these skills.

There are some conditions where the individual's vision may be better one day over another, depending on fatigue and other factors.

It is impossible to generalize visual impairments into one problem with one solution. People with congenital visual impairments (impairments present from birth) may have skills in reading braille and tactile orientation aids. However, people who have lost their sight later in life usually have visual memories of color and scale, and concepts such as reflections, that people who have been blind since birth do not have.

The process of aging also affects our visual perception. Both visual acuity and opacity are affected. Visual acuity influences how we perceive objects at a distance, and opacity of the lens determines the way light is transmitted, affecting perception of colors and textures.

Generally, elderly people perceive almost 20 percent less keenly than those with normal vision. Colors often blend together and closely related textures cannot be discerned.

Glare is a major problem for many people, particularly the elderly. Do not confuse the term "glare" with "light level." Low light levels cast heavy shadows, making it difficult for many low vision people to perceive hazards such as stairs, changes in floor surface, etc. Glare usually results when too much light bounces off of light colored walls and floors, making it difficult and uncomfortable to navigate a long corridor or around a room.

Many visually impaired children have been overprotected by parents, friends, and teachers; as a result, they may not have had the opportunity to explore their environment during early childhood. These children need to explore as much of their environment as possible to build concepts that their peers acquire through sight.

Children who are blind or have severe visual impairments may lack skills in body control, balance, coordination and physical abilities. Poor posture is another characteristic of many people with severe visual impairment. They may develop faulty carriage because of the inability to orient their posture to their surroundings. They have a tendency to lean forward with their arms outstretched to avoid hitting objects. Some blind children are very tense, walking rigidly with their heads tilted backward.

Early detection of blindness or visual impairment is essential for treatment and education of children. The main objectives of treatment are to restore or improve sight and to prevent further deterioration of vision.

Education of visually impaired children may take place in a special school, special classroom or in a mainstream setting. With a totally blind child, auditory instruction and reading by touch using the braille system are emphasized. Children with partial vision may attend regular school, providing the teacher is trained to meet their special needs. Parents also receive training to better meet the needs of their visually impaired child.

As adults, the greatest emphasis in rehabilitation is independent mobility training (skills in moving about and in coping with environmental factors). Following World War II, the Veteran's Administration began to train blinded veterans in the use of the white cane system. This system developed after observing that for various reasons many blind people could not, or did not wish to, adjust their lives to using guide dogs.

It is important to note that many blind adults do not read braille. In fact, less than 10 percent of the people who are blind or who have severe visual impairments are able to read this system. Many adults choose to get written information transcribed onto audio cassettes and listen to the material.

A.3.2 Hearing Impairments

People with hearing impairments are unable to respond normally to sound in most social situations. There are two main classifications of hearing impairments, each with subdivisions.

a.   Hard of Hearing:

1)   Mild. People with a mild hearing loss learn speech by ear and are able to function almost normally in group and individual conversations. These

people may have difficulty discerning singular and plural forms of words and in hearing subtle tone changes.

2) Marginal. People with marginal hearing impairments usually have difficulty understanding speech from a distance of more than a few feet and in following group conversation.

3) Moderate. People with moderate hearing impairments have enough hearing to learn language and speech with amplification of sound through a hearing aid when the auditory sense is aided by visual information.

b. Deaf:

1) Severe. People with severe hearing impairments have trainable residual hearing with amplification of sound through one or two hearing aids. Their language and speech do not develop spontaneously so they must learn communication through specialized techniques.

2) Profound. People with profound hearing impairments cannot learn to understand language and speech by ear alone, even with amplification of sound. Sign language is usually needed for communication.

The time at which hearing loss occurs in a person's life has a profound affect on the development of communication and social skills. Congenital impairments (impairments present at birth) are often caused by certain contagious diseases such as rubella, mumps and influenza during the mother's pregnancy. Acquired hearing impairments may develop any time during one's life after certain childhood diseases, injuries, ear infections, etc.

A.3.3 Developmental Disabilities

In people described as developmentally disabled, learning ability develops slower than average. Reasoning and judgement capabilities may also develop at a slower pace. For most people with mental retardation, it is not the ability to learn that is missing, but the speed and ease with which things are learned that is lessened.

The range and capabilities in people with developmental disabilities is probably greater than in any other disablility group, and it is with mental retardation and emotional impairments that the general public has the most apprehension and misconceptions.

People with developmental disabilities are often overprotected and discouraged from exploring the world or interacting with others. Often these people are limited to programs that are designed "especially for their needs," and allowed to socialize only with "their own kind." After finishing a specialized education program as a child or young adult, many may spend their adult years in inactivity.

Fortunately, the practice of institutionalizing mentally retarded people is changing. With more appropriate training and education, many people learn to become independent citizens, managing their own homes or apartments and money. Many are able to obtain and hold a non-skilled or semi-skilled job.

Many people with developmental disabilities have problems with coordination, balance, agility, strength, body awareness and self image. These problems are often the result of inactivity and lack of opportunity to participate in group activities.

Mildly to moderately retarded people will usually not behave very differently from their peers. They may be interested in things that we perceive to be more appropriate for younger people and some social skills may be below their expected age level.

While learning skills of a person with developmental disabilities may be more concrete, more repetitive and perhaps less focused than their nonretarded peers, their emotional life, sense of humor and sensitivity to others may be more sophisticated than expected.

A.3.4 Emotional Impairments

There are many situations or behaviors that may lead us to label someone as emotionally impaired. These behaviors may develop as part of an individual's "coping strategy" to survive in their environment. People with emotional impairments have adapted methods to interact with their surroundings with a "fight for survival approach."

Someone simply may be of an ethnic minority whose lifestyle and needs are different from the prevailing "norm." Others may have a variety of behavior problems and may act them out, may become aggressive and perhaps harmful to themselves and/or others. Still others may be people whose lives are filled with extreme fears, withdrawal, depression, anxiety and stresses. Some people have developed problems as a result of alcohol and drug abuse.

Conditions that may be labeled as autistic, schizophrenic, psychotic and other severe impairments may appear to give people a "lack of contact with the real world," and an inability to relate to others. These people may have severe language impairments, a strong need for predictability in their daily lives and repetitive behaviors.

Sometimes the greatest barriers in working with a group that has been labeled as emotionally impaired are the fears and expectations other people have about their behavior. These fears and expectations may affect the approach and design of programs.

Knowing the cause or definition behind a label does not improve our services or skills. What is important to remember is that people with emotional impairments are just like any other group.

A.3.5 Epilepsy

Epilepsy means seizure, but not all convulsive seizures are due to epilepsy. Seizures are classified by variations in severity, duration, frequency and warning of impending attacks.

a. **Grand Mal.** This is easily recognized by rigidity, loss of consciousness and falling. Biting of the tongue may occur from strong contraction of the jaw muscles. Jerking, twisting, involuntary cries and complete amnesia are also characteristic of this type of seizure. The seizure itself may only last a few minutes, but the deep sleep that follows may last several hours. Upon waking from a grand mal seizure, the person may experience weakness, mental dullness or headaches.

b. **Petite Mal.** This is a short lapse of unconsciousness followed by immediate recovery. The eyes blink or roll and fix upon some object, and fine muscular twitchings may be unnoticed except by the epileptic.

c. **Psychomotor Attack.** This condition is characterized by sudden strange behavior in which there is consciousness without apparent recall. The person experiencing this type of rare attack may go out of the room without reason, may have a sudden temper tantrum, or appear to act out a bad dream. During the seizure the person is apt to be injurious to others. Most often these types of attacks are associated with psychosis.

An epileptic person may participate in activities designed for the general population provided the person is supervised by a leader who is considerate of the person's special needs and educated in such a way to effectively meet those needs. An epileptic's seizure threshold seems to be lower when experiencing emotional upsets, bodily discomfort or if the blood sugar level is lowered due to hunger. Many studies indicate however that lying around and constantly resting seem to spark emotional upsets. It is advisable for an epileptic to get a reasonable amount of physical and mental activity. It has been shown that seizures rarely occur when the person is alert and active.

A.3.6 Mobility Impairments

We have all experienced limited mobility at some point during our lives. As toddlers, the built environment and much of the natural world presented hurdles that made it difficult and tiring for independent navigation. Steps were too high, streets too long, chair seats were too far from the floor. Most of us do not think of toddlers as mobility impaired people, nor do we tend to include pregnant women as people with limited mobility. However, advanced pregancy may place extra burdens on a woman as she navigates through her environment.

Too often we focus on the disability or limitations of that disability as we perceive it. Our reactions, conversation and interactions are often aimed at the disability and not at the person. Many people with a disability refer to their "condition" as an inconvenience, rather than a handicap or limitation. This inconvenience may require the individual to be creative in moving around the environment and in accomplishing tasks of everyday living.

The following descriptions list conditions that may affect an individual's mobility and independence within the environment.

a.   **People Who Use Wheelchairs for Mobility.** Wheelchairs allow people with many disabling conditions mobility that they might otherwise not have, or would find greatly reduced. Congenital impairments, accidents and illness can all leave parts of our bodies in different stages of weakness, paralysis or absence. Paralysis may not only affect motor control of certain parts of our body, but may also affect responses to external stimuli, such as touch, temperature, pain and sometimes, even awareness of body position.

Some environmental concerns of people who use wheelchairs include obvious things such as ramped entrances and elevators instead of stairs, adequate parking in convenient areas, level walks with firm surfaces, and wide aisles in stores and classrooms. Not only are accessible toilet facilities a must, but so is the availability of drinking water. Due to immobility, it is imperative that large amounts of water be consumed. Renal infection and failure are the leading cause of death in paraplegic and quadraplegic men and women.

Many people with severe upper and lower limb impairments, or with greatly reduced stamina, use electrically powered wheelchairs for mobility. Uneven surfaces, such as cobblestones, can cause a moving chair to jolt and the fine control required to operate an electrical wheelchair may become erratic or even stop. Uneven surfaces can also aggravate extreme pain in some people.

Many people with impaired mobility also have faulty internal thermostats and are unable to adjust their body temperature needs to meet external demands. In hot weather they may not be able to perspire freely, and thus may suffer heat stroke at a relatively low temperature. In some conditions pain and/or muscle and joint flexibility may be affected by cold and dampness. Thus, people with mobility limitations need opportunities to escape from uncomfortable climatic conditions, which may become life threatening for some.

b.   **People Who Have Difficulty in Walking.** People who have difficulty in walking may (or may not) walk with aids such as crutches, a cane, a walker, braces, artificial limbs, or even holding onto a friend's arm. Reduced agility, speed of movement, difficulty in balance, reduced endurance, or even a combination of these may contribute to impaired mobility. Energy reserves are often used faster than average. A person who walks with difficulty may be required to spend their energy in trying to keep their balance or otherwise meet challenges of the environment as it confronts their limitations.

Some environmental elements of concern to people with walking difficulties include uneven walking surfaces, walks interrupted with raised or uneven expansion joints, slippery surfaces such as highly polished floors or wet shower rooms, walks filled with debris, areas that collect standing water, sand and/or ice, etc.

People who wear leg braces or artificial limbs may find stairs with square nosing a great hazard. Their toe may get caught by the nosing, making it difficult to pass from one level to the next and possibly precipitating a trip or fall.

Handrails on both sides of stairs and ramps are particularly helpful to people with walking difficulty. Handrails are needed on both sides, as someone may be stronger on one side over the other, and not everyone is "right-handed." Often people who may be using a wheelchair will use handrails along the ramp as an assist up the incline.

Heavy doors are often a problem for everyone, but people who use crutches, canes or walkers may have another problem. The door may close too quickly and trap the crutch or tip below the bottom of the door.

c.   **People With Upper Limb Impairments.** While we don't normally think of some-one with "two good legs" having a mobility problem, the environment requires extensive and complex manipulative skills and strength for people to function independently.

Environmental concerns of people with upper limb impairments include styles of knobs, buttons and handles to operate doors, drinking fountains, coin operated vending machines, telephones, elevator controls, the weight of exterior doors, etc.

Fixtures to operate doors, drinking fountains and and other equipment should be lever style with a non-slip finish. They should be large. Shut-off springs or quick self-closing devices should be avoided.

People with upper limb impairments may have some difficulty with balance, especially when climbing stairs or walking up inclines. Handrails along both sides of the risers will be helpful in providing support when the individual leans against them.

d.   **People With Less Than Average Agility, Stamina and Slower Reaction Time.** Many people have multiple health problems which may include cardiovascular and cardiopulmonary diseases, hypertension and degenerative conditions of aging. Pregnant women and young children may also have difficulty with limited agility, stamina and slower than average reaction times.

There are many environmental elements that require people to make quick decisions and/or to be strong and agile. Such elements include revolving doors, escalators, street crossings, boarding buses and street cars, etc. Not only do elderly people have difficulty with these facilities, but most children are also impeded.

A.3.7 Some Common Physical Disabilities

a.   **Cerebral Palsy.** Cerebral palsy is a neurological disorder resulting from damage to the brain before, during or after birth. Control of the muscles is lost or impaired, ranging in degree from mild to severe. Four general groups of cerebral palsy are spastic, athetoid, ataxic and rigid. Persons with cerebral palsy (CP) may fall into more than one of these categories.

b.   **Spinal Cord Injuries.** Spinal cord injuries are generally caused by trauma rather than congenitally. Diving and motorcycle accidents are the most frequent causes of trauma, followed by auto accidents and falls.

Depending on the level of injury, a person is either a quadraplegic (quad meaning four) where all limbs are impaired or paralyzed, or a paraplegic (para meaning two) where two limbs are affected. When the cord is damaged or severed, sensory and motor nerves are not able to send impulses below the level of the injury. Some of the nerves that are damaged relate to loss of bladder and bowel control.

c.   **Poliomylitis.** This is a disease which affects motor cells in the spinal cord, which in turn destroys the nerve impulses in certain muscles. Residual effects of polio are varied. If nerves are not completely destroyed there will usually be a certain amount of recovery. Some persons will have mild effects of the disease while others can become quadraplegics.

d.   **Stroke.** This is destruction of brain substance resulting from a rupture of a cerebral blood vessel, an occlusion of a cerebral blood vessel or vascular insufficiency. Hemiplegia and speech disturbance are specific symptoms.

e.   **Multiple Sclerosis.** This is a slowly progressive disease of the central nervous system characterized by partial paralysis involving one or more limbs, visual disturbances, or heaviness of the limbs.

f.   **Arthritis.** Joints of the body are inflamed and may become enlarged and painful to move, causing a loss of range of motion.

g.   **Spina Bifida.** A congenital malformation of the spinal column in which some portion of the vertebra fails to form over the spinal cord (thus leaving it exposed). This can be corrected with surgery. Spinal cord involvement may occur producing varying degrees of neurological impairment affecting strength and movement of the legs as well as bowel and bladder control.

h.   **Muscular Dystrophy.** Muscular dystrophy is a chronic, progressive disease of the muscles manifested by the gradual weakening of the voluntary muscles. Muscular dystrophy (MD) itself is not fatal. However, eventually all of the voluntary muscles become involved and are unable to perform their functions in respiration and circulation.

A.3.8 Amputees

Individuals who have lost a limb(s) or part of a limb are included in this group. A large number of amputations are a result of automobile, machinery or explosion accidents.

Certain diseases like diabetes also cause many amputations. Some terms used to describe the location of the amputation are:

a.   Unilateral - one arm or leg

b.   Bilateral - two arms or legs

c.   Double - one arm and one leg

d.   Multiple - more than two limbs

A person who loses an arm or leg experiences not only physical loss but psychological damage as well. It is desirable that the injured person adjust to the loss. Perhaps the most important action in developing an adjustment to a loss is a process of re-evaluation. The person must rearrange thinking and place added value on those things, such as personality or social contribution, that previously may have been of little concern or value. At the same time the person must try to do their best to devalue, if possible, those things that they are unable to do because of their physical condition.

Persons bothered by their appearance may increase their scope of values to include surface appearance within their personality appearance. Because many people quite naturally judge a person's attractiveness in terms of personality, it is reasonable to expect this rearrangement of values to add to the adjustment of the loss.

Injured persons who have adjusted to the loss will consider themselves equally worthy members of a group of able-bodied persons. They have widened their scope of values, count their improvements in terms of their performance after the injury rather than before the injury, and realize that although their productive capacity has been altered, their personal contributions are at a maximum because of their efforts to apply themselves. Consequently, as people, they are no different than the able-bodied.

It is important that the able-bodied person thinks of the disabled as a "normal being," one who has "difficulties," rather than thinking of the disabled person as "inferior."

A.3.9 Disfigurement

Disfigurement can result from a number of causes, including birth defects, burns and accidental injury. An important factor to remember is that the degree of disfigurement does not indicate the degree of difficulty that an individual may have in adapting to his or her disability. Often an individual with a "minor" disfigurement has a more difficult adjustment than an individual whose disability appears more severe.

B. ORGANIZATIONS AND INSTITUTIONS INVOLVED IN PLAY FOR ALL

The following is a list of organizations and institutions involved in *Play For All* who continue to lend support to the program in many ways.

Access California, Oakland Social Services Dept., Oakland, CA

Adaptive Environments Center, Boston, MA

Airspace U.S.A., Asheville, NC

American Alliance for Health, Physical Education, Recreation and Dance (AAHPERD), Reston, VA

American Association for Leisure & Recreation, Reston, VA

American Foundation for the Blind, Inc., New York, NY

American Hotel & Motel Association, New York, NY

American Occupational Therapy Association, Rockville, MD

American Society for Deaf Children, Silver Spring, MD

American Society of Landscape Architects, Washington, DC

Association for Play Therapy, Yonkers, NY

Balsam America Sports Facilities, Inc., Houston, TX

Barrier Free Environments, Inc., Raleigh, NC

Bay area Outreach Recreation Program, Berkeley, CA

Beckwith Associates, Forestville, CA

BigToys, Tacoma, WA

Bing Nursery School, Stanford University, CA

Brazoria County Park Commission, Angleton, TX

Breakfall Inc., Milwaukee, WI

Bureau of Engineering, City of San Francisco, CA

Bureau of Parks and Recreation, Portland, OR

California Parks and Recreation Society, Sacramento, CA

Callander Associates, San Mateo, CA

Cam-Turf, Spring, TX

Center for Childcare Alternatives, Ltd, Washington, DC

Center for Human Environments, New York, NY

Center for Human Policy, Syracuse, NY

Center for Independent Living, Berkeley, CA

CHILDESIGN, Inc., New York, NY

Childhood City Network, New York, NY

Children's Environments Quarterly, New York, NY

Children's Playgrounds, Inc., Cambridge, MA

Children's World, Golden, CO

College of Social and Behavioral Sciences, University of Texas, San Antonio, TX

Community Development Dept., City of Buffalo, NY

Community Playgrounds, Novato, CA

Community Services Department, City of Escondido, CA

Community Services Department, City of Byran, TX

Community Services Department, City of Fremont, CA

Consumer Product Safety Commission (CPSC), Bethesda, MD

Curriculum in Recreation Administration, University of North Carolina, Chapel Hill, NC

Cypress Enterprises, Inc., San Jose, CA

Daly City Parks and Recreation, Daly City, CA

Denver Parks and Recreation, City of Denver, CO

Dept. of Architecture, New York State University, Buffalo, NY

Dept. of Architecture, University of California, Berkeley, CA

Dept. of Architecture, University of Florida, Gainesville, FL

Dept. of Art, Southwest Texas State University, San Marcos, TX

Dept. of Community Development, City of Buffalo, NY

Dept. of Environmental Design, University of California, Davis, CA

Dept. of Environmental Management, County of San Mateo, Redwood City, CA

Dept. of Education, University of Texas, Austin, TX

Dept. of Environmental Psychology, City University of New York, NY

Dept. of Landscape Architecture, University of California, Berkeley, CA

Dept. of Parks, City of Redding, CA

Dept. of Parks and Marina, City of Berkeley, CA

Dept. of Parks and Recreation, City of Austin, TX

Dept. of Parks and Recreation, City of Bloomington, IN

Dept. of Parks and Recreation, City of Dallas, TX

Dept. of Parks and Recreation, City of Escondido, CA

Dept. of Parks and Recreation, City of Lafayette, CA

Dept. of Parks and Recreation, City of Napa, CA

Dept. of Parks and Recreation, City of San Francisco, CA

Dept. of Parks and Recreation, City of San Ramon, CA

Dept. of Parks and Recreation, City of Santa Cruz, CA

Dept. of Parks and Recreation, City of Seattle, WA

Dept. of Parks and Recreation, City of Sunnyvale, CA

Dept. of Physical Education, University of Southern Florida, Gainsville, FL

Dept. of Recreation, City of Dublin, CA

Dept. of Recreation, City of Folsom, CA

Dept. of Recreation, City of Kentwood, MI

Dept. of Recreation, City of Plano, TX

Dept. of Recreation, City of Scottsdale, AZ

Dept. of Recreation, City of Washington, DC

Dept. of Recreation and Leisure Studies, San Francisco State University, San Francisco, CA

Dept. of Recreation and Parks, City of Baltimore, MD

Disabled Children's Computer Group, Richmond, CA

Diversified Recreation, Little Rock, AR

Division of Environmental Planning and Management, University of California, Davis, CA

Division of Parks, City of Anaheim, CA

Division of Physical Education, North Texas State University, Denton, TX

East Bay Regional Parks District, Oakland, CA

Elaine Day LaTourelle & Associates, Seattle, WA

Environmental Design Dept., Wheelock College, Cambridge, MA

Environmental Design Research Association (EDRA), Washington, DC

Federal Home Loan Bank, Washington, DC

FPE Group, Lafayette, CA

HAGS PLAY, Sweden

Handicapped Adventure Play Association, United Kingdom

Hayward Area Recreation & Park District, Hayward, CA

Henn, Etzel and Mellon, San Francisco, CA

Human Services and Parks Commission, Culver City, CA

Industrial Design Magazine, New York, NY

International Association for the Study of People and Their Physical Surroundings, London, England

International Association of the Child's Right to Play, (IPA), Stockholm, Sweden

Iron Mountain Forge, Farmington, MO

John Carrol University, Cleveland, OH

Kinder-Care Learning Center, Inc., Montgomery, AL

King County Natural Resources and Parks Division, Mercer Island, WA

Kompan, Inc,. Windsor Locks, CT

Lafayette Community Center, City of Lafayette, CA

Landscape Architecture Magazine, Washington, DC

Landscape Structures, Inc./Mexico Forge, Delano, MN

Let's Play to Grow, Washington, D.C.

Lisle Park District, City of Lisle, IL

Log Rhythms Playground Specialists Inc., Boulder, CO

Los Angeles Department of Recreation and Parks, City of Los Angeles, CA

Mafer Children's Hospital, Brisbane, Australia

Massachusetts Architectural Barriers Compliance Board, Boston, MA

Matrix Design Consortium, Canyon Lake, TX

Metropolitan Dade County Park & Recreation Dept., Miami, FL

Moore Iacofano Goltsman, Berkeley, CA

Naperville Park District, Naperville, IL

National Association for Children with Autism, Washington, DC

National Community Education Association

National Endowment for the Arts, Washington, DC

National Easter Seal Society, Washington, D.C.

National Playing Fields Association, London, England

National Safety Council, Chicago, IL

National Theraputic Recreation Society, Washington, D.C.

New Orleans Parkway and Park Commission, New Orleans, LA

New York City Department of Parks and Recreation, NY

North Bakersfield Recreation & Park Dist., Bakersfield, CA

Northern Suburban Special Recreation Association, Highland Park, IL

Office of State Architect, Access Compliance Section, Sacramento, CA

Pacific Early Childhood Institute, Daly City, CA

Pacific Oaks College, Topanga, CA

Pacific Playground, Inc., Tacoma, WA

Palo Alto Recreation Department, City of Palo Alto, CA

Parks, Beaches & Recreation Dept., City of Pacifica, CA

Parks and Recreation Dept., City of Gilroy, CA

Pentes Design Inc., Charlotte, NC

PLAE, Inc., Berkeley, CA

Play Works, Milwaukee, WI

Playcatering Ltd., Baltimore, MD

Playground Clearinghouse, Phoenixville, PA

Playground Review Committee, Escondido, CA

Playscapes Children's Environments, Madison, WI

Playworld Systems, New Berlin, PA

Program on Urban Studies, Stanford University, Stanford, CA

Public Works Department, Division of Architectural Engineering, City of San Jose, CA

Recreation Center for the Handicapped, San Francisco, CA

Recreation Environments Co., Annapolis, MD

Recreation Plus, Aurora, CO

Reese Industries, Inc., Prospect Heights, IL

Ross Recreation Equipment, Novato, CA

San Diego County Office of Education, San Diego, CA

San Francisco Foundation, San Francisco, CA

School of Architecture and Urban Planning, University of Wisconsin, Milwaukee, WI

School of Design, North Carolina State University, Raleigh, NC

School of Design, University of Washington, Seattle, WA

School of Health, Physical Education and Recreation, University of Northern Iowa, Cedar Falls, IA

Summit Supply Corporation of Colorado, Durango, CO

Super Tots, Washington, DC

The Markfield Project, London, England

Tiger Hug Toys, Denver, CO

United Cerebral Palsy Association, Washington, DC

United States Association for the Child's Right to Play, Austin, TX

United States Consumer Product Safety Commission, Seattle, WA

Universal Play Systems, Inc., New Rochelle, NY

University of Texas, San Antonio, TX

Vagelatos Associates Landscape Architecture Ltd., Vancouver, B.C.

Walt Rankin and Assoc., La Mesa, CA

Wellesley College, Center for Research on Women, Wellesley, MA

Whole Access, Redwood City, CA

World Leisure and Recreation Association, Canada

World Rehabilitation Fund, Inc., New York, NY

Wooden Environments, Inc., Speonk, NY

BIBLIOGRAPHY

SELECTED BIBLIOGRAPHY

Below are listed works consulted in the preparation of this document. Where appropriate, in support of specific points, they are cited in the text. The following organizational abbreviations are used:

AEC (Adaptive Environments Center), Boston, MA

American National Standards Institute (ANSI), Washington, DC

BFE (Barrier Free Environments, Incorporated), Raleigh, NC

CCCY (Canadian Council on Children and Youth), Ottowa, Canada

CMHC (Canadian Central Mortgage and Housing Corporation), Ottowa, Canada

Consumer Product Safety Commission (CPSC), Bethesda, MD

FPC (Fair Play for Children), London, U.K.

HAPA (Handicapped Adventure Playground Association), London, U.K.

HUD (U.S. Department of Housing and Urban Development), Washington, DC

IPA (International Association for the Child's Right to Play) Stockholm, Sweden

NCBFE (National Center for a Barrier-Free Environment), no longer in existence

NPFA (National Playing Fields Association), London, U.K.

PLAE (Playing and Learning in Adaptable Environments, Inc.), Berkeley, CA

Abernethy, W.D. (n.d.). *Playgrounds.* London: NPFA

———. (n.d.). *Playleadership.* London: NPFA

Adaptive Environments Center (1980). Environments for All Children. *Access Information Bulletin.* Washington, DC: NCBFE.

Allen, Lady, of Hurtwood (1968). *Planning for Play.* Cambridge, MA: MIT Press.

Allison, L. (1975). *The Reasons for Seasons.* Canada: Little, Brown and Company.

Andel, J. van. (1986). Physical Changes in an Elementary Schoolyard. *Children's Environments Quarterly* 3(3), 40–51.

Andrews, J.S. (1981). Negligence: As it Applies to a Recreation Leader. *Australian Parks and Recreation.* 22:3, 15–17.

ANSI (1980). A117.1

Appleyard, D. (1981). *Livable Streets.* Berkeley, CA: U.C. Press.

ASTM (1986). F-355/86. Standard Test Method for Shock-Absorbing Properties of Play Surface Systems and Materials.

Balmforth, N. & Nelson, W. (1978). *Jubilee Street.* London: British Broadcasting Corporation.

Barrier Free Environments, Inc. (1980). Doors and Entrances. *Access Information Bulletin.* Washington, DC: NCBFE.

Beamish, A. (1980). Child–Pedestrian Safety in Residential Environments. Ottawa: CMHC.

Beckwith, J. (1985). Play Environments for All Children. *Journal of Physical Education, Recreation and Dance.* May/June, 10–35.

Bird Book Ortho – Herb.

Bengtsson, A. (1972). *Adventure Playgrounds.* London: Crosby Lockwood.

———. (1970). *Environmental Planning for Children's Play.* New York: Praeger.

Benk, H. (1986/87). Playground Injuries. *Australian Parks and Recreation.* 23(2), 14–17.

Björklid, P. (1984–85). Environmental Diversity on Housing Estates as a Factor in Child Development. *Children's Environmental Quarterly.* 1(4), 7–13.

———. (1986). A Developmental – Ecological Approach to Child–Environment Interaction. Stockholm: Stockholm Institute of Education.

Blakely, K. (Ed.) (1985). Safety in Outdoor Play. Special issue of *Children's Environments Quarterly.* 2(4), Winter 1985.

Blue, G.F. (1986). The Value of Pets in Children's Lives. *Childhood Education.* 63:2, 85–90.

Boehm,E. (1980). Youth Farms. In Wilkinson, P.F. (Ed). *Innovation in Play Environments.* London: Croom Helm.

Boyce, W.T., Sobolewski, S., Sprunger, L., & Schaefer, C. (1984). Playground Equipment Injuries in a Large, Urban School District. *American Journal of Public Health.* 74:9, 984–6.

Brink, S. (1980). Design Criteria for the Development of Sheltered Play Spaces in Medium to High Density Housing Projects. Ottawa: CMHC.

———. (n.d.). Environmental Safety and the Prevention of Childhood Accidents. Ottawa: CMHC.

British Standard Institute. (1979). BS5696 Play Equipment Intended for Permanent Installation Outdoors. London: BSI.

Broadway, C. (1979). *Animals and Adventure Playgrounds: A Guide for Play Leaders and their Managements.* Leicester: Highfields Adventure Playground Assoc. (76 Hartington Road, Leicester).

Brower, S. (1977). *The Design of Neighborhood Parks.* Baltimore, MD: Dept. of Planning.

———. (1977). *Streetfronts and Backyards.* Baltimore, MD: Dept. of Planning.

Bunin, N., Jasperse, D., & Cooper, S. (1980). *A Guide to Designing Accessible Outdoor Recreation Facilities.* Washington, DC: U.S. Dept. of the Interior, Heritage, Recreation and Conservation Service (Lake Central Regional Office, Ann Arbor, MI).

Canadian Council on Children and Youth (1980). *Play Space Guidelines.* Ottawa: CCCY.

Cangemi, P. (1987). Correspondence.

Cary, J. (1978). *How to Create Interiors for the Disabled: A Guidebook for Family & Friends.* NY: Pantheon Books.

Central Mortgage and Housing Corporation (1979). *Play Opportunities for School-Aged Children, 6–14 Years of Age.* Ottawa: CMHC.

———. (1978). *Play Spaces for Preschoolers.* Ottawa: CMHC.

———. (1977). *Creative Playground Information Information Kit.* Ottawa: CMHC.

A Child's Garden. (1980). San Francisco: Chevron Chemical Company (Public Affairs Department, Box 3744, San Francisco, CA 94119).

Childhood City Newsletter. (1980). Participation 1. No.22.

———. (1981). Participation 2: Survey of Projects, Programs and Organizations. No.23.

———. (1982–83). Participation 3: Techniques. 9(4)/10(1).

Children's Environments Quarterly. (1984). Children and Animals. 1(3).

Chilton, T. (1985). *Children's Play in Newcastle-Upon-Tyne.* Birmingham: Play Board.

City Farmer, published by the National Federation of City Farms. (The Old Vicarage, 66 Fraser St., Windmill Hill, Bedminster, Bristol BS3 4LY, England).

City of Seattle, Department of Parks and Recreation (1986). *Guidelines for Play Areas: Recommendations for Planning, Design and Maintenance.* Seattle, WA: Department of Parks and Recreation.

Cooper Marcus, C. (1974). Children's Play Behavior in Low-Rise, Inner-City Housing Developments. In Robin C. Moore (Ed.). *Man-Environment Interactions Vol 12: Childhood City.* Washington, DC: EDRA.

Cooper Marcus, C. (1986). Design Guidelines: A Bridge Between Research and Decision-Making. In Ittelson, W., Asai, M. & Ker, M. (Eds.). *Cross Cultural Research in Environment and Behavior. Proceedings of the Second United States–Japan Seminar.* Tucson, AZ: University of Arizona.

——— & Sarkissian, W. (1986). *Housing as if People Mattered : Site Guidelines for Medium Density Family Housing.* Berkeley, CA: UC Press

Coyle, T. (1980). *Incentives as an Aid for Improving the Quality of the Family Housing Environment: A Position Paper.* Ottawa: CMHC

Cunningham, C. (1984). Planning for Small Natural Areas: a Case for Kids. *Proceedings.* Symposium on Small Natural Areas: the Conservation and Management. Trust of New South Wales National.

———. (1987). The Geography of Children's Play: Australian Case Studies. Paper presented to 56th ANZAAS Conference and 14th New Zealand Geography Conference, Palmerston North, New Zealand, January 1987.

DIN7926 (FRG norms) Parts 1–5 (1985). Playground Equipment for Children; Concepts, Safety Requirements, Testing. Linford Wood, Milton Keynes: British Standards Institution (Technical Help for Exporters). Issued by Deutsche Institut für Normung (DIN), Postfach 110, D-1000 Berlin 30, FRG).

Duncan, J., Calasha, G., Mulholland, M.E. & Townsend, A. (1977). Environmental Modifications for the Visually Impaired: A Handbook. *Visual Impairmant and Blindness.* December, 1977. 444–452.

Eikos Group (1980). *Children's Perceptions of Play Environments.* Ottawa: CMHC.

Eriksen, A. (1985). *Playground Design.* New York: Van Nostrand Reinhold Company.

Esbensen, S.B. (1979). An International Inventory and Comparative Study of Legislation and Guidelines for Children's Play Spaces in the Residential Environment. Ottawa: CMHC.

Fair Play for Children (n.d.). *Safety Checklist.* London: FPC and NPFA.

———. (1976). *Training for Leadership.* London: FPC.

Fitzgerald, A. (1982). *We Can Do It: A Training Manual for Integrating Disabled People into Recreation Programs*. Berkeley, CA: Bay Area Outreach Recreation Program.

Freedberg, L. (1983). *America's Poisoned Playgrounds: Children and Toxic Chemicals*. Oakland: Youth News.

Frost, J.L. & Klein, B.L. (1983). *Children's Play and Playgrounds*. Austin, TX: Playscapes International.

——— & Sunderlin, S. (1985). *When Children Play*. Weaton, MD: Association for Childhood Education International.

Gehlbach, R.D. (1986). Children's Play and Self-Education. *Curriculum Inquiry*. 16:2, 203–13.

Gold, S.M. (1972). Non-use of Urban Parks. *Journal of the American Institute of Planners*, 38(Nov), 369–78.

———. (1981). Designing Public Playgrounds for User Safety. *Australian Parks and Recreation*. 22:3, 10–14.

Goltsman, S., Moore, R., and Iacofano, D. (1982). Project PLAE: Using Arts and Environment to Promote Integration of All Children With and Without Disabilities. *IPA Newsletter*. 8:2, 2–8.

Gordon, F. (1985). *The Playleader, Her Role in Scottish Pre-School Playgroups*. Glasgow: Scottish Pre-school Play Association.

Gordon, R. (1972). *The Design of a Pre-School Therapeutic Playground and Outdoor "Learning Laboratory"*. New York: Institute of Rehabilitation Medicine New York University Medical Center.

Gray, A. (1974). *Learning Through Play*. Aukland, New Zealand: New Zealand Playcentre Association.

Gray, La V. & Brower, S. (1977). *Activities of Children in an Urban Neighborhood*. Baltimore, MD: Dept. of Planning.

Gröning, G. (1986). An Attempt to Improve a School Yard. *Children's Environments Quarterly*. 3(3), 12–19.

Hanan, E. & Lucking, G. (n.d.). *Playgrounds and Play*. Dunedin Playground Advisory Committee and Christchurch Playground Advisory Committee.

Handicapped Adventure Playground Association (1978). - *Adventure Playgrounds for Handicapped Children*. London: HAPA.

Harkness, S. & Groom, J. (1976). Building without Barriers for the Disabled. NY: Watson-Guptill Publications.

Hart, R. (1979). *Children's Experience of Place*. New York: Irvington.

Heseltine, P. (1985b). *A Review of Playground Surveys*. Birmingham: Play Board.

Heusser, C.P. (1986). How Children Use Their Elementary School Playgrounds. *Children's Environments Quarterly*. 3(3): 3–11.

Hewes, J.J. (1974). *Build Your Own Playground!* Boston: Houghton Mifflin Company.

Hill, P. (1979). *Play Opportunities for School-Age Children, 6 to 14 Years of Age*. Ottawa, Ontario: CMHC.

Hogan, P. (1982). *The Nuts and Bolts of Playground Construction*. West Point, NY: Leisure Press.

Hole, V. (1966). *Children's Play on Housing Estates*. London: Her Majesty's Stationary Office.

Iacofano, D., Goltsman, S., McIntyre, S., and Moreland, G. (1985). Project PLAE: Using the Arts and Environment to Promote Integration of All Children. *California Parks and Recreation*. 41:4.

International Association for the Child's Right to Play. (1977). *Declaration of the Child's Right to Play*. IPA: Birmingham, UK.

Jeavons, S. (1987). Criteria for Assessment of Play Environments. *Australian Parks and Recreation*. 23(2), 7–13.

Kiewel, H.D. (1980). Ramps, Stairs and Floor Treatments. - *Access Information Bulletin*. Washington, DC: NCBFE.

King, F. (1980). *Towards a Safer Adventure Playground*. London: NPFA.

Kirkby, M.A. (1984). *Young Children's Attraction to Refuge in the Landscape: An Opportunity for Dramatic Play*. Landscape Architecture Thesis. Seattle, WA: University of Washington, Center for Planning and Research.

Kompan (1984). *Playgrounds and Safety: Comparison Between Various Playground Equipment Standards*. Windsor Locks, CT: Kompan.

Lambert, J. & Pearson, J. (1974). *Adventure Playgrounds*. Harmondsworth, Middlesex, England: Penquin.

Langley, J.D. (1984). Two Safety Aspects of Public Playground Climbing Equipment. *New Zealand Medical Journal*. 97:404–6.

———. (1982). School Playground Climbing Equipment—Safe or Unsafe. *New Zealand Medical Journal*. 95: 540–2.

———, Silva, P.A. & Williams, S.M. (1981). Primary School Accidents. *New Zealand Medical Journal*. November, 1981. 336–339.

Lawrence, R.J. (1982). Designers' Dilemma: Participatory Design Methods. Bart, P., Alexander, C., & Francescato, G. (Eds). *Knowledge for Design*. Proceedings of the 13th International Conference of the Environmental Design Research Association, College Park, MD.

Leedy, D.L. (1982). Planning for Wildlife in Cities and Suburbs. *Urban Wildlife*. Washington, DC: The Superintendent of Documents, U.S. Government Printing Office.

Le Fevre, D.N. (1983). *Playing for the Fun of It*. Stockholm, Sweden: Vattumannen Bookshop.

Lifchez, R., Williams, D., Yip, C., Larson, M. & Taylor, J. (1979). *Getting There*. Sacramento, CA: California Dept. of Rehabilitation.

Linberg, L. (1986). *Facility Design for Early Childhood Programs*. Washington, DC: National Association of Young Children.

Los Angeles, City of (1984). Design Standards for Children's Play Areas and Equipment. Los Angeles, Department of Parks and Recreation.

Lynch, K. (1961). *Image of the City*. Cambridge, MA: MIT Press.

——— & Hack, G. (1984, 3rd.ed.). *Site Planning*. Cambridge, MA: MIT Press.

Mason, J. (1982). *The Environment of Play*. West Point, NY: Leisure Press.

Massingham, B. (1972). *Gardening for the Handicapped*. Aylesbury, Bucks: Shire Publications, Ltd.

Melvin, J.H. (1980). *Play Spaces to Accommodate Disabled Children*. Ottawa: CMHC.

Miller, J. 1987). The Work of the Play Leader. *Australian Parks and Recreation*, 23(2), 27–32.

Miller, P.L. (1972). *Creative Outdoor Play Areas*. Englewood Cliffs, NJ: Prentice–Hall.

de Monchaux, S. (1981). *Planning with Children in Mind*. (a notebook for local planners and policy makers.) Sydney: NSW Dept. of Environment and Planning.

Moore, G.T., Cohen, U., Oertel, J. & van Ryzin, L. (1979). *Designing Environments for Handicapped Children*. New York: Educational Facilities Laboratories

Moore, R.C. (in press). Before and After Asphalt: Diversity as a Measure of Ecological Quality in Children's Play Environments. In Bloch, M. & Pellegrini, T. (Eds.). *The Ecological Context of Children's Play*. Ablex Publishing.

———— & Wong, H.H. (in press). *Another Way of Learning: Child Development in Natural Settings*. San Francisco, Sierra Club Books.

————. (1986a). The Power of Nature: Orientations of Girls and Boys Toward Biotic and Abiotic Settings on a Reconstructed Schoolyard. *Children's Environments Quarterly*. 3(3), 52–69.

————. (1986b). Plant Parts as Play Props. *Playworld Journal* 1, 3–6.

————. (1986c). *Childhood's Domain: Play and Place in Child Development*. London: Croom Helm.

————. (1980). Learning from the Yard: Generating Relevant Urban Childhood Places. In Wilkinson, P.F. (Ed). *Play in Human Settlements*. London: Croom Helm.

————. (1978a). A WEY to Design. *Journal of Architectural Education*. XXXI(4), 27–30.

————. (1978b). Meanings and Measures of Child/Environment Quality: Some Findings from the Environmental Yard. In Rogers, W.E. & Ittelson, W.H. (Eds). *New Directions in Environmental Design Research*. Washington, DC: Environmental Design Research Association.

————. (1976). The Environmental Design of Children–Environment Relations. In *Children, Nature and the Urban Environment*. Proceedings of a Symposium–Fair. Darby, PA: U.S.

Forest Experiment Station (Publication #19028).

————. (1975). The Place of Adventure Play in Urban Planning for Children's Leisure. In *Adventure Playgrounds and Children's Creativity*. Proceedings of the 6th World Congress of the International Association for the Child's Right to Play, Milan, Italy. Birmingham, UK: IPA.

————. (1974a). Open Space Learning Place. In Coates, G. *Alternative Learning Environments*. Stroudsburg, PA: Dowden, Hutchinson and Ross.

————. (1974b). Patterns of Activity in Time and Space. In Canter, D. & Lee, T (Eds). *Psychology and the Built Environment*. London: Architectural Press.

————. Moore, R.C. (1966). An Experiment in Playground Design. Masters Thesis. Massachusetts Institute of Technology, Department of City and Regional Planning.

———— & Wochiler, A. (1975). An Assessment of a Redeveloped School Yard Based on Drawings Made by Child Users. In Moore, R.C. (Ed.). *Man – Environment Interactions. Vol 12: Childhood City*. Washington, DC: EDRA.

———— & Young, D. (1978). Childhood Outdoors: Toward a Social Ecology of the Landscape. In Altman, I. & Wohlwill, J. (Eds). *Children and the Environment*. New York: Plenum Press.

Moreland, G., McIntyre, S., Iacofano, D., Goltsman, S. (1985). The Risky Business of Children's Play: Balancing Safety and Challenge in Programs and Environments for All Children. *Children's Environments Quarterly*. 2(4), 24–28.

National Playing Fields Association (1986). *Grass Seed Mixtures for Children's Play Areas*. London: NPFA.

————. (1985). *Kick-About Areas*. London: NPFA (1st ed. 1977).

———. (1983). *Playground Management for Local Councils.* London: NPFA.

———. (1980). *Towards a Safer Adventure Playground.* - London: NPFA.

———. (1978a). *Play Mounds.* London: NPFA.

———. (1978b). *Play Mounds.* London: NPFA.

———. (1977). *Hard Surfaces for Play Areas.* London: NPFA.

National Safety Council. (1985). *Accident Facts: 1985 Edition.* Chicago: National Safety Council (444 N. Michigan Ave., Chicago, IL 60611).

Newman, Oscar (1972). *Defensible Space.* New York: MacMillan.

Nordhaus, R.S., Kantrowitz, M. & Siembieda, W.J. (1984). - *Accessible Fishing: A Planning Handbook.* Santa Fe, NM: New Mexico Natural Resources Dept.

Norén-Björn, E. (1982). *The Impossible Playground.* West Point, NY: Leisure Press.

Orlick, T. (1978). *The Cooperative Sports and Games Book: Challenge Without Competition.* New York: Pantheon.

——— & Botterill, C. (1975). *Every Kid Can Win.* Chicago: Nelson-Hill.

Osmon, F.L. (1971). *Patterns for Designing Children's Centers.* New York: Educational Facilities Laboratories, Inc.

Ostroff, E. (1978). *Humanizing Environments.* Cambridge, MA: The Word Guild.

Peoples Housing, Inc. (1983). *Retrofitting Public Restrooms for Accessibility.* Sacramento, CA: California Department of Rehabilitation.

Peters, G.A. (1986). Warning Signs and Safety Instructions: Covering all the Bases. *Security and Fire News.* Jan/Feb. 1986.

Playing and Learning in Adaptable Environments (PLAE, Inc.) Program Documentation. Berkeley, CA, 1981–1987.

Play Board (1986). *Learning by Playing.* Birmingham: Play Board (in association with Fisher–Price Toys and *Nursery World*).

———. (1985). Play and Children with Special Needs. (information pack). Birmingham: Play Board.

———. (1985). *Play and Playgrounds in Rotterdam – A Research Approach.* Birmingham, UK: Play Board.

———. (1984). Playdata Sheets: Playground Surfacing (nd). Birmingham: Play Board.

———. (n.d.). Playground Surfacing. Birmingham, UK: Play Board.

Preece, J. (nd). *Play and Education – South Aston Play Centre.* Birmingham: Play Board.

Pre-School Playgroups Association (n.d.). *Guidelines for Playgroups with a Handicapped Child.* London: PPA.

Robinette, G. (1985). *Barrier-Free Site Design: Anyone Can Go Anywhere.* New York: Van Nostrand Reinhold.

Root, J. (1983). *Play Without Pain.* Melbourne: Child Accident Prevention Foundation of Australia.

Ross, W. (1978). *Children's Experimental Workshop.* Washington, DC: U.S. Dept. of the Interior, National Parks Service.

Rothenburg, M., Hayward, D.G & Beasley, R.R. (1974). Playgrounds: For Whom? In Moore, R.C. (Ed.). *Man – Environment Interactions Vol 12: Childhood City.* Washington, DC: EDRA.

Royal Australian Institute of Parks and Recreation. (1981). National Seminar on Playground Design and Safety. RIPPR: Lyneham, A.C.T.

Ruddy, N. (1981). ANSI A117.1 (1980) Survey Checklist. *Access Information Bulletin*. Washington, DC: NCBFE.

Rudolph, N. (1974). *Workyards*. New York: Columbia University, Teachers College Press.

Rutledge, A. & Molnar, D.J. (1986, 2nd.ed.). *Anatomy of a Park: The Essentials of Recreation Area Planning and Design*. New York: McGraw Hill.

Sandels, S. (1968). *Children in Traffic*. London: Paul Elek.

Sanoff, H. (1986). Planning Outdoor Play in the Context of Community Politics. *Children's Environments Quarterly*. 3(3), 20–25.

Schicker, L. (1986). *Children, Wildlife and Residential Developments*. (Masters Thesis in Landscape Architecture). Raleigh, NC: School of Design, NCSU.

Schneekloth, L. (1985). *Play Environments for Disabled Children: Design Guidelines*. Unpublished ms.

———. (1978). Schools Council. (1974). *Animal Accommodation for Schools*. London: English University Press.

———. (1974). *Environments for Visually Impaired Children: Design Guidelines*. College of Architecture, Virginia Polytechnic Institute and State University, Blacksburg, VA. Unpublished ms.

——— & Day, D. (1980). *Comparison of Environmental Interactions and Motor Activity of Visually Handicapped and Sighted Children*. College of Architecture, Virginia Polytechnic Institute and State University, Blacksburg, VA. Unpublished ms.

The School Outdoor Resource Area. London: Longman.

Scott, A.H. (1980). Play in a Cold Climate. In Wilkinson, P.F. (Ed). *Innovation in Play Environments*. London: Croom Helm.

Seattle, City of. (1986). Draft Play Area Design Guidelines. Seattle, WA: Department of Parks and Recreation.

Shaw, L.G. (1980). Design Guidelines for Handicapped Children's Play Environments. In Wilkinson, P.F. (Ed). *In Celebration of Play*. London: Croom Helm.

Shier, H. (1984). *Adventure Playgrounds*. London: NPFA

Shildrick, J. (1986). *Grass Seed Mixtures for Children's Play Areas*. London: NPFA

Simm, D. (1985). *Damage on Playground Equipment*. London: NPFA.

Standards Association of New Zealand (1986). *NZS 5828: Part 1: General Guidelines for New and Existing Playgrounds – Equipment and Surfacing*. Wellington, New Zealand: Standards Association.

Standels, S. (1968). *Children in Traffic*. London: Paul Elek.

Sullivan, M. (1982). *Feeling Strong, Feeling Free: Movement Exploration for Young Children*. Washington, DC: National Association for the Education of Young Children.

Sutherland, A.T. & Soames, P. (1984). *Adventure Play with Handicapped Children*. London: Souvenir Press.

Sutton, S. (1985). *Learning Through the Built Environment: An Ecological Approach to Child Development*. New York: Irvigton.

Sweeney, T. (1987). Playgrounds and Head Injuries: A Problem for the School Business Manager. *School Business Affairs*, 53(1), 28–31.

————. (1979). Playground Accidents: A New Perspective. *Trial.* 15(4), 40–44.

Thompsen, C.H. & Borowieka, A. (1980). *Winter and Play.* Ottawa: CMHC.

Turner, M. (1983). *Play Education and the Arts.* London: NPFA.

U.K. Department of the Environment (1973). *Children at Play.* London: HMSO.

U.S. Consumer Product Safety Council. (1981) *A Handbook for Public Playground Safety. Vol I: General Guidelines for New and Existing Playgrounds. Vol II: Technical Guidelines for Equipment and Surfacing.* Washington, DC: CPSC.

U.S. Department of Housing and Urban Development (1978). *A Playground for All Children: Resource Book.* Washington, DC: Superintendent of Documents.

Watkins, B. (1980). Play Environments in Arid Lands. In Wilkinson, P.F. (Ed). *Innovation in Play Environments.* London: Croom Helm.

Westland, C. & Knight, J. (1982). *Playing Living Learning: A Worldwide Perspective on Children's Play.* State College, PA: Venture Publishing.

Wilkinson, P.F. & Lockhart, R.S. (1980). Safety in Children's Formal Play Environments. In Wilkinson, P.F. (Ed). *Innovation in Play Environments.* London: Croom Helm.

————. Lockhart, R.S. & Luhtanen. (1980). The Winter Use of Playgrounds. In Wilkinson, P.F. (Ed). *Innovation in Play Environments.* London: Croom Helm.

Zirpolo, N. (1987). Plan Checking Report, Flood Park Barrier Free Access Design Project, San Mateo County Parks and Recreation Division, Department of Environmental Management, San Mateo County, CA.

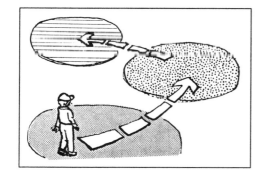

INDEX

PLAY FOR ALL™ News

Play For All News is a quarterly newsletter to support communication among the PLAY FOR ALL network members. Each issue features news from around the country in the field of children's environments, new ideas and a case study of an exemplary children's environment or program.

SUBSCRIBE!

Yes, I want to subscribe to *Play For All News!*

_____
Name

_____
Address

_____
City   State   ZIP

Enclosed is $ _____ for _____ subscription(s).

Subscription rate is $25 for 4 issues.

Please send a free copy of *Play For All News* to:

_____
Name

_____
Address

_____
City   State   ZIP

Return this form with your check, payable to:
PLAE, Inc.
1824 A Fourth Street
Berkeley, CA 94710

A Project of
PLAE, Inc.
1824 Fourth Street
Berkeley, CA 94710

Published by
MIG Communications

ISBN 0-944661-00-9